Character Animation
with 3D Studio
MAX

STEPHANIE REESE

CORIOLIS GROUP BOOKS

Publisher	Keith Weiskamp
Project Editor	Denise Constantine
Cover Design/Artist	Anthony Stock
Layout Design	Bradley O. Grannis
Layout Production	April Nielsen
Technical Editor	Andrew Reese
Copy Editor	Joanne Slike
Proofreader	Stephanie Hoon

The Coriolis Group, Inc.
7339 E. Acoma Drive, Suite 7
Scottsdale, AZ 85260
Phone: (602) 483-0192
Fax: (602) 483-0193
WWW: http://www.coriolis.com

ISBN 1-57610-054-5: $39.99
Printed in the United States of America

10 9 8 7 6 5 4 3 2 1

I'd like to thank my wonderful husband Andrew who was my technical and developmental editor on this book and without whose love and support this book would not have become a reality. Also our children who are always supportive and loving, Christopher, Steven, Elisabeth but especially Caytlin, who had to be patient while both mom and dad worked night and day.

Acknowledgments

A book is a collaborative effort by many, many people. If I've unintentionally omitted your name, please don't shoot me. Anyway, I've moved!

Thanks to Denise Constantine, my project editor, who was patient even though I'm sure she has much less hair now than she did when we started. And to Keith Weiskamp for believing in this project. Also a special thanks to April Nielsen, my typesetter, who went through hell to lay out this book.

A special thanks goes to Michael Girard, who generously provided so much of his time to answer my many questions about the hidden workings of Character Studio, and who provided great artwork and animation for this book—I know he's glad this book is done.

Thanks also to Beau Perschall at Digimation who worked tirelessly to make sure I had all my many questions answered about Bones Pro MAX and who also provided animations for the CD-ROM.

Thanks, as always, to Gary Yost of the Yost Group, and Phillip Miller and Tanya Berkin at Kinetix for all their help.

Also to Sean Hammon, Mary, and Phil at Viewpoint Datalabs International, who made sure I had the meshes for this book and CD-ROM, my humble gratitude.

Thanks to Albert Yang of CompInt and Jeff Cooley of Cerious Software for letting me put their software on the CD-ROM.

A very special thanks to Jessica Hodgins and her team at Georgia Tech for allowing me to use their state-of-the-art dynamic simulations on the CD-ROM and for information and artwork for this book.

Thanks to Judy Conner at Pacific Data Images, who had to keep answering my phone calls, and who gave me permission to use their artwork and animations even though it was done on their proprietary software and not in MAX.

Thanks to Matt Elson for permission to use Stanley and Stella in Breaking the Ice and to Suzanne Datz at Rhythm and Hues for the making of the Coca-Cola Polar Bears commercials sequence.

Thanks to Professor Norman Badler from the University of Pennsylvania School of Engineering and Applied Science Computer and Information Science Department for his help in the area of facial animation.

Most of all I wish to thank all other artists who provided their work for all to learn from: Martin Foster, Jim Biebl, Frank Robbins, John Goodman, Glenn Melenhorst, Ron Lussier, Cyrus Lum, Stephen Seefeld, Jeff Cook, and Pedro P. Uz.

I wish to thank the following companies and people who generously provided equipment, services and software for the writing of this book: Clive Maxfield and Intergraph Computer Systems, Melanie Swanson and Wacom Co., Ltd., Mara Pratt at McLean Public Relations and Fractal Design Corp., Apple Computer, CompuServe Information Service, and everyone at Kinetix and the Yost Group for creating 3D Studio MAX in the first place!

Contents

Introduction

Before starting this book, I was amazed to find that few 3D artists knew much about anatomy, proportions, or how living things moved in the real world. Many had learned their craft a bit at a time using home software. Most spent hours in front of their computers, building great-looking spaceships and blowing them up more or less spectacularly...or creating monsters as video game villains. Some artists had actual fine art backgrounds, but they were small in number compared with the many who studied programming instead of art.

For myself, I started out as an art major, but was sidetracked into the medical field and spent nearly twenty years as an X-ray technician and nurse. Although I never lost the desire to be artistic and creative, it was difficult to make a living through art alone. In 1987, my husband and I started a forensic animation company, producing graphics for courtroom use. We were using Atari ST and Commodore Amiga computers at home and an Aurora paint box system at the local TV station to turn out the work. For its time, the Aurora was a high-end system, but by today's standards, it ran on a laughably slow 286 PC with an enormous 10 MB disk pack (the size of a compact refrigerator).

3D graphics were just beginning to make a splash back then. We went to SIGGRAPH in 1987 and saw amazing 3D animations like *Breaking the Ice*, the Symbolic tale of forbidden love between a bird named Stanley and a fish named Stella. (It's on the companion CD-ROM.) Looking back, those animations seem pretty primitive compared to present standards—and that's only a decade past.

While still involved with computer graphics, I decided to try my hand at sculpting. I found it was a great way to be creative and to take advantage of my medical knowledge at the same time. I became especially adept at sculpting plasticene clays. Eventually, I was creating 2D and 3D animations with one hand while sculpting original character figures with the other—okay, not at the same time, but almost. The transfer of information from one medium to the other was automatic.

As 3D became more popular, I saw a lack of in-depth information available to 3D artists on human and animal anatomy, proportion, and movement. Things that were impossible to overlook by traditional 2D artists were not a priority for 3D artists. After all, the models were built, not drawn—all you needed was software, right? Well, not really. Animators must know how humans and animals look and move in the real world to be able to recreate them in 3D. Even fantasy figures need some basis in reality.

This book came about as a way to give some of my knowledge, hard-won over the years, to others in the growing craft of 3D animation. I tried to make this book useful for all 3D computer artists, not just MAX junkies.

The first half of the book is an in-depth workshop on anatomy, proportions, and movement that any computer artist can use with any computer program. The second half of the book gives 3D Studio MAX users a better understanding of two new plug-ins, Character Studio and Bones Pro

MAX. Each chapter features tutorials that explain both the ordinary and some of the unusual techniques required to make the results effective and lively. On the accompanying CD-ROM, you'll find all the tutorial files for Chapters 7 through 12. Instructions for loading them can be found in Chapter 6.

Note: In order to take full advantage of the tutorials, you must have purchased and authorized both Character Studio and Bones Pro MAX. Some of the tutorials feature Character Studio, others concentrate on Bones Pro MAX, and a few require both.

Also included on the CD-ROM are many samples of character animation for your pleasure, as well as for educational purposes. They are in AVI, MPEG, or QuickTime format. Not all the examples were created using 3D Studio MAX—they're just good examples of quality character animation. You'll find a behind-the-scenes look at the making of the Coca-Cola polar bears, courtesy of Rhythm & Hues; a clip from *Total Recall,* the Carolco sci-fi movie, courtesy of MetroLight Studios; and parts of this year's Kinetix SIGGRAPH reel from Unreal Pictures, Inc., to name just a few. You'll also find animations from Pacific Data Images, John Goodman of Rhythm & Hues, Ron Lussier of LucasArts, and some of the most up-to-date animations by users of Character Studio. Finally, Georgia Tech's Graphics, Visualization, & Usability Center has contributed some fantastic state-of-the-art simulations of human athletic activity.

Five special programs (plus a surprise bonus) are also on the CD-ROM, through the courtesy of their creators:

- Bones Pro MAX demo version, courtesy of Digimation, that lets you see the interface and action of this remarkable program.

- Thumbs Plus 32, courtesy of Cerious Software, is the latest version of this dynamite image processor/manager. Now in 32-bit for more speed.

- Photo4D evaluation version, courtesy of CompInt, that lets you create 3D models from photographs.

- Two 3D Studio MAX plug-ins that let you render directly to your printer and capture the active viewport to an image file.

See the Readme documents in each folder for more information on these programs.

Unreal Pictures and Kinetix have generously contributed the Character Studio MAX files used for their 1996 SIGGRAPH demo. If you have 3D Studio MAX version 1.1, Character Studio is included on the program CD-ROM. You may install Character Studio and view these files in MAX.

Mesh files from Viewpoint DataLabs, as well as from Kinetix and individual model builders, have also been included for you to play with. Please check acknowledgments for modeling and animation credits.

Quick Time for Windows and a shareware evaluation version of Vidfun 1.8 have also been included on the CD-ROM to let you view the animations.

There's a lot in the book and more still on the CD-ROM—I hope you enjoy it. It's been a labor of love for me.

Special Note: For those who want to use 3D Studio MAX and its plug-ins for production work, I strongly recommend the Intergraph TDZ series of computers. I was fortunate to have a TDZ400 to use for the writing of this book. It would have been *very* difficult without the dual Pentium Pro/200 processors with 128 MB of RAM, not to mention the 4 GB hard drive and the 21-inch monitor. Let me tell you, this machine screams!

Part One

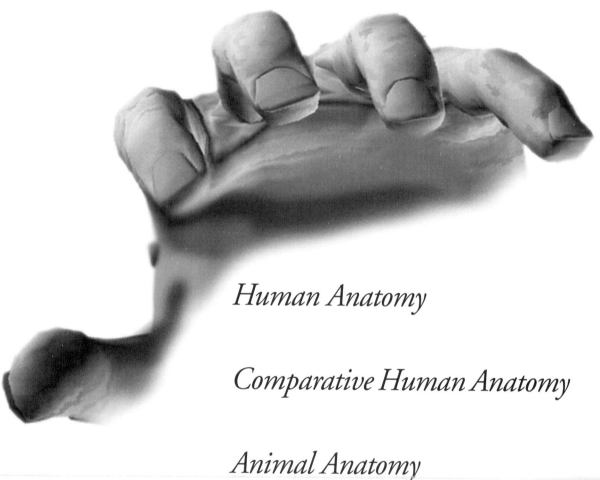

Human Anatomy

Comparative Human Anatomy

Animal Anatomy

Fantasyland

The Nature of Motion

Chapter 1

Human Anatomy

In this chapter, we will look at human anatomy and physiology, beginning with the human skeleton. After all, most of the 3D modeling programs you will be using in your work, such as Kinetix 3D Studio MAX with its Character Studio plug-in, also have skeletons or "bones" on which to build models. And even if your 3D model isn't human at all—maybe you're creating an alien humanoid or a dinosaur with a bowling shirt—if it's supposed to move like a human, you first must learn how the human body is built and how it moves. And that's the point of this chapter.

If you feel comfortable with your knowledge of human anatomy and physiology, you can skip this chapter. But I'd rather that you at least skimmed it—there are gems in here that were never taught to you in your Anatomy for Artists classes!

The State of the Art

When was the last time you heard someone say, "Gee, I can't tell if that's a real person or a 3D model on the screen?" My guess is never. Our eyes have become so accustomed to how a live human being looks, moves, and reacts that we can see in an instant if something is not quite right. This is one reason that 3D animators have stayed away from the human form. It is so difficult to fool the eye that the magic of animation is lost. Instead, people like *Toy Story* director John Lasseter of Pixar have concentrated on the nonhuman form. It was easier to give a personality to a desk lamp in *Luxo Jr.* or make the sad little unicycle in *Red's Dream* come to life than to animate a human. Even the clown in *Red's Dream* was very cartoon-like. *Tin Toy* was Lasseter's first attempt to create a life-like human baby, and despite his remarkable talent, the results were definitely mixed.

Of course, that was a few years ago. Look around today and what do you see making the big splash in 3D animation? Toys, of course! In *Toy Story*, the humans are almost caricatures and are usually shown on the periphery to lessen the viewers' distraction. The big stars are the toys.

Animals also are big—really big! As big as the dinosaurs in *Jurassic Park*. What wonderful effects Industrial Light and Magic (ILM) created; the realistic look of lizard skin moving over the ribs as the T-Rex breathed, and the herd of dinosaurs running around and over the cast! And don't forget *Jumanji* and all its 3D animals. And, of course, *Babe,* which, along with the movie *Hocus Pocus*, demonstrated Rhythm and Hues' great techniques to make real animals move their mouths and talk on-screen.

The latest to make a splash on the movie screens is *Dragonheart*. It features a state-of-the-art 3D dragon that took the ILM animators more than a year to create. It is the best yet of the 3D illusions. The biggest challenge for the animators was making the dragon's mouth move in synch with Sean Connery's voice. Considering the differences in structure and shape between Draco's mouth and that of a human, the results are spectacular.

Even though these 3D wonders aren't perfect human models—or even human at all—they have *character*. For years 2D and cel animators have used the secrets of character animation to breathe life into their animations. As 3D modeling has become more accessible to the non-artist, more and more people are using it for everything from games to Web advertising. Many started out as computer enthusiasts rather than artists. As the 3D programs have become more and more sophisticated, the models they produce are also becoming more polished. Unfortunately, however, because many of the people producing them have not received classical training in fine art, most of the 3D models and animations look very mechanical.

In this chapter, you will go through each section of the body in order to learn how the structure works. I can't teach you everything there is to know about the body here, but after this chapter, you will have a better understanding about how it all works together. To create a lifelike human form, an artist must follow certain basic formulas for most body dimensions. They aren't cast in stone, but they are a good starting point. As we proceed through the body structure in this chapter, keep these rules of thumb in mind to remind you how one part's size relates to another.

And now, into the body.

Skeleton

The wonder of the human skeleton is how it all works together so effortlessly. With more than 200 separate bones, it forms the framework for flesh and muscle and provides the system that protects all the internal organs. Without a skeleton, as shown in Figure 1.1, our bodies would be little more than Jabba the Hut lookalikes.

Even if you don't recognize it at first glance, the skeleton is easily noticeable through the surface of the skin. Protruding ribs, hips, shoulder blades (scapulas), collar bones (clavicles), and kneecaps (patellas) give the body additional dimension. Also, the movement of these bones can be seen easily as the body moves.

Since the muscle, fat, and skin are only the upholstery of the skeleton, any deformities in the skeletal system, such as a hunched back or a shorter leg bone on one side, will show up in the finished model. You can't conceal a defective skeleton with flesh; even if it looks OK while stationary, when it moves, the concealed defects become evident.

It is important to note some of the key bones and structures so that you can understand how to create and control your 3D model.

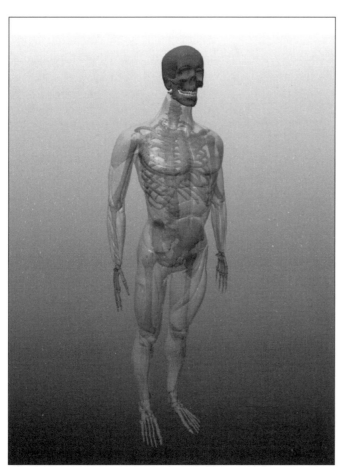

3D Models provided by Viewpoint Datalabs International, Inc.

Figure 1.1

The human skeleton is the framework that holds our bodies together and keeps us from dissolving into amoeba-like blobs of protoplasm.

Skull

The skull is comprised of 22 bones, 8 of which are plate-like and encase and protect the brain. As shown in Figure 1.2, when viewed from the top, the skull is egg-shaped, with the larger end toward the back.

There is very little flesh on the typical human head (fatheads excluded), so the skull provides much of the shape of the head and face. Figure 1.3 shows how the skull shapes the head.

Years ago, I was hired to create the box art for an Atari ST 3D program called *Cyber Sculpt* (written by *3D Studio MAX* co-author Tom Hudson). I sculpted a head

emerging from a stone block, one triangular face at a time, working primarily from the side view. Incidentally, we chose the half-head concept because during development, the program couldn't handle the number of faces necessary to create an entire head. Am I glad that 3D programs have made so much progress since then! (There's a lesson here also about learning to work within the limits of your available tools.)

You'll seldom be required to create a skull to fit within your 3D head—except for the occasional 3D horror video game with flesh-ripping special effects. Start with a good commercial skull, like the one shown from Viewpoint Datalabs, and add geometry over the skull as necessary.

3D Models provided by Viewpoint Datalabs International, Inc.

Figure 1.2

The human skull is not round. It's not even elliptical—it's egg-shaped.

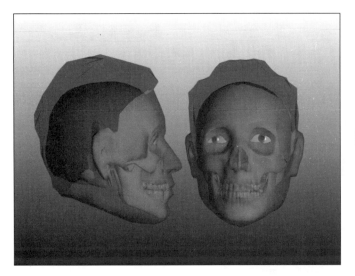

Figure 1.3

The contour shape of the skull shapes the head and the facial features because of the relative lack of flesh on the head.

Spine

The spine is made up of twenty-four vertebrae divided into three groups: the *cervical* (neck) with seven vertebrae, including the atlas and axis; the *thoracic* (upper back) with twelve vertebrae; and the *lumbar* (lower back) with five vertebrae. Between each pair of vertebrae are cartilage-like discs that cushion the interaction between the vertebrae and provide a shock-absorber effect for the entire spine.

The spine is the primary support column for the entire body; all other bones are connected directly or indirectly to the spine. It also protects the spinal cord, which could be described as the "informa-

tion superhighway" of the nervous system. The spinal cord runs through a channel called the *vertebral arch* at the rear of each of the vertebral bodies.

The spine is connected to the skull via the first and second vertebrae. As shown in Figure 1.4, the first vertebra is called the *atlas* because, like the mythical figure who shoulders the world, it holds up the head. It also allows rocking motion from side to side and front to back. The second vertebra is called the *axis*; it connects with the first vertebra. Together, the *atlas* and the *axis* provide the swivel motion of the head.

For 3D artists, it's most important to remember two things. First, the spine is not

When creating your 3D head, you'll find that it's easier to create an accurate face from the side than from the front. Defects in structure or placement are more evident in frontal view. But if your work requires you to create accurate 3D portraits of real people, try to obtain as many views as possible from which to work. (Better yet, have them digitized!)

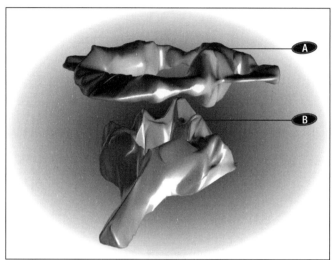

Figure 1.4

The first two cervical vertebrae, the atlas and axis, interconnect to allow head movement. The bony protrusion at the back of the axis fits into the opening in the atlas to help locate the head and keep it attached.

A Atlas
B Axis

3D Models provided by Viewpoint Datalabs International, Inc.

straight. As shown in Figure 1.5, it has four curves: the rearward curves in the spine create the chest and pelvic cavities, while the forward curves help with balance.

Second, the spine is flexible all along its length; one of the key areas where 3D character animation fails is in not providing enough flexibility along the length of the spine.

Cervical Vertebrae

The *cervical vertebrae* are the smallest and most flexible of all the spinal vertebrae. They can move backward, forward, and from side to side. The cervical vertebrae begin at the base of the skull with the atlas and axis and include the vertebrae down to the seventh cervical protrusion. (That's that little bump on your back where the neck ends and the upper back begins.)

Thoracic Vertebrae

The *thoracic vertebrae* include the 12 vertebrae in the upper-back region. The

thoracic vertebrae are capable of all the same movements as the cervical vertebrae, but only to a much smaller degree. Each of the *thoracic vertebrae* has a rib attached to it, which limits motion substantially. However, there is still some movement; you cannot ignore the thoracic area and expect to reproduce normal human motion.

Lumbar Vertebrae

The *lumbar vertebrae* are the vertebrae of the lower back. Because they are the largest and carry the most weight from the upper body, these are frequently the vertebrae that are damaged when someone says "Oh, my aching back!" The lumbar vertebrae allow the most forward movement of any in the spine, but allow no rotating motion and very little other motion.

At the base of the lumbar vertebrae are the sacrum and coccyx, or the "tailbone." They are fused and form the back of the pelvis.

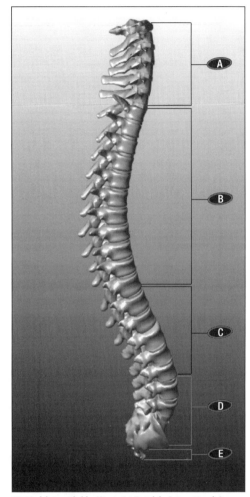

3D Models provided by Viewpoint Datalabs International, Inc.

Figure 1.5

The spinal column consists of the cervical, thoracic, and lumbar vertebrae. With four separate curves, it is far from being straight.

A Cervical Vertebrae

B Thoracic Vertebrae

C Lumbar Vertebrae

D Sacrum Vertebrae

E Coccyx Vertebra

These are the vestigial remains that connect us to our ape relatives.

Pelvis

The pelvis is a relatively large structure formed by the fusion of the hip bones, the sacrum, and the coccyx, as shown in Figure 1.6.

The male and female pelvis are very different. The male's pelvis is narrow and shallow, while the female's is wider and deeper with a larger central passage to allow childbirth. The side plates of the pelvis protect the inner organs, while the lower structures give the body a place to sit. The spine transfers all of the upper-body weight onto the pelvis. It's then

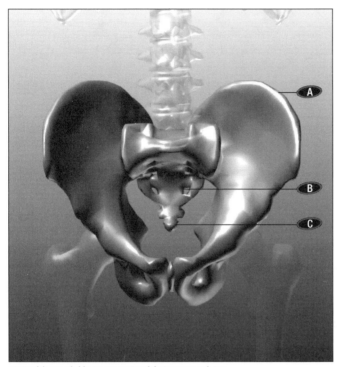

Figure 1.6

The pelvis is made up of the hip bones, the sacrum, and the coccyx.

A Hip bone

B Sacrum

C Coccyx

3D Models provided by Viewpoint Datalabs International, Inc.

transferred to one or both femurs (thigh bones), depending on the stance.

The pelvis is comparatively large in proportion to the rest of the skeleton. Yet, for all its size, there are few points where it shows on the body surface. The most conspicuous place where the pelvis points show is at the hips, especially on a slim-figured person. If you are modeling a very obese person, then the pelvis points will be pretty much covered.

Femurs

The femurs are the largest bones in the body. The top end of the femur includes two projections called *trochanters*, and a ball and neck that are attached at an angle to the main shaft. The ball sits in a cup-like surface on the pelvis, creating the ball-and-socket joint. See Figure 1.7.

The larger of the two trochanters, which sits at the root of the femur's neck, can

In order to locate the top of a person's pelvis, look for the navel. Even on the most obese person, it's virtually always on the same line as the top of the pelvis.

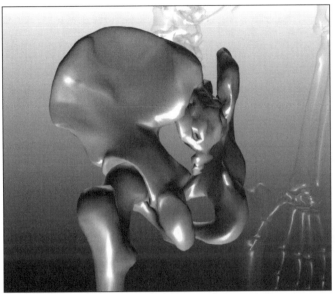

Figure 1.7

The femur and pelvis come together to form a ball-and-socket joint at the hip. The trochanters are the projections from the femur.

easily be felt at the surface of the hip. On the male body, the width between the right and left trochanters is the widest part of the hip. On the female, it is lower because of fat deposits, sometimes called "those dreaded saddlebags."

Because of the angle at which the head and neck are located on the shaft, the femurs are angled inward toward the knees, as shown in Figure 1.8. A common mistake of 3D animators is to bring the femurs straight down from the pelvis, thus giving their 3D models that Robby-the-Robot look.

As the femur approaches the knee, its shaft becomes wider and heavier, forming four rounded protuberances called the *condyles* and *epicondyles*. This end of the femur is thus much larger than the hip end, and with the tibia, it forms the largest joint in the body: the knee as shown in Figure 1.9. Remember that the knee joints support all

of the upper-body weight through the femurs. The knee joints each have a little shock-absorber pad filled with fluid called the *meniscus*. This lets the knee give a little with the added weight, and this give should be considered when animating a 3D model.

Bones of the Feet

Another area of the body that needs additional attention from 3D modelers is the foot. No, a rigid box won't work—not even for that robot! The feet are a flexible and complex part of human anatomy. When they aren't constructed right or move improperly, it really shows. The foot and ankle have less movement than the hand and wrist, but are otherwise quite similar in construction. As shown in Figure 1.10, three groups of bones make up the foot: the *tarsals*, the *metatarsals*, and the *phalanges*.

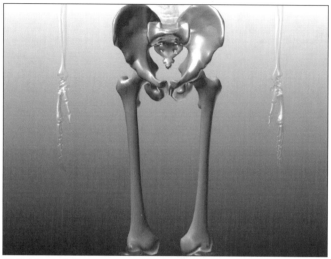

3D Models provided by Viewpoint Datalabs International, Inc.

Figure 1.8

As the femurs come
down from the pelvis,
they are angled toward
the knee.

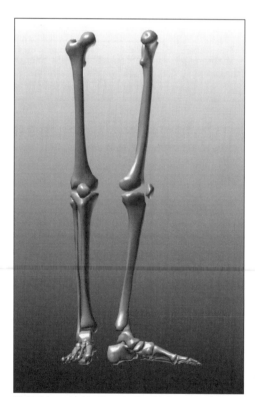

3D Models provided by Viewpoint Datalabs International, Inc.

Figure 1.9

The femur and the tibia form the knee
joint, the largest joint in the body.

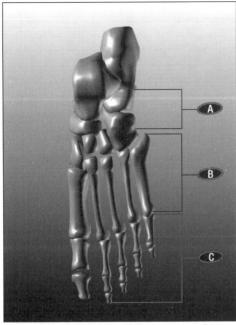

3D Models provided by Viewpoint Datalabs International, Inc.

Figure 1.10

The foot consists of the tarsals, the metatarsals, and the phalanges.

A Tarsals

B Metatarsals

C Phalanges

Tarsal Bones

The *tarsal bones* are the seven irregularly shaped bones of the ankle. They interlock to form both a movement system and a support system for the foot. The most obvious ankle movements include rocking forward and back, and lifting and pointing the toes. The ankle also bends inward and outward to a lesser degree, and the foot turns to point the toes in or out. All of these movements must be allowed to create an accurate 3D foot model.

Metatarsal Bones

There are five *metatarsal bones* in each foot. They run parallel to each other and converge slightly toward the heel. Except for the metatarsal of the big toe, all of the metatarsals are approximately the same size. The metatarsal of the big toe is much shorter.

The metatarsals join with the ankle at the back and the toes on the front, as shown in Figure 1.11. The fifth metatarsal on the outside of the foot is horizontal to the ground plane. Metatarsals four through one are positioned higher in the foot with the first metatarsal being the highest, creating the arch of the foot. The heads of the metatarsals compose the ball of the foot.

Phalanges

There are fourteen *phalanges* distributed three to each toe, with the exception of the big toe, which has two. The toes have less flexibility than the fingers certainly, but when a person is on tiptoes, the toes do spread against the floor.

Take your shoes and socks off and look at your feet. You'll notice that the toes

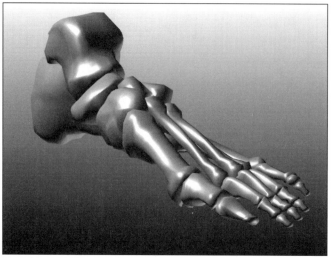

Figure 1.11

The metatarsals are attached to the ankle at the back of the foot and attached to the toes at the front. This is a view from the side of the foot.

3D Models provided by Viewpoint Datalabs International, Inc.

are much shorter than the rest of the foot. (By comparison, the fingers are a much greater percentage of the hand's length.) The foot must carry more weight and therefore has more shock absorption in the long metatarsals. The toes, although somewhat flexible, don't have the flexibility of fingers. (Otherwise, we could climb vines and type on computer keyboards with our feet!)

Viewed from the top, the toes attach to the foot on a curve, making the fifth toe, the little one, shorter and located back approximately one-fourth the length of the

entire foot. On some people, however, it may be as far as one-third the length of the foot back from the rest, while on others it may be less.

Now look at your feet in a mirror; notice that they don't stick straight out from your legs—they normally turn out slightly. Walk around a bit. Your feet are still turned out slightly. In addition, there is a slight outward bend at the ankle that compensates for the angle at which the leg leaves the hip joint. This lets the bottom of the foot rest flat on the floor, as shown in Figure 1.12.

TIP

Be accurate when constructing the skin and flesh of the foot. If you curl the toes, the fleshy pad and the skin of the arch wrinkle, but the skin of the heel always remains smooth.

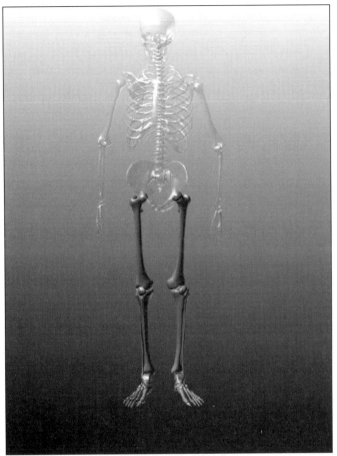

3D Models provided by Viewpoint Datalabs International, Inc.

Figure 1.12

Contrary to popular opinion, legs aren't straight. The femurs leave the hip joint at an angle, and the ankle joint must compensate to allow the foot to be flat on the floor.

Shoulder

Usually people think of the shoulder as part of the torso, but in reality, the shoulder is a key element of the body *separate* from the torso itself. The shoulder is made up of the *scapula* (shoulder blade) and the *clavicle* (collarbone), as shown in Figure 1.13.

The only stationary part of the shoulder is the end of the clavicle, which is attached by ligaments to the *sternum* (breastbone). The rest of the shoulder is very mobile.

Clavicle

The clavicles lie across the front of the upper torso from the top of the sternum to the top of the shoulder. Usually the clavicles slant downward slightly toward the sternum as shown in Figure 1.14, but not always.

The ends of the clavicles at the sternum are usually separated by about 1 inch. This forms the "pit" of the neck. The clavicles are attached to the sternum by ligaments, allowing limited flexibility. At the other end, they attach to the *acromion process* of

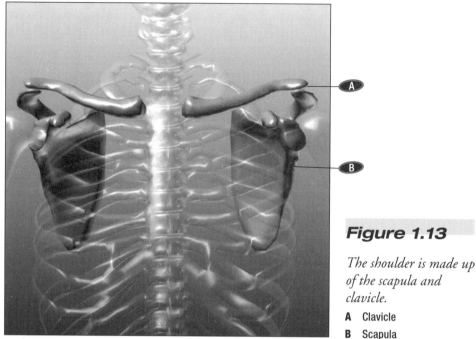

Figure 1.13

The shoulder is made up of the scapula and clavicle.

A Clavicle
B Scapula

3D Models provided by Viewpoint Datalabs International, Inc.

the scapula. This gives lateral movement to the arm. The ball-and-socket joint formed by the shoulder and upper arm allows the arm great range of motion.

Scapula

The scapulas usually lie between the second and sixth or seventh rib on each side of the back. They will be about as long vertically as the sternum is in front.

The scapula provides a socket for the head of the *humerus* (the upper arm bone) and when the body is standing with the arms down to the side, the scapulas lie flat against the back. As the arms are pulled forward, as when the shoulders are rolled forward for a chest x-ray, the scapulas are pulled around to the side of the back ribs. (Now you understand why they put you

in that position for a chest x-ray; to get your scapulas out of the way.)

When the arm is swung out to the side, the scapula swings into an outward position as well, gliding and wheeling about the ribs, as shown in Figure 1.15. Consequently, when a person's torso is moving, say during one of those really wild dances of the 60s or 70s, the scapulas are moving wildly as well.

Even though the scapula moves when the arm moves, it does not move at the same time and the same speed. When the arm is higher than its horizontal plane, the arm motion diminishes, and the wheeling of the scapula starts to help the arm continue its upward movement.

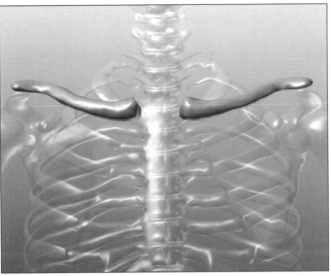

3D Models provided by Viewpoint Datalabs International, Inc.

Figure 1.14

The clavicles usually slant slightly downward toward the sternum.

3D Models provided by Viewpoint Datalabs International, Inc.

Figure 1.15

The scapula wheels and glides about the ribs as the arm is moved.

Bones of the Hand

The hand and wrist consist of twenty-seven bones, as shown in Figure 1.16. In the wrist are eight irregularly shaped bones called the *carpal* bones. These are analogous to the tarsal bones in the foot. The palm of the hand is made up of five long,

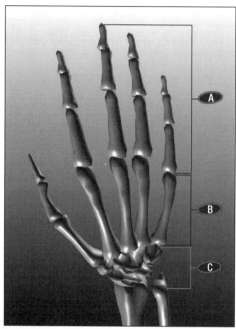

Figure 1.16

The wrist and hand are comprised of the carpals, metacarpals, and phalanges.

A Phalanges

B Metacarpal

C Carpals

slender bones with rounded ends called *metacarpals*, which are analogous to the metatarsals in the foot. Last but not least, the fingers and thumb are made up of fourteen short bones with the ends squared off called *phalanges*, again analogous to the phalanges in the foot.

Carpal Bones

The *carpal bones* are clustered in the wrist and fit like a jigsaw puzzle with each other, with the metacarpals on their lower ends and the *radius* and *ulna* (bones of the forearm) on their upper ends. The joint with the *most* mobility is at the base of the thumb. This includes the first metacarpal and the *navicular bone* in the wrist. There is also some mobility at the base of the fifth metacarpal (the pinky finger) and the

hamate bone in the wrist. The rest of the wrist bones have little or no movement with the hand bones.

Metacarpal Bones

The *metacarpal bones* make up the palm area of the hand. The four metacarpals directly under the four fingers of the hand cannot be separated or moved from each other. Only the first metacarpal under the thumb can be moved separately.

Phalanges

The *phalanges* make up the fingers. There are three bones in each finger and two in the thumb. Notice that each bone in the fingers is a little smaller and more tapered toward the fingertip. The shapes of these bones influence the shape of the fingers.

Remember always: there are no straight lines on the body. Every part of the body has some curve, some arch to it. For example, the knuckles in the fist form two curves.

The phalanges have no side-to-side movement—well, not intentionally, anyway. However, the joints between the metacarpals in the palm and the first phalanges in the fingers do have some side-to-side movement over the rounded edges of the metacarpals.

The squared ends of the phalanges show as knuckles on the back of the fingers when a fist is made. The ends of the metacarpals also show on the back of the hand when a fist is made, but they are a more rounded surface than the knuckles on the fingers.

Make a fist and study your hand. The metacarpal joints are not in a straight line but form an arch across the back of the hand, as shown in Figure 1.17. Notice also that the first two joints at the first and second fingers are more apparent and the third and fourth joints appear to flatten

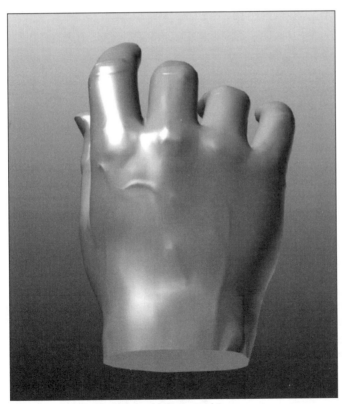

3D Models provided by Viewpoint Datalabs International, Inc.

Figure 1.17

When the hand is in a fist, you can see how the metacarpals and phalanges shape the knuckles differently.

out. (On fleshier hands, they might disappear altogether or form dimples where the joints are.)

Either the first or second knuckle sticks out further than the rest, depending on individual differences. Notice also that when the fist is clenched, the skin on the back of the hands smoothes out and the veins and tendons are compressed.

Each pair of fingers has a web in between that separates them and is slightly squared. The web between the thumb and the first finger is the most noticeable and allows the thumb greater mobility.

Look at the shape of your own hand and notice that, once again, there are no straight lines. The hand viewed from the edge can be seen most simply as a tapered trapezoid. The outer edge of the hand is thinner than the thumb side. If you lay your hand flat and stick your thumb out, you'll notice that it starts almost at the base of the palm.

Put your thumb alongside the rest of your fingers and notice that the thumbnail is in a different plane than the rest of your fingernails. This is because the thumb's first metacarpal bone is attached to the wrist on a plane nearly perpendicular to the other metacarpals in the hand.

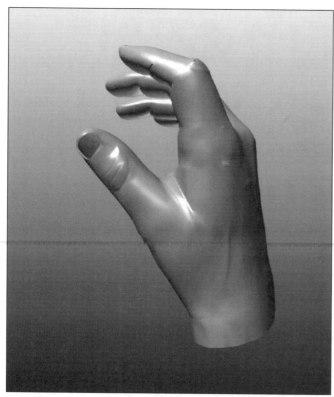

3D Models provided by Viewpoint Datalabs International, Inc.

Figure 1.18

When the hand is held in this position, you can see that the thumb and first finger are in the same plane.

As you hold your hand on its side, resting on the edge of the hand, you can hold your thumb out, creating an "L" shape. Notice that in this position, the thumb and first finger are in the same plane, as shown in Figure 1.18. It is the only finger that lies in the same plane as the thumb.

Lay your hand flat and examine the tapered fingers. The middle, or third, finger is typically longer than the rest. One reason for this is that it has slightly longer phalanges, but it is also set higher on the palm than the other fingers. Thus, the line on the palm at the base of the fingers is, once again, a curve. The first and fourth fingers are about the same size but are shorter than the middle finger by nearly one-half a segment. The smallest finger, or fifth finger, is shorter than the fourth finger by a full segment.

Straighten your hand again and lay the fingers side by side. Notice that your fingers lie snugly against one another because the knuckles are staggered. (What great design!) This results from the curve of the palm and the different lengths of the fingers. See Figure 1.19.

The middle finger is not only the longest but also the straightest and largest of the fingers. The other fingers taper toward it, making the hand more oval in shape and

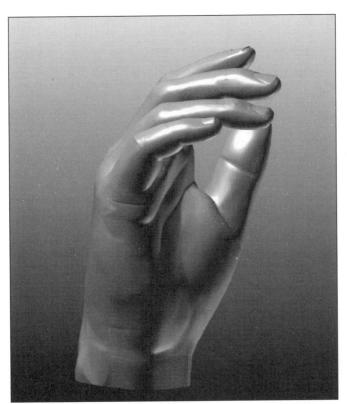

3D Models provided by Viewpoint Datalabs International, Inc.

Figure 1.19

Notice the relationship between the fingers and the curve of the hand.

less rectangular. The fingers also bend slightly toward the palm. Try to hold your fingers out straight and note that it is uncomfortable to hold it for long.

The palm consists of four major fleshy pads. The first is at the base of the thumb. This ball-shaped pad is the most powerful part of the thumb. Next are the little pads that lie at the base of the fingers. The last two are inside the palm and heel of the palm at the wrist below the fourth and fifth fingers. These last two are the flattest; when you bring the thumb together with the fin-

gers on one hand, you'll notice that these pads are mostly obscured by the other two.

The lines on the palm do more than make it amusing to go to a palm reader. They also allow your hand to bend naturally, as shown in Figure 1.20.

Look at your own hand; bend your fingers open and closed. The fat pads contract, bunch up, and fold over onto themselves. Notice the lines at your wrists at the base of the palm. The skin folds up onto itself to allow movement there as well.

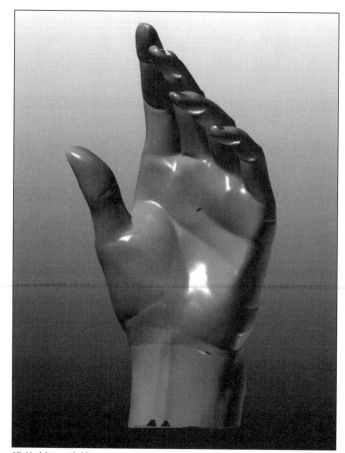

3D Models provided by Viewpoint Datalabs International, Inc.

Figure 1.20

The lines on the palm side of the hand allow the hand to be flexible.

TIP *Movement constraints depend in large part on the presumed age, sex, health, and so forth of the subject, so be sure to consider who or what you are modeling when setting up your animation constraints.*

Body Joints

Bones are connected to each other by joints to make the body mobile and flexible. One of the most common mistakes made by 3D modelers is in not making the body flexible enough to allow lifelike movement. If the back is locked in a straight position or only bends in the diaphragm area, no matter how you try, smooth, flexible movement is impossible. Yet if you give *too* much flexibility in the joints, you'll again have unnatural movement, such as the knees bending the wrong way.

The three basic categories of joints are *immovable, slightly movable,* and *freely movable.*

Immovable Joints

Immovable joints, like the skull and breastbones, protect vital organs such as the brain and heart.

Slightly Movable Joints

Slightly movable joints, like the discs of cartilage between the vertebrae, are vital to allowing the bend and arch of the spine. Including this flexibility in a 3D model is important to produce more fluid movement.

Freely Movable Joints

Freely movable joints include a number of types that account for most of the mobility in the body. You should understand the different types of joints, but more importantly, you should know where each type of joint is found and its limitations.

- *Sliding joints,* as in the wrists and ankles, are held in place by the surrounding ligaments, as shown in Figure 1.21.

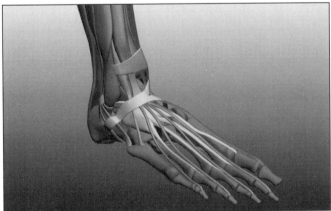

3D Models provided by Viewpoint Datalabs International, Inc.

Figure 1.21

The ankle joint is an example of a sliding joint.

- *Hinge joints,* found in the elbows and knees, work like the hinges of a door, as shown in Figure 1.22. They bend on one axis only and do not rotate. The *patella* (kneecap) itself is a *floating* or *sesamoid* bone; as the knee bends, it slides up and creates a flat surface at the joint.

- *Saddle joints,* found in the thumbs where they connect to the wrist, allow free movement so that we can grasp and hold things with our hands. See Figure 1.23.

- *Pivot joints* are two bones moving within a ring, such as in the elbow. See Figure 1.24.

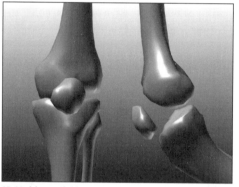

Figure 1.22

The knee joint is an example of a hinge joint.

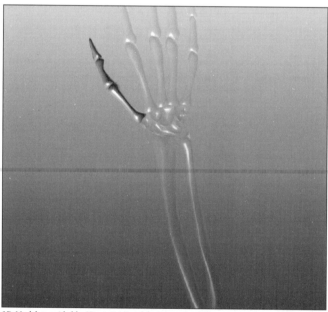

Figure 1.23

The thumb has a saddle joint where it connects to the wrist.

Character Animation with 3D Studio MAX

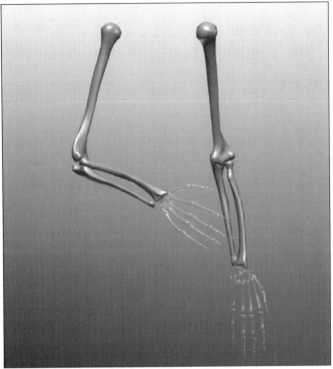

3D Models provided by Viewpoint Datalabs International, Inc.

Figure 1.24

A pivot joint is shown in this illustration of an elbow.

- *Ball-and-socket joints,* found in the hips and shoulders, have the most movement, as shown in Figure 1.25. The ball sits in a cup-like socket and rotates.

- *Condyloid joints* are just like ball-and-socket joints, except that they don't permit rotation, as shown in Figure 1.26. They are found in the first row of

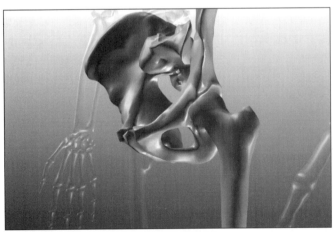

3D Models provided by Viewpoint Datalabs International, Inc.

Figure 1.25

The hip is shown here with a ball-and-socket joint. The shoulder has the same type of joint.

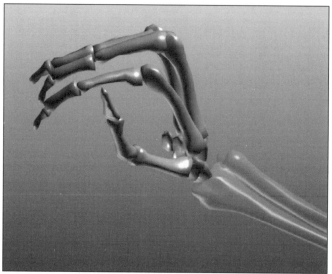

Figure 1.26

Condyloid joints are shown here in the knuckles where the hand attaches to the fingers.

knuckles (the metacarpal-phalangeal joints) on the hand.

- *Ellipsoid joints* are a modified ball-socket in which the connecting surfaces are elliptical rather than spherical, such as in the wrist. There is not as much rotation as with a ball-and-socket joint.

The joints all have specific limitations. In order for your 3D model to have a normal range of motion, you must set limits or constraints on the joints. Each joint must be set up properly according to the sex and condition of the subject.

Body Form

The first step in creating realistic human form and movement is to understand how the body is shaped. Any artist who has tried to draw or sculpt a lifelike human form

has learned that the proportions of the body are very important. The correct proportions will keep your 3D model from looking like an "ape boy." We don't want any knuckle-draggers here—unless that's what your boss or client wants.

Understanding how the body is measured is critical. Generally, the human form is measured in head-lengths (HL). The average adult human is 7 1/2 to 8 HL tall. Therefore, the model's head size should always determine the length of the body. However, this can change with race, age, or physical deformity. The relationship between age and proportion is shown in the table in Figure 1.27.

Some Observations on the Human Form

The differences between the sexes must be considered when creating a 3D model.

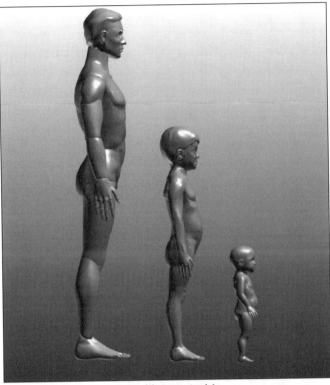

3D Models provided by Viewpoint Datalabs International, Inc.

Figure 1.27

The chart shows human proportions from infant to adult.

Other than the more apparent sex-linked differences, men usually are taller, have wider shoulders and narrower hips, and tend to have more body muscle and less body fat. Women tend to be smaller in stature than men, with wider hips and narrower shoulders. In general, women have a smoother, rounder appearance than men. As with any rule, of course, there are exceptions. Examine Figure 1.28 to see the more subtle differences.

Here are some simple measurements to remember:

- The male form usually has wider shoulders: two head-*lengths* for the male, compared to two head-*widths* for the female.

- The male has narrower hips; two head-widths, compared to the female's two-and-one-half head-widths.

- If you want to make the female figure shorter, typically the thighs will be reduced in length (up to one-half head-length), as well as the upper arm (up to one-third head-length).

- The elbow is usually just above the waist. (Remember that ape-boy look!)

- The wrist is at the crotch level.

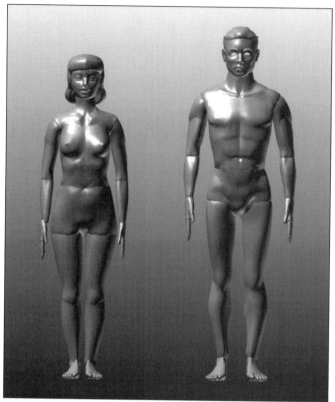

Figure 1.28

Male and female figures have different proportions that must be taken into account when creating their 3D counterparts.

- The head and torso are usually one-half the body length.

- The hand in its longest dimension is the same length as the distance from chin to mid-forehead.

- The forearm from inside the elbow to the wrist is the same length as the foot.

- The head is usually five eye-widths wide.

Muscles

The muscles are intertwined about the body, encompassing the skeleton. They are the driving force that moves the body. Each muscle is made up of elastic fibers that contract and relax in response to nerve impulses. Their ends are attached to bones with tough ligaments.

Different muscles have different purposes. *Prime mover muscles* have a specific movement. *Fixation muscles* stabilize the prime movers, and *synergist muscles* steady joints as the other muscles are brought into play. When all these muscles are working together properly, we call this *body tone*.

When a muscle contracts, its deformation can be seen on the body surface. For example, when the bicep muscles pull the lower arm up and bend the elbow, the bicep bulges as it contracts. As the arm straightens, the muscle thins out again and becomes less noticeable. (If you want to see the maximum level of muscle deformation, you can watch a body-building competition.)

Body Shape

Musculature can also determine body shape. If everyone looked like Mr. or Mrs. America, we wouldn't worry about the amount of muscle and fat on our 3D models—they would all look alike. Since most of us don't qualify as perfect specimens (Okay, *you* do!), there are four types of bodies to remember.

Average Body Type

This type has a fairly even distribution of fat, giving a sleek appearance. There is a good proportion of muscle; however, it is not as overly defined or angular as in the muscular type. See Figure 1.29.

Muscular Body Type

This is the Arnold Schwarzenegger of body types, an exaggeration of normal musculature. Some of the features of this type are larger upper body, large thighs, large neck, and excessive muscle definition in the back. Usually this body type cannot lay the arms down at the sides because of the bulging muscles. Remember that this type cannot stand or move like the average type. There must be some compensation for the bulging muscles.

Obese Body Type

Just as the muscular type was a departure from normal in muscle, the obese type is a departure from normal in body fat. It is characterized by a round, voluminous shape. The body weight is centered in the abdomen, and the tissue jiggles with movement. Fat rolls are apparent around the neck and legs, keeping the thighs from coming together. Fat in the chest, torso area, and arms prevents the arms from coming down to the sides. Usually the wrists and ankles are near-normal size. However, they can also be heavy because of disease or water retention.

Very Thin Body Type

This is the Twiggy of body types. (Remember her?) Characterized by a frail appearance, this body type lacks most fat and muscle, leaving only a thinly covered skeletal figure. The thighs on this type don't come together at the crotch. The joints look overly large, as does the pelvis. You'll also notice on this type that the ribs and breastbone are very noticeable.

Facial Muscles

Most body muscles stretch from one bone to another, usually over a joint. When the muscles contract, they pull the two bones together. The facial muscles, on the other hand, are the only muscles in the body that don't follow this rule. The facial muscles

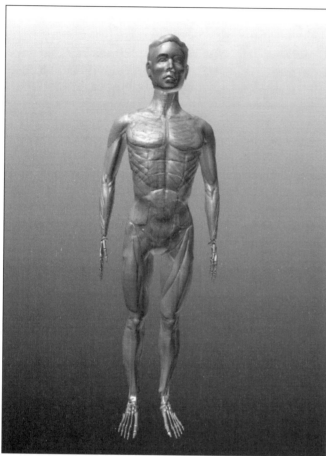

Figure 1.29

This is a basic body shape showing the external muscles. Notice that the skeleton cannot be seen.

have one fixed end attached to a bone of the skull, while the other end is attached to the skin or another muscle that's attached to the skin.

When a facial muscle contracts, it moves skin, not bone. The end of the muscle attached to the skin always pulls closer to the end attached to bone. Often when the skin is pulled back, bulges and wrinkles appear as the skin folds onto itself.

The facial muscles all work together to form expressions, as shown in Figure 1.30. For example, try smiling your biggest, most winning smile without raising your cheeks and squinting your eyes. It's impossible! When you smile, more than just your lips are involved in the movement: your cheeks move up, your eyes close slightly as the lids are squeezed together, and your brows rise. In an all-out laugh, the brows tend to come *down* as the eyes

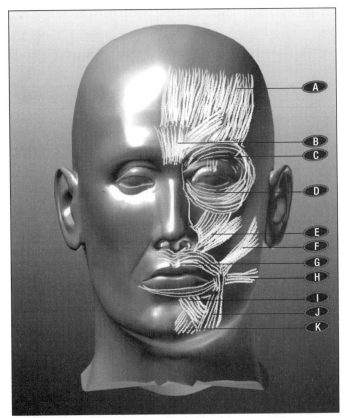

3D Models provided by Viewpoint Datalabs International, Inc.

Figure 1.30

These are the facial muscles most commonly used in expression.

A Frontalis

B Corrugator

C Levator Palpebrae

D Obicularis Oculi

E Levator Labii Superioris

F Zygomatic Major

G Obicularis Oris

H Bisorius Platysma

I Depressor Labii Inferioris

J Trangularis

K Mentalis

are squeezed almost shut. When a heavy or obese person smiles, he or she often has that "jolly look," with round cheeks and eyes squeezed together, because there is more fat in the face to move.

A fat or obese person also usually has dimples and a smooth face free of most wrinkles. A very thin person, on the other hand, has more lines in his or her face when he or she smiles. If wrinkles are already present, they will become more prominent with a smile.

Wrinkles and bulges that appear with facial movement are organic in nature. Although they are not the same in everyone, they do make faces appear much less stiff and mechanical.

Head and Face

Our faces are what make each of us distinct from each other. They are our principle vehicles of communication and what separates us from the billions of other people on this planet. Two people are never exactly alike—even twins usually have some small detectable differences. The reason for this phenomenon is that there is an infinite number of combinations of facial characteristics. Yet everyone is normally limited to two eyes, a nose, and a mouth, all set in a very small area of face.

With all of the differences in faces, there are many more similarities than differences. This lets us give standard dimensions for feature placement on a head. The first way to make feature placement easier is to draw a line down the center of the head from top to bottom. This is your midline.

Next, draw a line horizontally across the head midway between the top of the head and the bottom. This line is where the eyes

will be centered. The next step is to divide the face into thirds from the top of the forehead (where the hairline will be, not at the top of the skull) to the bottom of the chin. The area between the top line and the second line is the forehead area, with the second line being the brow line. The second and third lines include the area from the brow to the base of the nose. The area between the third and fourth lines spans the area from the base of the nose to the chin. See Figure 1.31.

The head is usually the most difficult part of a human to model realistically in 3D. We are so accustomed to seeing heads and

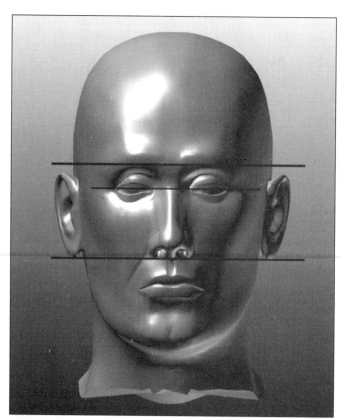

3D Models provided by Viewpoint Datalabs International, Inc.

Figure 1.31

Typically, the features can be divided as shown. The horizontal midline locates the eyes, while the face is divided into thirds.

Character Animation with 3D Studio MAX

faces from the moment we are born that we can detect any irregularities in the look of a modeled head without even understanding what the problem is. Following are some of the most common mistakes made when modeling a head in clay or in 3D:

- Not enough forehead. Remember the eyes should be in the vertical center of the face.

- The ears are too high or too low. The ears should lie midway between the front of the face and the back of the head between the top of the eye and the bottom of the nose.

- The eyes are in a straight line. Remember, everything on the body has a curve and there are no straight lines or flat planes on the human form. The outer corners of the eyes should be higher than the inner corners.

- Facial features are from different ages. All of the features should be from the same age and sex person. A grown woman would look pretty strange with a two-year-old's nose and an eighty-year-old's eyes. Well, so would your 3D model!

- The mouth is too small or too large. The mouth should never extend beyond an imaginary line drawn straight down from the centers of the eyes.

- The nose is too long or too short. There is only one eye-length between the inside corner of the eye to the top of the side nostril on the nose.

- The eyeball protrudes too far forward on the face. The eyeball is the point furthest back on a face. All other features are built forward from the eye.

Look at Figure 1.32 to see where the features should be.

Eyes and Brows

Depending on what source you consult, you will find that there are twenty-six

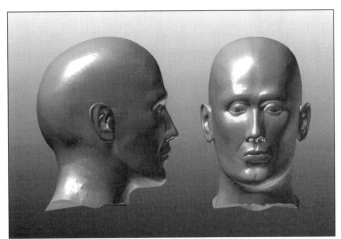

3D Models provided by Viewpoint Datalabs International, Inc.

Figure 1.32

The head from the front and side illustrates where facial features should be.

muscles (more or less) in the face used for expression. Most are attached to the eyes, brows, or mouth. It's obvious that since this is where the most subtle muscle control occurs, these areas are the most expressive areas of the face.

The eyes are also the most interesting part of the face. You can tell how a person is thinking or feeling by the many expressive movements of the eyes. A single look can speak a thousand words, like the one your mother gave you when you flushed the car keys down the toilet. (I still get looks like that, even years later!) Even when the eyes are the only part of a face visible, feelings of happiness, fear, sadness, or anger are easily detectable.

The eyes don't lie in a straight line on the face; the inside corners of the eyes are on the horizontal midline between the top of the head and the chin. The outside corner of the eyes lie a little above the midline.

Also, there are no flat surfaces on the face—the eye does not sit flatly on the surface. Rather, the surface surrounds the eye and forms to its shape.

The eyes are one eye-length apart, and the vertical opening of a normally opened eye is usually one-half its length. The iris width is approximately one-third of the total eye width. Eyes also are asymmetrical; the upper and lower lids have their own distinct shape. Moreover, the high point of the upper lid does not line up vertically with the low point of the lower lid. The result is that the eye opening is not just a simple oval. Rather, the upper lid is more arched and appears to come down over the lower lid on the outside corner. Finally, both of the lids are shaped by the round eyeball underneath. Examine Figure 1.33 carefully to see these details.

When a person shuts an eye, the top eyelid seems to do all the work, coming down

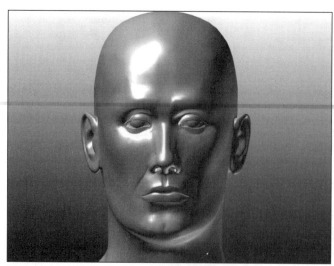

3D Models provided by Viewpoint Datalabs International, Inc.

Figure 1.33

The eye and lids are not simple shapes. They are asymmetrical and rather difficult to model properly.

over the eye and resting on the lash line of the lid below. However, the top lid cannot move without some movement of the bottom lid, even if the lower-lid movement is minute. In fact, the lower lid has a much smaller range of movement than the upper. In resting or normal position, the lower lid usually just touches the lower edge of the iris. If a person is crying or laughing, the squinting motion raises the lower lids up much higher to cover part of the pupil from below. The lower lid almost never moves *below* its normal position.

To understand how the upper eyelid moves, the relationship between the upper lid and the iris is important to remember. The upper lid in the normal position is just above the pupil. If the upper lid touches the pupil at all, the whole look of the eye changes from alert to, well, anything that's not. The normal position of the upper lid can be anywhere from the top of the iris to just above the pupil. However, each eye has its own normal lid position and always returns to it, as shown in Figures 1.34a through 1.34c.

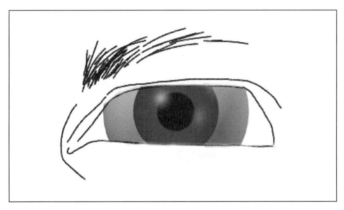

Figure 1.34

The positions of the eyelid for different moods.

a.

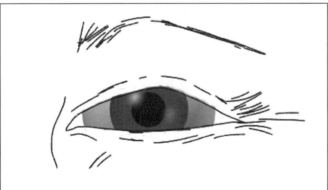

b.

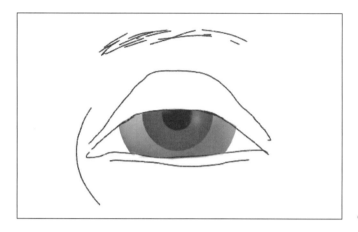

c.

When the eye is not moving or focused correctly, it is immediately noticeable. When someone looks right at you and then diverts his or her eyes even slightly, you recognize that the eyes are no longer focused on you. When looking at an object, the irises of both eyes turn inward until they are directed at the object. The pupil is always centered in the iris. The further the object is from the eyes, the less the irises must turn inward to focus. An unfocused gaze or that glazed look your teenager gets when you ask them, well, almost anything is demonstrated with both irises looking straight ahead. See Figure 1.35 for examples of different eye foci.

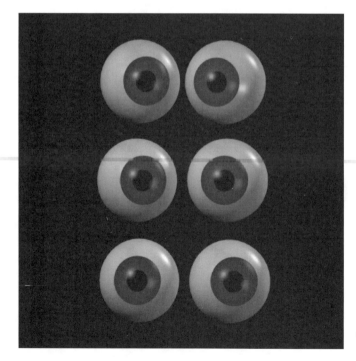

Figure 1.35

Illustrations show eye focus up close, far away, and a blank stare.

The eyebrow is a band of short hairs that grow in an arch above the eye and follow the edge of the skull's orbit. It is also a very expressive facial feature. Figure 1.36 illustrates where typical eyebrows are placed, but the variety of types, sizes, and arches produces endless possibilities.

The inside one-third of the brow is the area where most action occurs and where there is the most subtle muscle control. In a neutral position, this part of the brow is usually even or slightly lower than the rest of the brow. (I can't be responsible for those ladies who draw their brows on in an interesting manner.) It never naturally grows in an upward sweep, so any upward movement of the inner portion of the brow can easily be detected as an expression of distress.

The main part of the eyebrow always rests somewhere above the skinfold that marks the top of the upper lid. If the muscles

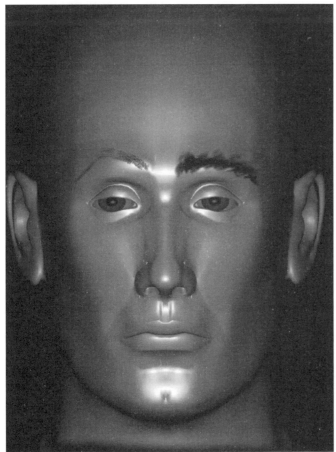

3D Models provided by Viewpoint Datalabs International, Inc.

Figure 1.36

There are a number of differences between male and female eyebrows.

pull the inner brow down over this point, a frown appears, creating an angry or disturbed look, as shown in Figure 1.37.

The arch of the brow usually starts about two-thirds of the way from the inner end. This is also where the face begins to curve to the side plane.

Brow shapes depend on sex and age. The male brow tends to be heavier and closer to the eye, while the female brow tends to be thinner and higher. In both, the eyebrow follows the orbital ridge of the skull. The male brow usually appears to sit on the downslope of the ridge, while the female brow appears to sit on the ridge's

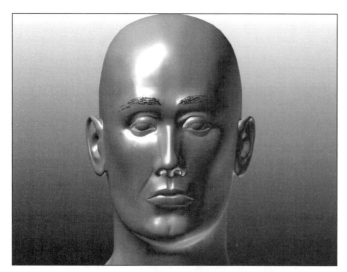

a.

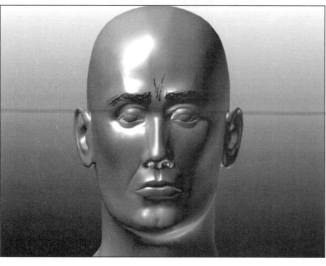

b.

Figure 1.37

Illustration of eyebrow at rest and frown.

upslope. The male eyebrow also tends to stick out more from the face than the female's, giving it a bushier appearance. Finally, brows change as we age, becoming thinner and less prominent on the face.

Mouth

The mouth encompasses twelve muscles, but only seven are involved in expression. These muscles let us move our mouths in a wide variety of ways. Take a few minutes to stand in front of your mirror and move your mouth, watching only your mouth. Pretty scary, huh? The mouth is attached to the skull only indirectly, so it moves quite freely. See Figure 1.38 for an illustration of the muscles of the mouth.

There is one eye-length between the base of the nose and the bottom of the lower lip. Whether the mouth is in resting position or smiling, this measurement

remains the same, because a smile—even open-mouthed—shortens the distance between the upper lip and the base of the nose. This rule does not apply if an uproarious laugh or yell is expressed with the jaw forced open.

The lips which define the mouth also come in many different shapes and determine much of the look of the mouth. The corners of the mouth are interesting because many facial muscles converge at this point, creating a little bulge and sometimes even lending a slight downward appearance to the mouth.

The Neck

The neck is an often misunderstood part of the body. Its most common 3D form seems to be a stem-like appendage that does little more than hold the head off

Figure 1.38

Of the twelve mouth muscles, only seven are used for expression.

A Sneering Muscles
B Smiling Muscle
C Lip Tightener
D Frown Muscle
E Pouting Muscle
F Lower Lip-curl Muscle

3D Models provided by Viewpoint Datalabs International, Inc.

the chest. Looking at the neck from the side, however, notice that the neck tilts forward as it emerges from the shoulders, as shown in Figure 1.39. This tilt is usually more pronounced in a woman than in a man because there is less developed muscle in a woman's neck. This tilt is particularly noticeable in a weightlifter, football player, or anyone with a muscular body. Because the neck tilts forward, the back of the neck is shorter than the front.

From the front, the sides of the neck do not go up into the head in a straight line like a cylinder. Instead, the lines taper up toward the head, as shown in Figure 1.40. This can vary according to the body type and sex. The female neck is usually more slender and graceful than a man's, and a man is more likely to have a pronounced Adam's apple.

From the back, the muscles of the neck attach to the skull in three places: the base

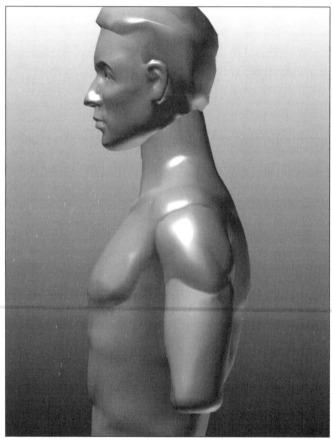

3D Models provided by Viewpoint Datalabs International, Inc.

Figure 1.39

The neck tilts toward the front as it emerges from the shoulders.

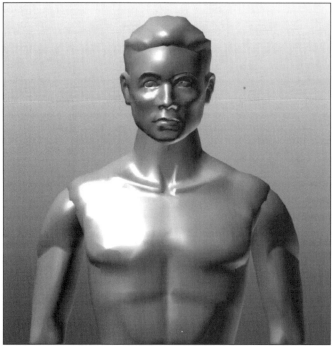

3D Models provided by Viewpoint Datalabs International, Inc.

Figure 1.40

Front view of the neck shows the neck is not a straight cylinder.

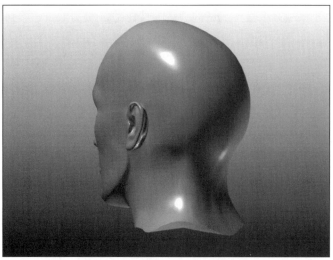

3D Models provided by Viewpoint Datalabs International, Inc.

Figure 1.41

Back view of the neck. You can see the depression down the middle where both sides of the trapezius muscle come together.

of the skull and on the *mastoid* bone behind each ear, as shown in Figure 1.41. On the back of the neck where both *trapezius* muscles attach to the base of the skull, a depression is formed between them from the back of the neck to the seventh cervical vertebra notch.

The two muscles that have the most to do with the look of the neck are the *sterno-mastoid* that rise from the sternum to below and in back of the ears, and the trapezius that we just described in the back view.

Weight and Gravity

The body maintains a delicate balance that enables it to stand or move without falling over. To maintain this equilibrium, an object must keep its center of gravity positioned over its line of support at all times. In an upright human body (or any body walking on two legs), the center of gravity must therefore be positioned over the feet. It is important to note also that the center of gravity is usually somewhat lower in the female because her torso is heavier in the hips than the male. The male has more torso weight in the chest. However, there are exceptions, of course, but I decline to name any particular subject....

A straight line down from the pit of the neck to the floor (or the line of gravity) shows where the feet should be to hold the body upright in a standing position, as shown in Figure 1.42.

If, however, the body is bent to the side at the waist, the feet must move and the head and shoulders would have to shift to the opposite side to maintain balance. In that position, the center of gravity would be shifted to compensate for the shift in body weight, making the line of gravity start somewhere between the shoulders and hips and come straight down to the feet. If the line of gravity is moved beyond the limits for support, the person will fall.

Remember also that the smaller the line of support is, the more finely balanced a model must be. The line of support is the size of the support area on the supporting surface. A ballerina poised on the toes of one foot has an extremely small line of support and is thus much more complicated to balance than a clown with two great big feet on the ground.

Consider also the size of your 3D subject. An obese model is much more difficult to animate and maintain its apparent balance than a normal body type because the larger the person is, the slower he or she must move. Obese people also have a harder time controlling where their weight takes them.

Normally, the body compensates continuously and automatically to maintain its equilibrium. If you shift your body weight to one foot, your torso shifts, raising the hip and lowering the shoulder on the weighted side. The degree of body shift depends on how much of the body weight is shifted to one leg. The more weight borne by the weighted leg, the more the body must tilt to compensate. Although many times a person appears to standing with equal weight on both legs, this is rarely the case. Usually, one leg carries more weight than the other. Examine Figures 1.43a and 1.43b for weight distribution in different poses.

As body movement and direction change the center of gravity, so does influence

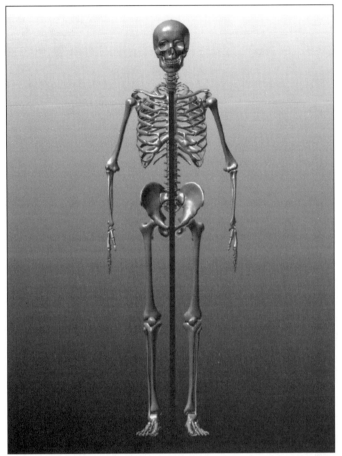

3D Models provided by Viewpoint Datalabs International, Inc.

Figure 1.42

The body is shown here standing upright with the line of gravity from the pit of the neck to the feet.

from outside. A person who has picked up a heavy object has just added its weight to his own body weight and shifted his center of gravity to include it. If the weight is carried in front, the person must compensate for the extra weight by bending backward from the waist. This makes the line of gravity start in between the object and the person and run downward. If the weight is carried on the hip, another set of body movements follow to compensate for the side weight, as shown in Figures 1.44a through d.

Obviously, there are more things to consider when you are modeling a person carrying weight. Is the subject big or small, strong or weak? Is he thin or heavy? All these things affect how the model carries the weight.

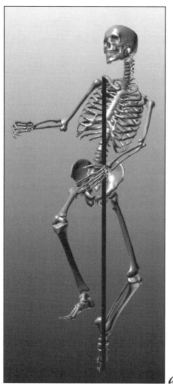 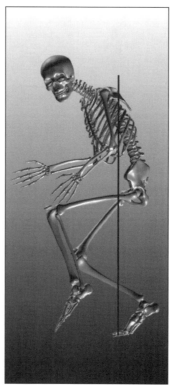

Figure 1.43

Shows how the body weight and line of gravity shifts in different poses.

a. b.

3D Models provided by Viewpoint Datalabs International, Inc.

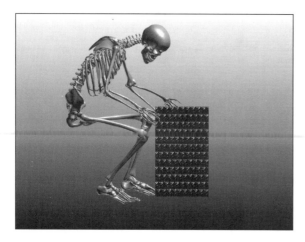

Figure 1.44

Shows how weight shifts as a person picks up weight.

a.

Character Animation with 3D Studio MAX

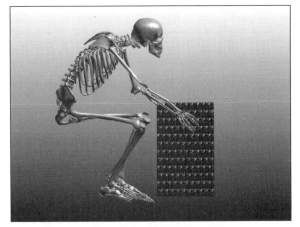

b.

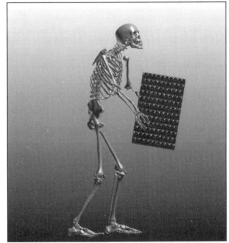

c.

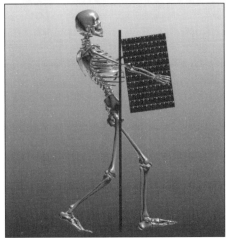

d.

3D Models provided by Viewpoint Datalabs International, Inc.

Next Chapter...

In this chapter, we have covered basic human anatomy, particularly as it applies to 3D modeling and animation. Creating models to approximate a lifelike appearance is extremely difficult, but if you are conscious of what makes a person look real, you can then see when something is wrong *and* how to change it.

In our next chapter, we will take it one more step and see how the human form changes because of age, sex, and race. We'll also see how to modify a human form for that sideshow look. Step right up....

Chapter 2

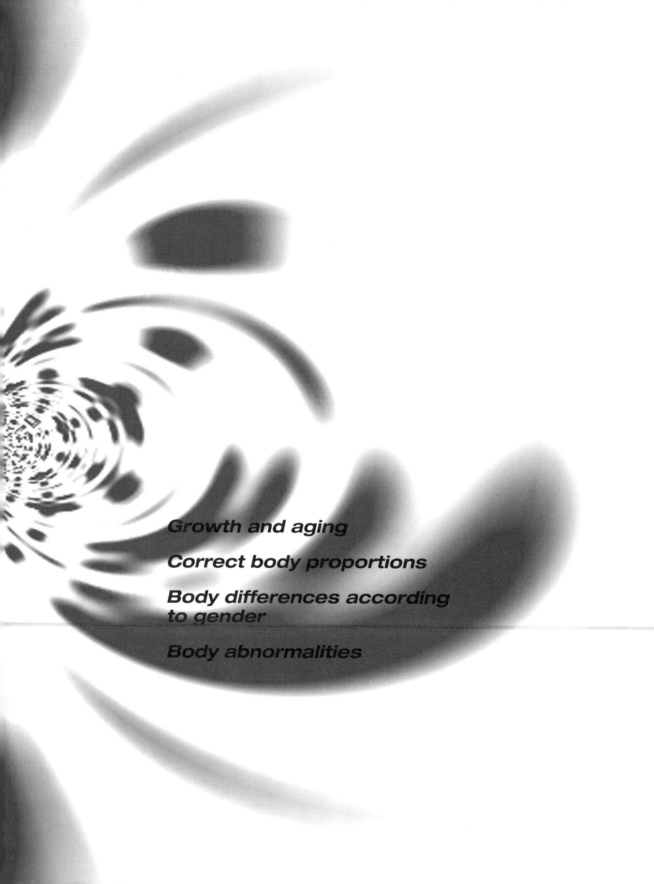

Growth and aging

Correct body proportions

Body differences according
to gender

Body abnormalities

Comparative Human Anatomy

In Chapter 1, we looked at human anatomy and physiology in general, focusing on those areas that are most important to the 3D artist and animator. In this chapter, we'll build on the basic knowledge gained in Chapter 1 to enable you to customize your 3D people to fit special needs. By the end of this chapter, you'll understand the differences that arise through the growth and aging processes, sex-linked differences, changes caused by disease or abnormality, and differences among ethnic groups. "It takes all kinds" really sums up this chapter!

Before you begin the process of creating a 3D human model, you must ask yourself a number of questions about it:

- What body type will the character have?

- Will the character be male, female, or asexual?

- What will be the age of the character: young, old, or in-between?

- What will be the race or ethnic group of the character?

- Does the character have any abnormalities, including deformities, genetic defects, disease processes, or amputations?

These are all things that affect your 3D model. In Chapter 1, I described the differences among physical types (see the section entitled "Body Shape" for a discussion of the different general body types and their proportions). In this chapter, I'll describe and show you how to change the look of your 3D people. Before you can create these distinctions, you must first know what the differences are and second, how to make those differences believable, whether the subject is an Asian man, Caucasian woman, old crone, toddler, or superhero.

Growth and Aging

Most 3D human subjects are from a fairly narrow age range, loosely labeled "adult." This encompasses the rough period between, say, ages 18 and 45. Before this, the growth process accounts for substantial changes from infancy to adulthood. After this period, the aging process takes its toll, reshaping the body in predictable (and sometimes almost whimsical) ways. The very best way to learn the differences among these groups is to *study* people, people of all ages, races, and so on. Sit down with your nephew or grandmother and watch how he or she moves, their proportions, how they sit, stand, walk, and run. Put on those Foster Grants and watch people in the park, walking on icy streets, or hobbling up the steps to a fifth-floor walkup. Following are some things to look for.

The Child and Age Definition

The differences between an infant and an adult are fairly obvious, but the differences from age to age are much more subtle. A six-year-old child and a two-year-old child may not at first seem that different, but there are a number of differences that must be observed when you create your 3D kid.

As you saw in Chapter 1, a child's body is not proportioned the same as an adult. The head is usually much larger in proportion to the rest of the body at birth. As a baby grows, its head size becomes more balanced with the rest of the body, as shown in Figure 2.1.

Body Proportions

The body of a child is also proportioned differently than an adult's. The geometric center of an infant's body is near the navel until approximately age two, while an adult's geometric center is at the pubic bone. By geometric center, I mean the approximate midpoint in height. An adult's legs are thus roughly equal in length to the distance between the pubic bone and top of the head. Since the infant does not use its legs for locomotion or weight carriage, they are a much smaller proportion of its total length.

In the following paragraphs, remember that a child's head changes in size as he or she grows. An infant's head is usually one-half the length of an average adult's head,

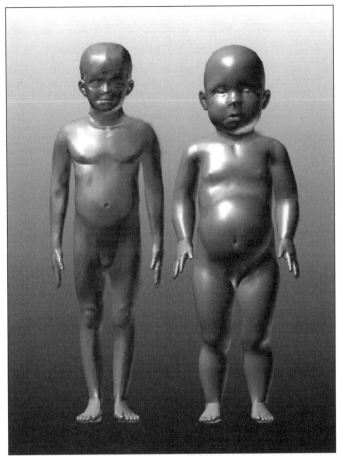

3D Models provided by Viewpoint Datalabs International, Inc.

Figure 2.1

As a child grows, the body-to-head proportions become more balanced.

but by the time a child is six years old, the child's head size has grown to approximately three-fourths the length of an average adult's. A child's proportions are generally described in relation to head-length (HL), but since that head-length is constantly changing, the numbers that follow may occasionally seem odd. See Figure 2.2 for a graphical depiction of this data.

An infant is approximately four head-lengths in length, or one-fourth of an adult's height. Viewed another way, if an average infant could stand, the infant would come up to the knee of an average adult. By age three, the child has grown to 5 HL and stands one-half of an average adult's height, or up to the height of the adult pubic bone. (Of course, a graph of the distribution of heights in the general population follows a typical bell-shaped curve, so there are bound to be exceptions to this rule. For example, some children can be as tall as the adult navel at this age.)

By age six, a child will be 6 HL tall and by age ten will be 6 1/2 HL tall, or three-fourths the size of an average adult. At age ten, the child will typically be as tall as the center of the adult chest, or can be as tall as the adult's nose.

By age 16, the child will stand a full seven heads high and will usually have reached his or her adult height. By age 20, the average person has reached adult height and full stature is attained, as shown in Figure 2.2.

Facial Features

It's easy to mix up facial features from different ages when you are drawing or modeling younger people. When you do, your model suddenly just doesn't look quite right. You may be unable to put your finger on the exact problem, but you *know* there's something wrong. The following is a list of tips to remember while modeling children's heads.

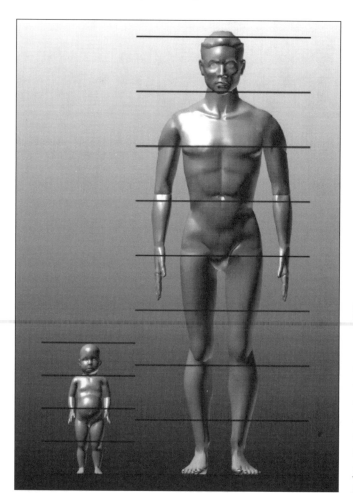

3D Models provided by Viewpoint Datalabs International, Inc.

Figure 2.2

The length or height of a child is not measured in adult head-lengths, but in head-lengths of his or her own age. This makes it easy to determine the correct proportions for a particular age.

- An infant's face is relatively small in proportion with the head. Where the adult eye lies on the horizontal midplane, the child's eye lies just below the midplane.

- An infant's lower jaw is almost horizontal along the lower edge of the skull. As he or she matures, the jaw begins to angle downward, giving the head a longer look, as shown in Figure 2.3.

- Since the infant's jaw is not angled down, the chin is smaller.

- The infant's nose is small and turned up to allow the infant to breathe while nursing. The bridge of the nose is flattened as well.

- The back of an infant's head sticks out further than an adult's from the backplane of the neck, and the neck itself is thinner than an adult's. (So much so that a newborn infant typically does not even have the strength to hold its head up.)

- Because an infant's or child's face is smaller than an adult's in relation to the head, their eyes appear to be further apart than an adult's.

- The iris of a child's eye appears to be larger than an adult's. An infant's iris is actually adult-size at birth, but the eye opening in the face is smaller. Thus, as the child's face grows and the eye openings enlarge, the irises seems to shrink, as shown in Figure 2.4.

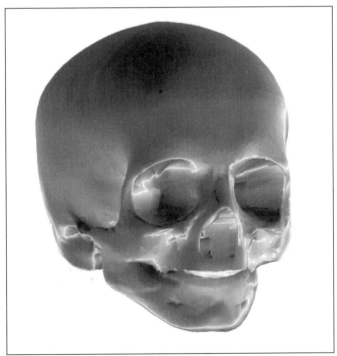

3D Models provided by Viewpoint Datalabs International, Inc.

Figure 2.3

The infant's jaw lies almost in a horizontal plane, along the base of the skull. As the infant ages, the jaw angles downward.

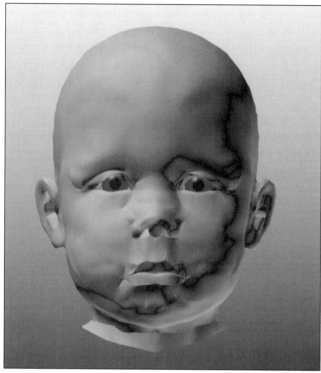

3D Models provided by Viewpoint Datalabs International, Inc.

Figure 2.4

The child's eye appears to have a very large iris because the iris is almost adult size at birth; only the eye opening is smaller.

- A child's eyelashes appear longer than an adult's, but again, this is because of the relative face sizes.

- A child's eyebrows are thinner.

- A child's upper lip has what is called a "milk lip," that is, a small protrusion in the center of the top lip.

- A child's lips appear fuller, more pouty, and have more of an indention at the corners.

- A child's chin is smaller and the cheeks are rounder than an adult's.

Old Age—You Can't Get Around It!

Fortunately or unfortunately, we don't stay the same age forever. Forget what you hear in the beauty ads on TV—the (not so) shocking truth is that we all age, and some much better than others, I fear. It's one thing when age creeps up on *you*, but what do you do as a 3D artist if it's supposed to creep up on your 3D character instead?

The body does treacherous things as it ages. Hair seems to move *to* places where it never appeared before and *from* places where it *was* in abundance. It also turns

TIP *Remember when modeling a child's face, there are no distinct lines or folds. Every expression is subtle and everything is rounded. Add one crease along the side of the mouth or around the eyes and your child will look like an eighty-year-old in a two-year-old's body.*

57

Chapter 2: Comparative Human Anatomy

gray and changes texture. Noses and ears start to appear larger, and spots, blemishes, and wrinkles start to blotch that youthful appearance. Once-toned muscles start to sag and the jawline begins to droop. It's time either to admit old age is upon you or go see your neighborhood cosmetic surgeon. Even if the latter is your choice, the miracles of technology won't make your *inside* any younger. Even though you've had the outside stretched, shrunk, peeled, and patched, the rigors of age are still weakening the inside framework.

Body Shape and Proportions

As humans age, several processes occur. The spine compresses and shortens as the vertebral disks degenerate and thin out. Osteoporosis and other diseases associated with aging can also cause the bones themselves to compress, especially in the vertebrae. The spine then assumes a more pronounced curvature, producing a more hunched appearance, as shown in Figure 2.5.

As the curvature increases with age, the neck appears to sink into the chest. As a result of these processes, a person can expect to lose somewhere between one-half and one full head-length in height. These changes also produce a much more frail appearance.

In addition to the skeletal framework changing, more subtle changes also occur in the human body. The skin becomes thinner, making it much easier to bruise and tear. After years of being in the sun and the elements, blotches often called "liver spots" start to appear. These are small discolorations that appear mostly on the hands, arms, and face. Not only does the skin become thinner, it also loses some of its elasticity and begins to sag.

The result of these changes is that the flesh on an older person does not "fit" the skeleton nearly as well. The flesh tends to hang from the bones, while the skin appears more mottled in appearance. You can seldom use the same skin material on a 3D model of an older subject that you use on a younger one. At the same time, choosing the material well helps to "sell" the illusion of advanced age.

Wrinkles and Other Skin Texturing

The same elements that cause skin spots and sagging also help the skin form noticeable wrinkles in the face, arms, and hands. Wrinkles begin as laugh lines around the eyes and mouth, but with age, they become more permanent and widespread. Other factors can also contribute to skin wrinkling besides sun, the

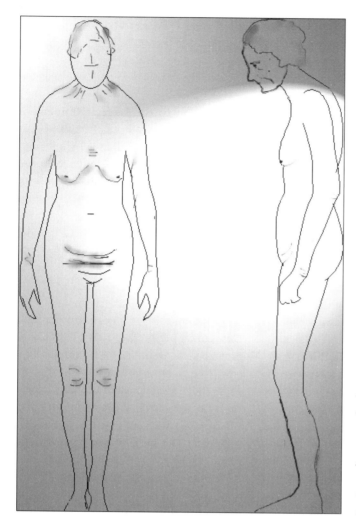

Figure 2.5

With aging, the disks in the spine—and some-times the vertebrae themselves—compress, producing a much more pronounced curvature. Depending on the extent of these processes, a person can lose some-where between one-half and one full head-length in height!

elements, and the natural progression of age. Smoking has also been found to be a factor in early skin wrinkling. Still, the largest single determinant of the degree of skin wrinkling is family genetics. Look at your older relatives and you'll have a pretty good idea what your own future holds—wrinklewise, that is.

Wrinkling is usually marked in the mouth, eye, and forehead areas where expression, and consequently, flexing is greatest. These are the areas where the skin is stretched and relaxed repeatedly as expressions change. Wrinkling does not always have to be represented by large rolls of skin or heavy, deep lines. Some-times it appears on the skin only as delicate hatch marks or crisscross lines. This is most often apparent on skin that isn't pulled and folded onto itself as much with expression changes. Skin on the cheeks is a common area where these hatch marks appear.

Vertical lines that deepen with age also appear around the lips. You've seen them, I'm sure, on little old ladies whose lipstick just doesn't seem to stay within their liplines anymore. Last but not least, the neck often also shows lines and creases with age as the skin loses its elasticity.

Now all this about wrinkling may seem relatively unimportant for 3D modeling. But it should give you some idea of the *look* of a human face as it ages. Moreover, it should also suggest ways to match your 3D characters to the story line of the animation sequence. For example, say the story is about a classic clipper ship captained by an old seafarer. He'd look rather odd with the smooth creamy skin of a computer android or generic 3D human!

Many of the 3D human models available generally seem to be generic, smooth-skinned young people with little character or age in their faces and whose skins literally look like plastic. Look at those people around you and notice the skin textures. How does the beard affect the skin texture? Remember, our skin is neither shiny nor perfectly smooth. You must attempt to re-create these qualities with your 3D character.

The most important thing to notice about real, live humans is the variation in skin coloring. I'm not talking here about racial differences, weathering, or tattoos, but the natural variation in coloring from place to place on the body. Everyone's skin—even an infant's—is composed of many colors and hues. Watch an infant cry and notice how its color changes, even to the point of becoming mottled on occasion. Sun tanning and burning also add to the variation—are you going to reproduce tanlines on your 3D characters? A 3D truck driver, for example, should probably have a darker left arm than right arm from exposure to sun out his rig's driver's-side window.

It just wouldn't look natural for your 3D folks to have a single uniform skin color—even if he or she wears pancake makeup! See Figure 2.6 for examples of different facial skin tones and textures.

The Aging Eye

The eyeball itself sits on a fat pad in the eye socket, but with age, this fat pad diminishes and the muscles around the eye start to sag. As the person loses facial muscle and fat, more and more of the underlying facial skeleton begins to show, and the eyes appear to sink into their sockets. The ridge of the orbit begins to appear, as well as the upper shape of the eyeball. Lines appear around the eyes, along with bags and wrinkles under the eyes, as the skin loses its elasticity, as shown in Figure 2.7.

Many times, eye color changes with age as well. The whites of the eyes appear less white, taking on a slightly more yellow or red tint, depending on age and disease. The iris seems to take on a more transparent quality, except that if cataracts have grown, a cloudy look appears. Old eyes just don't look like young eyes! An Aging Checklist

Figure 2.6

Study these pictures. The color and texture of these faces should give you insights into their personalities.

Here's a checklist of things to look for when creating an old 3D character:

- As described above, the spine is more curved, giving a hunchbacked appearance.

- The neck appears to sink into the chest and becomes more gaunt.

- The head is thrust more forward because of the spinal curvature.

- The hair is thinner than that of a young person even bald. And don't forget that a woman's hair also thins with age.

- The hairline changes—even in older women, you can see what is usually called "male pattern baldness."

- The hair turns white or gray, sometimes with a yellowish tinge.

- The hair texture coarsens.

- The eyebrows become more sparse or scraggly.

- Hair becomes more profuse in the ears and other previously unknown areas.

- Slight depressions may occur at the temples.

- A slight bluish tinge at temples and the inner eye appears where veins show through the thinning skin.

- The skull starts to protrude through the facial flesh as the fat deposits on the face decline. The cheekbones, orbits around the eyes, and the bones of the chin protrude.

- The flesh on the arms and legs tends to loosen and hang down more from the bones.

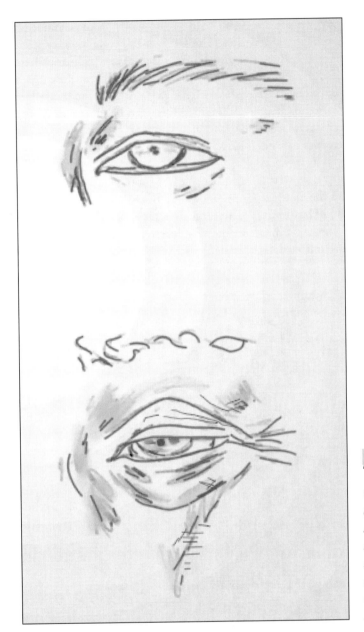

Figure 2.7

Compare the young eye on the top with the aging eye below it. With age, the eyes appear to sink into their sockets, and bags and wrinkles appear as the skin loses its elasticity.

- Some oldsters may appear to become more skeletal, with spindly arms and legs, as the body's fat deposits dwindle.

- The female bosom tends to sag as the pectoral muscles lose tone.

- With the decline of testosterone production in the male, there is a tendency to increase fatty deposits on the chest.

Wouldn't you just rather stay young forever?

The Differences Between the Sexes

The male and female bodies are alike in most gross aspects; that is, both have two arms, legs, and so on. The primary areas of difference lie in alignment and mass. There are other minor differences in skeletal areas such as the pelvis, as well, as mentioned in Chapter 1. As a rule, the female is smaller overall than the male except for at the hips. Her body has more fat covering her skeleton, and thus, her body is less angular and more rounded, as shown in Figure 2.8.

The head of the female is also smoother and rounder. Her brow is much less pronounced than that of the male and there is no prominence above the nose. As a whole a female's features tend to be smaller, although her lips can be fuller. See Figure 2.9 for a comparison of male and female facial features.

In the neck and shoulder area, the female appears much more slender and graceful. This is mostly caused by the shape and size of the shoulders. They are smaller in the female, and the clavicles tend to angle downward more toward the sternum, mak-

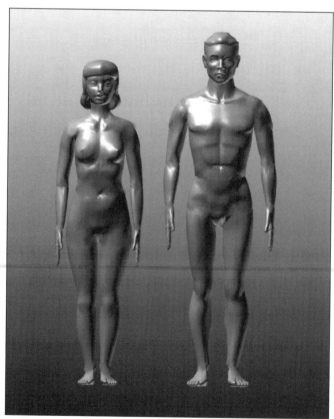

3D Models provided by Viewpoint Datalabs International, Inc.

Figure 2.8

The male is normally somewhat larger than the female and tends to have wider shoulders and narrower hips.

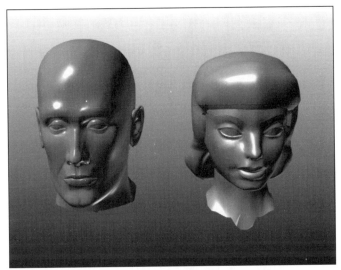

3D Models provided by Viewpoint Datalabs International, Inc.

Figure 2.9

The female face is smoother and rounder than the male, with additional subtle differences.

ing the shoulders look more rounded. In the male, the clavicles tend to be straighter, making the shoulders wider. He has a more squared look than a female, as shown in Figure 2.10.

The torso of the female is somewhat longer than that of a male in relation to the total body height. The chest is shorter and rounder on a female and shows the female breast development. The female pelvis is shorter but wider and deeper, and it tilts forward slightly to facilitate childbirth. This makes the female spinal lumbar curve a slightly deeper arch.

The female also usually has shorter arms and legs than the male. Be sure to take this into account if you want to attempt to adapt a male 3D model to be a female. Most of the height differences between females and males can be found in the upper arm (the humerus) and along the entire leg, as shown in Figure 2.11. Normally, the upper arm is shorter on a female anyway, placing her elbow a little higher than his. Her wrists and hands are also smaller.

The female thigh is shorter than the male's because of the femur's greater angle coming from the female's wider pelvis. This causes the more curved look of the female hips as they come down toward the knees.

Be sure to note that the lower leg is also a little shorter in the female than in the male. Because of distributed fat, the female leg tends to be smoother, and the swelling of the calf is also slightly lower on her leg. The female ankle is rounder and less prominent than that of the male, and her feet are smaller and narrower.

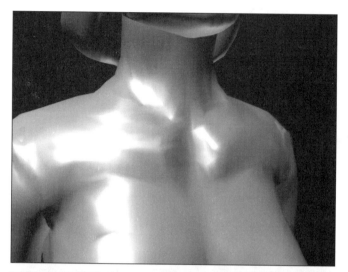

Figure 2.10

The neck and shoulder area display some of the most significant differences between male and female anatomy.

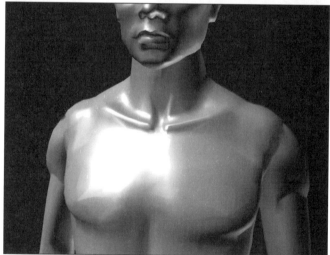

3D Models provided by Viewpoint Datalabs International, Inc.

While differences between the sexes can be seen in the skeleton, the most striking differences can be seen in the layer of body fat. Every woman who has been on a diet knows that the female body carries more fat than the male, and every area of the body is affected. It is what makes the female body round and voluptuous, as shown in Figure 2.12.

Distinct Racial Characteristics

Humanity originated in tribal groups around the world with each group, or race, having its own facial characteristics, color, and confirmation. As our world has evolved and developed, the races have come together so that today it is very dif-

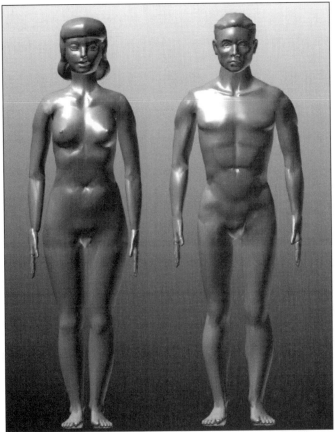

3D Models provided by Viewpoint Datalabs International, Inc.

Figure 2.11

You can't just uniformly scale down a male 3D model and have a properly proportioned female. The reduction in length must be taken from the upper arm and entire leg as shown.

ficult to find people who have remained isolated enough not to have some mixture in their genetic type. Because of this mixing, it is almost impossible to identify the exact makeup of any individual. All we can do here is to identify the characteristics relating to racial type.

A 3D world peopled by models of a uniform pink color would be bland and unrealistic. If you want to create interesting and realistic 3D worlds, you must take race into account in designing your characters. For example, a baseball simulation with all Caucasian players would

totally disregard the reality of the world around us.

I will discuss four general racial types here, although there are many subtypes: Caucasian, African, Asian, and Aboriginal. For our purposes here, I will concentrate on those areas that provide ready *visual* clues to racial identity, such as hair type, skin color, head shape, lower facial angle, as well as facial features such as eyes, nose, and lips.

All four types are illustrated in Figure 2.13.

Figure 2.12

Women painted by artists of the baroque era clearly depict the distribution of body fat on the female figure. Paintings by Peter Paul Rubens of generously figured women gave us the term "Rubenesque," still used today to describe the body shape.

Caucasian

The Caucasian race is usually referred to as white or having a light skin tone. Eye and hair color can both vary greatly. Hair texture is usually described as wavy, but in fact the hair can be anything from stick straight to very curly.

In a side view, the Caucasian head is medium-sized and the chin is usually closer to the spine than is the nose. The Caucasian nose is high and the lips are relatively thin, although cosmetic surgery and lipo injections have even made that unreliable!

African

The African race is usually referred to as black or having a brown to dark-brown skin. Hair texture is usually more consistent than Caucasian and is usually very curly with a wooly texture. The eyes and hair are predominantly dark brown or black.

In the side view, the African chin juts further forward than the nose, and the nose is flattened. The lips are usually relatively thick.

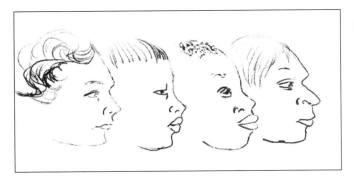

Figure 2.13

67

Chapter 2: Comparative Human Anatomy

The four primary racial groups differ visually in significant ways. From the left, the four types are Caucasian, Asian, African, and Aboriginal.

When you are modeling an African subject, remember that the facial features and angles will make all the difference between a correct, realistic character and a Caucasian with dark skin.

Asian

The Asian face is typically known for its distinct eye shape. Eyes in an Asian may or may not be slanted downward in the center, depending on the subgroup from which the subject comes. The upper eyelid disappears when the eye is open because of the epicanthic fold, which overlaps the lower lid slightly at the tear duct and also may overlap the lower lid at the outer corner of the eye.

Another striking characteristic of the Asian eye is the flatness of the orbit area. Beacause the bridge of the nose is low and the eye itself is prominent in Asians, the dip between the two planes is likely to be slight. It is important to note that usually the eyebrows are also slightly slanted upward and may taper off abruptly at the ends.

Asian skin is usually represented in yellow or brown tones, and the eye color is typically brown. Asian hair is straight and black.

The chin in the Asian face is typically slightly farther forward than the nose, but not as pronounced as in the African face. The nose is low but not flat, and the lips are of medium thickness.

Aboriginal

The Aboriginal face is characterized by the same marked face angle as in the African face—that is, the chin is typically further forward than the nose. However, the Aboriginal face has a more sloping forehead and receding chin. The brow is protruding, the nose is large and broad, and the lips are of medium thickness.

Aboriginal skin and eyes are dark brown, and the hair is black. Hair can be either straight or curly.

Exaggeration and Abnormality

I've now touched on some of the more common characteristics of different ages, sexes, and races of humans. It won't be enough to give you everything you need to create any type of 3D character, but it should give you a good start. The only way to create a completely authentic 3D character is to plan carefully and submerge yourself in research.

Exaggeration

Now that you know the typical human proportions that create body images that are not immediately jarring to our eyes, it's time to think of varying these proportions for specific effects. For example, if you are charged with creating a mythical mage, you might want to lengthen the figure to signify power and increase the head-length to suggest wisdom.

But sometimes it may not be a fantasy effect that is called for. For example, if your work calls for creation of a high-fashion look, then exaggeration can be very helpful to lengthen the body and create a more elegant line. While the prototypical human body may be roughly eight head-lengths tall, a more elegant fashion model's body might be up to fifteen heads tall, depending on the effect you're seeking.

Commentators have noted that Michelangelo created his figures in the unusual proportions of nine, ten, or even twelve heads in height, endeavoring to realize a grace and harmony not found in nature. Michelangelo is quoted as saying that it is necessary to have the compass in the eye, not in the hand.

By contrast with Michelangelo, some of Raphael's figures are only six heads high. If beauty is in the eye of the beholder, you as creator of your own 3D characters must create whatever kind of "beauty" is required. Once you know the basics of anatomy and proportion, however, you can project your own artistic talents onto your characters to create whatever look you want. Figure 2.14 illustrates exaggerated body proportions.

Abnormalities

Exaggeration can be produced by natural processes as well as artistic ones. For example, the body of a person with dwarfism may have proportions similar to a normal adult of average stature. Although such people are usually called *midgets;* technically, this term refers to well-proportioned dwarfs. It is more likely, however, that the torso is nearly normal size, while the arms and legs are somewhat shorter, as shown in Figure 2.15. Also, while the head size is typically normal or a little larger, the hands and feet are smaller.

At the other end of the scale, the so-called giant, or one with gigantism, can also manifest totally normal proportions. More typically, however, this body type displays an enlarged jaw and oversized hands and feet.

Physical ailments and genetic abnormalities can produce almost any variation in human form imaginable. Extreme examples do not usually survive long, but others may be in the human population and thus in the population of your 3D world. For example, Down's syndrome produces an enlarged head flattened on the front and back, a short, flat-bridged nose, almond-shaped eyes, a widened

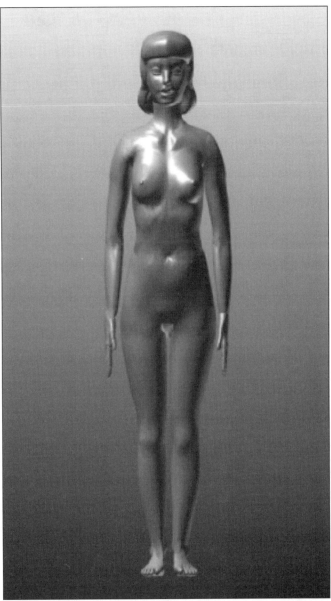

3D Models provided by Viewpoint Datalabs International, Inc.

Figure 2.14

An exaggerated figure can illustrate high fashion and elegance as long as balance is maintained.

space between the thumb and forefinger (and big and second toe), and relatively short stature. Rheumatoid arthritis is a relatively common ailment that often causes a distinctive hump in the back, compressing the chest cavity and freezing the back in place.

Other physical ailments may attack any part of the body and may afflict different people differently. If you are called upon to model a particular type, a great deal of research is called for.

Remember that exaggeration and stylization can be very useful in simplifying, caricaturizing, or symbolizing—or just making your character amusing.

How Age Affects Weight and Balance

Keeping the body in balance is a complex process. Any movement of the center of gravity must be counterbalanced by realigning the rest of the body to regain balance. Sometimes that means moving the head to one side or shifting the hip to compensate. It might mean putting a foot out to widen the area of the support line.

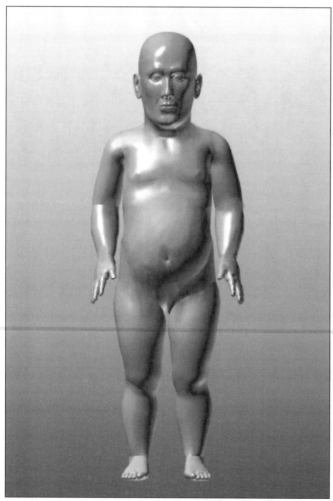

3D Models provided by Viewpoint Datalabs International, Inc.

Figure 2.15

A dwarf's proportions differ from those of a typical adult.

Character Animation with 3D Studio MAX

As infants grow, one of their major learning tasks is to balance their bodies. *Toddler* is the name given to that group of children just learning to balance on two feet. It's common for a toddler to walk with arms outstretched to provide an additional aid in balancing. The toddler also attempts to compensate for his or her top-heavy body (see Chapter 1) by taking short, rapid steps in order to keep—and regain—balance as he or she goes.

Interestingly, a child just learning to walk is typically unable to both look at something and walk. If something catches children's attention, they usually stop or suddenly sit down until they have quenched their curiosity, then continue on their way.

An old person can have different balance problems depending on how the rigors of old age have affected his or her body. If the spine has curved forward, the center of gravity moves forward as well. The head is also forced forward, producing a hump at the top of the back. The pelvis then must shift forward and the knees must be bent to counterbalance the forward movement of the top part of the body, as shown in Figure 2.16.

If the aging person also has hip problems such as arthritis or degenerative hip disease, the person will favor the ailing side and shift his or her weight to the good side. This shifts the pelvis and shoulders into an unnatural position and produces

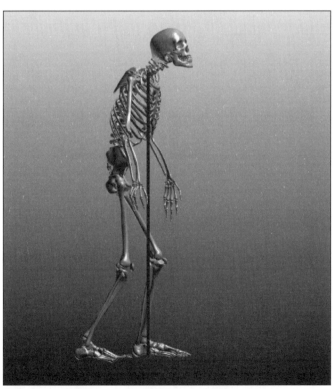

3D Models provided by Viewpoint Datalabs International, Inc.

Figure 2.16

The center of gravity shifts forward as the curve of the spine is shifted forward with old age.

the appearance that one leg is shorter than the other. The head must then lean a little to the weighted side so that balance can be regained.

Other diseases, trauma, and abnormalities affect the body balance. (See Figure 2.17.) A one-legged man must shift his body weight to the legged side, as the line of support is lessened. Abnormal curvature of the spine, or *scoliosis,* bends the spine in an S shape when viewed from the back. The affected person must shift his or her shoulders and pelvis to compensate for the abnormality, producing an apparent limp.

Using various appliances to help with balance will also change the center of gravity. Recall the discussion in Chapter 1 about how picking up extra weight affects the body balance. Using a cane or walker will also affect balance by expanding the line of support. This makes it easier for the affected person to balance and allows him or her to stand in a more normal position.

Note finally that all of these debilities will also affect a person's range of motion; an eighty-year-old man is not going to be as flexible and agile as a twenty-year-old gymnast!

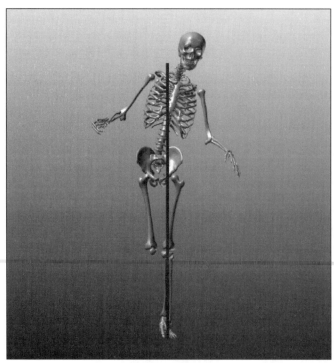

3D Models provided by Viewpoint Datalabs International, Inc.

Figure 2.17

Disease and body abnormalities affect the body's center of gravity. A one-legged person must shift his weight to compensate for lost support.

Next Chapter...

In the next chapter, we'll descend from the human to lower creatures. You may be called upon to create a stalking lion or flying bird—this will give you some idea how to do it.

Chapter **3**

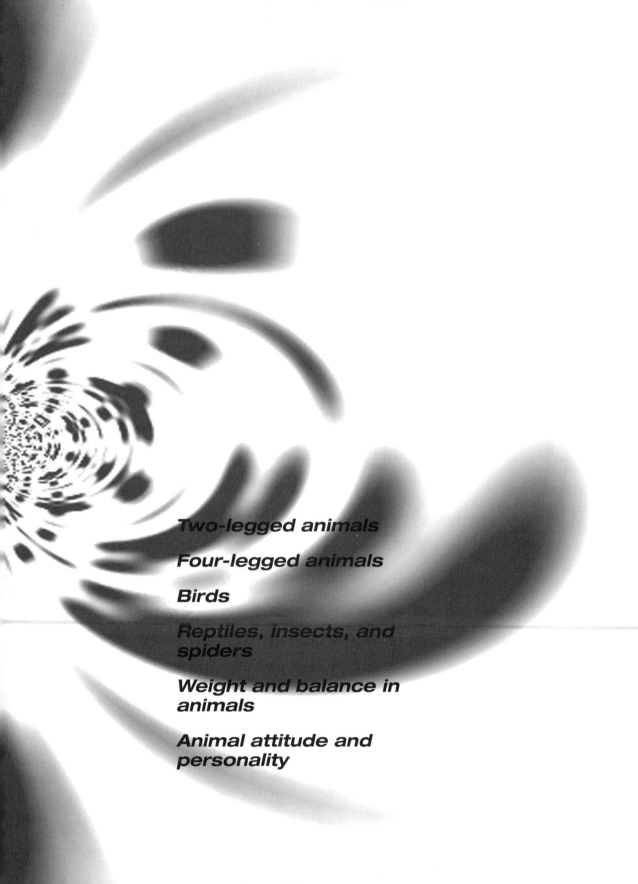

Animal Anatomy

In the first two chapters, we looked at human traits and anatomy. Now it's time to don our trusty pith helmets and explore the animal world. Although animal anatomy as a topic is far broader than can be covered in a single chapter, I've attempted here to describe the basic characteristics of the major characters of the 3D animal world. If you need to create a specific type of 3D critter that's not covered in this chapter, examine one of the books listed in the Resources appendix for assistance or talk to an expert in the field.

It is as important to study the shapes and movement of animals as it was for humans. However, you'll probably receive fewer glaring looks when you do so from animals than from other people. In fact, if you have a few treats, I'm sure Fido or Fluffy will be very pleased to cooperate to the fullest extent of their little pet abilities. Remember that there's nothing like watching live animals—or even looking at stills or videotapes—to give you the first-hand knowledge you need.

Animals

Non-human anatomy covers a very wide variety of types, from two-legged to four-legged animals and from birds that fly to insects. It is a trip on the evolutionary scale of living things. The best advice I can give (and you knew I would) is to study the animals you are interested in modeling. Watch them move (if they are not extinct), go to the zoo, watch some of the old Walt Disney True Life Adventures on videotape. National Geographic also has some excellent videos available. There are many places to go for research; you just have to look. See the Resources appendix for a sample.

The most comprehensive early visual studies of animal movement can be found in the sequential photographs taken by Eadweard Muybridge in the late 1800s. They provide a really good look at animals in motion and how the bodies compress and expand with every movement. However, Muybridge's photographs don't show the personality or expression that can make each of your own animal creations unique. Those qualities come from the artist's touch that brings your 3D model to life.

Be sure before you start your 3D creation that what you are being asked to create is an authentic animal and not just a human being in an animal suit, like Bugs Bunny or Mickey Mouse. If the latter type is what you want, refer back to Chapters 1 and 2 for guidance on how to model such a human. (Remember, though, that a bear that walks and talks like a human is more convincing if he's also *dressed* like a human. Otherwise, the audience will expect the bear to move and act like a bear. It may make us a tad uncomfortable to see a furry, natural-looking bear juggling and riding a unicycle, but put a circus coat and hat on him and he can be the next Bongo.)

With these things in mind, let's take a look at how a realistic animal is built and moves—just in case you don't have a circus hat.

Two-Legged Animals

Very few animals have just two legs. Of course, Sasquatch might be a possibility, if we could just get him out of the woods. Other animals with two legs, such as birds, are covered separately later in this chapter.

The tailless anthropoid apes are the only two-legged animals discussed in this section, as they're the only animals that walk in an upright (or at least semi-upright) position. Gorillas are the largest of these primates and are thus the most natural to compare with humans. Although most people usually consider gorillas as closely related to monkeys, in fact, this ape is more closely related to humans than to the orangutan.

Over time, the human thorax evolved to a shorter, wider shape than our ancestors'. This change facilitated better balance in an upright stance. The ape thorax also evolved, but into a squarer shape, which only allows them to walk in a semi-upright position. In fact, the ape still uses its forearms to assist in locomotion most of the time.

The human body is just not made to move on all fours, that is, on hands and feet. In this position, the front of the body angles downward toward the head and the pelvis rises because of the relatively short arms and long legs, as shown in Figure 3.1. With legs straight, the human in this position is physically unable to raise his or her head sufficiently to see well ahead. With legs bent, locomotion is even more difficult.

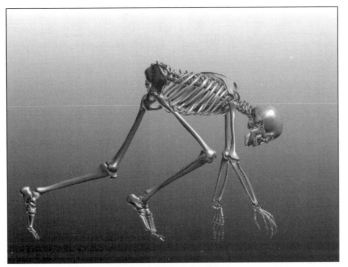

Figure 3.1

When a human is on all fours, he or she is not only unable to move efficiently, but can't see what predators might be ahead. The ape's relative arm and leg lengths, by contrast, are just the reverse of ours, making it a natural to move about on all fours.

3D Models provided by Viewpoint Datalabs International, Inc.

Apes, on the other hand, have arm and leg lengths just the reverse of ours. When they are on all fours, they have a downward slope from their heads to their pelvises allowing them to be in a natural position for locomotion and to see all areas ahead of them as well. Because apes' legs are short and their arms and hands long, they can use their bodies as pendulums as they grip, climb, hang, and swing.

Gorillas are built much differently than humans. The arm span of an average adult gorilla is eight feet. A gorilla's thumb and big toe each oppose the other digits, allowing it to grasp and manipulate objects with either hand or foot. Short legs help the ape brace itself when climbing, while its large (11 inches long and 6 inches wide) feet help to support its 400-pound-plus weight on the ground. See Figure 3.2.

Although the body of the gorilla shown here is shorter, it is also much more dense than a humans. Some things to remember when modeling a 3D gorilla are:

- The pelvis is nearly twice as wide and twice as long as that of a human.

- The chest is at least one-fourth larger than a human's in both width and length.

- Gorillas have a pot-bellied appearance because of the mass of intestines needed to accommodate and digest its bulky diet.

- The female gorilla is shorter than the adult male and weighs only about half as much. Adult females average 4 1/2 feet tall and weigh just under 200 pounds. Average adult males are 5 to 5 1/2 feet tall and weigh roughly 450 pounds.

- The head of a gorilla is massive, with a bony sagittal crest on top and a bulging forehead that overhangs the eyes.

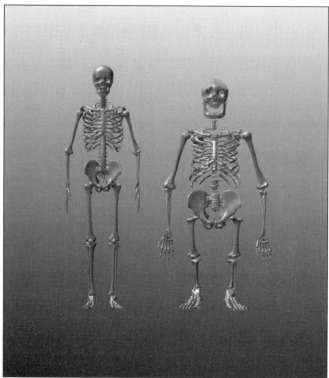

3D Models provided by Viewpoint Datalabs International, Inc.

Figure 3.2

Although ape and human anatomy have some similarities, they are very different in their proportions. The 3D gorilla skeleton was created from a human skeleton to illustrate typical gorilla proportions.

- The sagittal crest is especially apparent in males and provides an anchor for the large jaw muscles. See Figure 3.3.

- Gorilla faces vary from flat-nosed to prominent and from round to oval.

- Gorilla noses are very distinctive and are frequently used to differentiate one gorilla from another.

- Their ears lie close to the skull and their small eyes are usually dark brown.

- Gorillas have thirty-two teeth and the male's canines are much more developed than the female's. The molars are quite large in order to chew vegetation.

- Adult gorillas have no hair on their fingers, the soles of their hands and feet, or their armpits. Their hair is sparse on the upper chest, especially in the older males. The skin is black and covered with black to reddish brown hair. Male gorillas acquire a silver-gray saddle across their backs at the time of adulthood, beginning at about ten years of age, hence the name *silverback.*

- Newborns usually have pinkish-grey skin which darkens quickly, and a white patch of hair on their rumps that remains until they are a few years old.

- The normal gait of a gorilla is on all fours, but the hands are curled so that

Figure 3.3

This photo of a gorilla shows the massive head and stance.

the points of contact are on the knuckles of the hands and the soles of their feet. Although they are included in the two-legged animal category, two-legged locomotion is actually rare. They generally travel no more than 20 feet on two legs. Usually this upright stance is used for chest beating, observation, or to reach an object.

If you would like to try *being* a gorilla or to observe gorilla behavior and movement from the inside, as it were, visit Zoo Atlanta in Georgia and head toward their Virtual Gorilla Exhibit Project. (The Resources appendix lists the Web site location that describes this project.) Part of the Project is a virtual habitat that duplicates the real gorilla habitat at the zoo. It was created using Georgia Tech's SVE (Simple Virtual Environment) Toolkit, and allows visitors to enjoy an immersive interactive gorilla experience.

In the Project, you can observe characteristic gorilla locomotion modes and stances such as walking on four or three legs, standing, squatting, lying down, aggressive staring, and chest beating. You can even become one of the gorillas yourself and walk among and interact with other members of your gorilla family. Your actions as a gorilla will elicit appropriate responses from the other gorillas depending on your behavior and your assumed position within the family hierarchy. The lifelike virtual gorilla models in the Project have ten body parts and nine joints with a total of 20 degrees of freedom. Motions are keyframed, and the key positions were generated from video of actual gorillas and behavioral data of gorilla movements. It looks like a great place for a family vacation for the gorilla-minded.

Four-Legged Animals

As I said at the beginning of this chapter, detailing every animal type is much more complicated than we have room for in one chapter. Given the sheer numbers of animals that are included in this general category, I will only be able to provide the general form, structure, and function of four-legged animals. For other details, observation and research are the keys.

Simulating a walk with two legs is one thing, but add two more and it gets even more complicated. The animal skeleton isn't simply a human skeleton bent over walking on its hands and feet. The basic design of the four-legged animal skeleton is quite different from that of a human. Evolution has provided *quadrupeds,* those animals that walk with all four feet on the ground, with a design that better suits their needs.

The basic quadruped structure is similar to a bridge, as shown in Figure 3.4. The vertebrae act as the bridge span and are supported in the front and back by columns. These columns are made up of the shoulders and legs in the front and the pelvis and legs in the rear. The skeletal structure is secured in the front by the muscles in the neck and in the rear by muscles in the hindquarters. The pelvis sits in a downward slant. As the rear legs are straightened, this configuration helps transfer thrust to the vertebrae without losing power.

Although both the pelvis and shoulders support the weight of the animal, the front legs and shoulders support most of the body weight, roughly two-thirds. The other one-third of the body's weight is supported by the rear quarters.

Neck and head movement between the shoulders and chest is aided by a pivotal point on the shoulder blade that works like a counterweight on a crane. This is best typified by the up-and-down head movement of a horse as it walks.

Although these basic structural principles are true for any four-legged animal, quadrupeds differ significantly in detail,

Figure 3.4

The animal skeleton shows the bridge construction of a quadruped.

beginning with their proportions. While both a giraffe and a cow are herbivore quadrupeds, their proportions differ significantly. Examine an animal's proportions to learn how its body functions. For example, the giraffe is constructed so that it can graze in the tops of trees, while the cow gets its food from ground level. The giraffe gains most of its moisture from the foliage it eats; its long neck and legs make it quite difficult to drink from a ground-level pond. The cow, on the other hand, has a relatively short neck and legs that make it easy for it to drink from ground level.

Hind legs

The hind legs, as I noted earlier, join the pelvis to form the rear columns of the body bridge. This is called the body's *center of movement*. Depending on the body type, different evolutionary paths have changed the position and shape of the hind legs to meet the needs of the specific animal.

Whether the animal walks on paws (the ends of the metatarsus) or hooves (the end joints of the digits), the number and order of the joint angles are the same in all mammals, as shown in Figure 3.5.

The angles between the component bones vary, however, depending on the push-off function they perform. If the animal must push off strongly with its hind legs to hunt prey, such as a lion, for example, the angle of repose between the upper and lower legs is greater. An animal that grazes, such as a cow, need not push off from its hind legs strongly; thus, its hind legs are more likely to be straight than those of a predator. The angles of the hind legs are most noticeable in profile. The dynamic angles of the bones and the muscles associated with them combine to form the curving nature of these limbs. When the leg is flexing and extending, note that the compression and extension occur in the haunch (hip) and the toes,

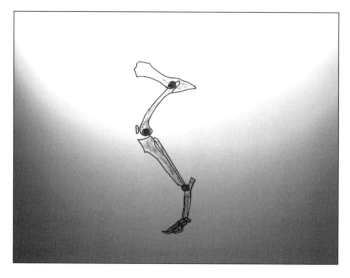

Figure 3.5

All mammals have the same number and order of joint angles in the hind leg.

Figure 3.6

Compression and extension in the legs of a running animal occur primarily in the haunch and toes.

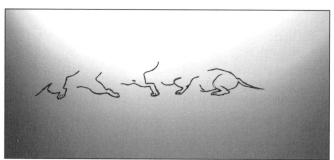

a.

b.

as shown in Figures 3.6a and 3.6b, and not in the bonier areas between.

When modeling a quadruped, remember also that the bones get smaller in diameter from the hip to the feet. The associated muscles of the haunch and leg also get smaller as they go down the leg. Thus, the hip muscles power all broad movements of the leg. In animals that run well, the hip joint movements are restricted to bending and stretching (flexion and extension) with little rotation. The muscles further down the legs provide little power but provide fine control over how the foot is used.

Forelegs

Animal foreleg construction can generally be divided into three categories: running animals, carnivores, and primates.

Carnivores, such as cats, need the ability to climb and cling to their prey and to uneven terrain, even the branches of trees.

They thus have freer use of the arm in general than running animals, as well as the ability to turn their paws. The humerus (upper arm) rotates in the shoulder joint, allowing them to use this flexibility to attack in a sideways swipe movement, as shown in Figure 3.7.

Compared to a dog, the angle of the metatarsus in a cat's paw is straighter. Also, evolution has resulted in the cat developing retractable phalanges, or claws; the dog's claws do not retract. See Figure 3.8. (An interesting side note is that a cheetah, the fastest-running cat, is built more like a dog than a cat, and the cheetah's claws don't retract. The claws provide traction for high-speed chases across relatively flat terrain.)

Animals that use flight as a means of escape—the runners—have no need to be able to rotate their humeri sideways, so their foreleg construction differs from the predators'. As typified by the horse,

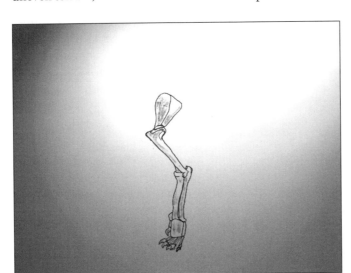

Figure 3.7

The free rotation of the humerus to the side lets the cat and other similar carnivores attack with a swiping motion.

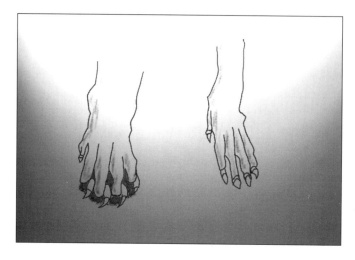

runners have no need to catch prey with their hooves and thus have little sideways rotation in their shoulder joints.

The anatomy of a deer, while basically similar, is slightly different from that of a horse. A deer's shoulders are almost in front of its rib cage, and its rear end is practically all leg and haunch. This structure not only gives the deer a more fluid appearance, but when the deer runs, its front legs can take on the body weight and steer it into a turn. See Figure 3.9.

Primates, on the other hand, have vast mobility in the hand, arm, and shoulder girdle, allowing them to use their hands to grip, swing, and climb.

In spite of the many differences among these groups, there *are* some common features:

• Number and sequence of joints.

• Direction of the angle of each limb segment.

• Shoulder and elbow joint positioning as related to the trunk.

• Distribution of the muscles in the musculature.

The following quadrupeds are examples of this basic form and function:

• *Hunter animals that lie in wait for their prey* tend to have massive skeletons and muscle structures. They have low trunks matched by short powerful heads and necks. The relationship of torso length to its height is rectangular. Their strong muscles allow them to have powerful short-distance sprinting power and the strength to pounce on their prey and bring it down. The elbows and knees of these animals are along the lower body line. Examples of this type are the African lion, the tiger, and the domestic cat. See Figure 3.10.

• *Hunter animals that pursue their prey* tend to be slim with a light build. This

Figure 3.9

The deer's shoulders are nearly in front of its ribs, and its rear is almost all legs and haunches, producing a more fluid look.

Figure 3.10

The difference between a quadruped that lies in wait for its prey and one that pursues its prey can be seen in their body types.

3D Models provided by Viewpoint Datalabs International, Inc.

type typically has long legs, a long slim head and neck, and large lungs, resulting in a deep chest. The relationship of torso length to its height is much more square than the first category. These are the long-distance light athletes who chase their prey to exhaustion. Examples of this type are dogs, wolves, foxes, and coyotes.

Remember, as an animal's legs become longer, so does its neck. Without this parallel growth, an animal would have a hard time getting food.

• *Herbivorous running animals* typically have trunks that sit high off the ground. Their main source of defense is their speed, as they do not usually have the horns or tusks for attack and defense. The relationship of torso length to its height tends toward the rectangular, but the relationship between the length of the torso and its height above the ground tends to be square. The lower line of the stomach lies roughly halfway between the top of the torso and the ground. Bodies in this category are well balanced and powerfully equipped for running and jumping. An example of this type is the horse, as shown in Figure 3.11. Other animals with this type of tall build include camels and horned species like deer and antelope.

Although the above proportions should give you a better idea of the body types in the four-legged world, the proportions of the thorax should not be neglected. All true quadrupeds have similar thoracic characteristics. The thorax is narrow or compressed, but with great depth between the vertebrae and the sternum, or breast bone. This allows the animal to move its legs unimpeded along the sides of the thorax.

Animal Weight and Balance

In most animals, the center of gravity is in the front third of the body. Just as in humans, the line of gravity is from the center of gravity to the line of support (the feet).

3D Models provided by Viewpoint Datalabs International, Inc.

Figure 3.11

The horse's body is well-balanced and powerfully equipped for running and jumping.

Compared to humans, however, animals generally have much better balance. This is because their center of gravity is much lower, and their line of support is much larger—they're standing on four feet, not two. See Figure 3.12.

If something causes the line of gravity to fall outside the line of support, the animal falls in the direction toward which the center of gravity was displaced. With grazing animals that have little sideways rotation in their shoulder and hip joints, pushing them past the point of recovery always results in a fall, thus making cow-tipping the favorite nocturnal pastime that it is.

As in humans, animals must shift their centers of gravity to stand on one fewer foot. If one forefoot is raised, the line of support is diminished and the body must shift the center of gravity at that end of the bridge over the leg that holds the weight. Because an animal's torso is usually horizontal, with four feet on the ground rather than two, when an animal raises its forefoot, a twist in the longitudinal axis of the torso must occur and the weight-bearing leg must slant inward to position the supporting foot or hoof under the front center of gravity, as shown in Figures 3.13a and 3.13b.

Birds

The genus of birds includes everything from songbirds to vultures, eagles to geese, and even includes non-plastic pink flamingos. One thing they all have in common

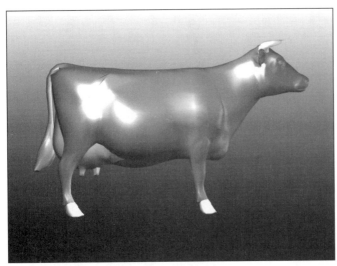

3D Models provided by Viewpoint Datalabs International, Inc.

Figure 3.12

Four-legged animals have better balance than humans because of their larger lines of support and lower centers of gravity.

Figure 3.13

With a forefoot raised, the center of gravity shifts over the weight-bearing leg. The torso twists along the longitudinal axis and the weight-bearing leg slants inward.

a.

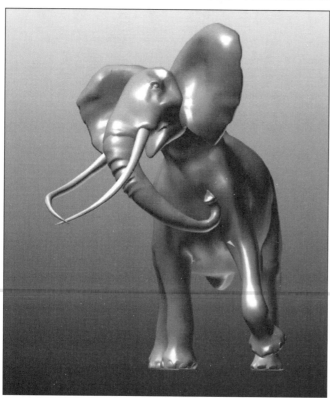

b.

is, of course, that they have wings. Humans have studied birds for millennia to learn the secrets of flight; if you want to model realistic flying birds, then grab your own binoculars and take to the hills. This is what the term *bird-watcher* is all about.

The animated birds of early cartoon days used a basic four-position wing cycle during flight. Obviously, two of the positions were at the extremes of the movement,

with wings up and wings down. See Figure 3.14. However the in-between positions of the wings were not that simple. Beginning with the wings up in the first position, the second position showed the wings horizontal. But because animators wanted to add flexibility and snap to the motion, the wing had a concave curve with wing tips turned slightly upward, thus showing the wind drag on the end feathers during the downward thrust. In the

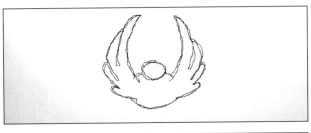

Figure 3.14

Simplified flight action is primarily for cartoons, it also can apply to realistic flight.

a.

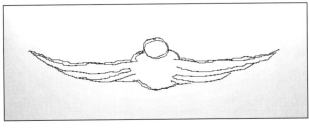

b.

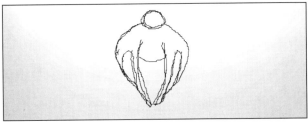

c.

d.

third position, the wings are in the down position, but the tips are slightly turned out, still showing the air resistance in the downward movement. The fourth position of the wings denotes the change of wing direction. It is, as I stated above, still in a downward position; however, the tips of the wings are now angled slightly inward, showing the wing suddenly reversing its direction to an upward motion. Even though in general, these wing positions do apply to realistic flight, if you want your 3D model to achieve a realistic smooth motion, you must take into consideration the real-life structural anatomy of the bird's wing. See Figure 3.15.

The real-life structure of the wing is a little more complicated than the solid wing in cartoons. A bird's wing is curved on the upper surface, allowing the air to flow rapidly over the feathers as the wing is raised. At the very ends of the wings, the feathers are spread apart like fingers. As a matter of fact, in cartooning, many birds use those feathers as human-looking hands. This spreading of the end feathers allows air to pass through, easily reducing the air currents that flow around the end of the wing when it's moving up and down. When the wing is on the upstroke, it has a quick flip forward. The air helps the wing to move back this way. The downstroke is the most important movement of the flap. As it moves down, the curve of the wing grips the air, and the bird propels itself forward.

The wing does not actually beat up and down. On the upstroke, it goes up and backward, while on the downstroke, it goes down and forward with the leading edge tilted down, as shown in Figure 3.16. This forces the air to move backward and allows the bird to push itself forward on the air beneath and behind its wings. Frequently during this downward motion, the wings are straight out, making this a slow and powerful motion.

Figure 3.15

The bird's wing is partially folded at the spots that correspond to your elbow and wrist. To reduce air friction, the wing curves in toward the body from the elbow.

Character Animation with 3D Studio MAX

Figure 3.16

This series of photos of a bird in flight show the forward swing to the wing on the downstroke.

Birds have something similar to airplane's propeller. In fact, the outer half of the wing, starting at the wrist, is sometimes referred to as a propeller. It does not make a complete circle like an airplane propeller, but as the wing flaps and the inner portion of the wing moves up and down, the tips of the wings actually describe a semicircular motion. This propeller action can actually reverse itself, a phenomenon most often seen when a bird lands. As the bird's wings raise, this motion slows down its descent, letting it land gently on its perch.

The goose wing motion is often studied because its wings are long and flap relatively slowly, making the wing structure more easily observed. The sequence of pictures, shown in Figures 3.17a through 3.17d, is from a remarkable series by David Goodnow.

- In the first image, the wings are in an upright position, ready to start the downstroke.

- In the second image, the wings are out to the side, but the thrust generated by

Figure 3.17

The goose is a relatively easy aerial subject to study, as its slow wing motion makes everything easy to see.

a.

b.

its primary feathers brings the wing forward until it nearly touches its bill.

- In the third image, the goose lifts its wrists above its body as it brings the tips inward toward its body.

- In the fourth image, the goose has completed the stroke by flicking its wrists and rotating them to open the fans of the primary feathers in preparation for the next downstroke.

c.

d.

Some birds have unusual wing positions in order to accommodate its body shape or size. The duck seems to pivot in midair as it begins its downstroke. From the front view, the weight and balance can be seen as the bird tilts its body to the right and leans its head to the left. Both wings appear to be shifted to the right side. See Figure 3.18.

One important thing to remember about bird flight is that the bird's body is pushed

Figure 3.18

The unusual position of the duck as it begins its downstroke accommodates its body size and shape.

upward slightly on each downward flap by the force of the wings against the air. When the wings rise, the body drops, resulting in an up-and-down movement as the bird flies, as shown in Figure 3.19.

With large, long-necked birds like swans and pelicans, there may also be a forward and backward movement of the head, such that the head and neck stretch forward on the downward flap and come back when the wings are raised.

The hummingbird is different from all other birds. Its whole wing works like a propeller blade and can turn completely around, forward and backward. This enables it to go up and down, back and forth, straight forward, or hover in one place. The

wing works on the same principle as a swivel joint. (Of course, the wing also beats fast enough that it is invisible to the naked human eye; you can re-create its motion easily in 3D using a semitransparent material, a few wing positions, and motion blur.)

Although a bird's wing structure is wonderful in and of itself, it would be worthless without feathers. The feathers bend and twist during flight to compensate for air currents and air pressure. On the wing, the feathers are long quills with barbs attached to the side like the teeth of a comb. The barbs attach to the shaft and angle forward toward the tip. This lets the feather spread, making it wider when needed. See Figure 3.20.

Figure 3.19

The bird's body moves up and down as it flaps its wings in flight.

Figure 3.20

The feather of a bird is a quill with barbs attached like teeth in a comb.

Every group of feathers has a different function and is controlled by muscles and membranes at the skin level. Scales or fur can't be moved by these muscles, so feathers give the bird a large advantage.

The tail feathers are another important part of the bird to discuss here. The tail feathers protrude from a muscle that can move up or down and open and close the tail feathers like a fan. When a bird closes its tail, it shifts its center of gravity to the rear and it rises in the air. When it opens its tail, its center of gravity shifts forward and it drops. Watch a bird come to eat from a bird feeder; it spreads its tail as it lands, using its tail almost as an air brake. In flight, it uses its tail for both balance and steering.

TIP

The larger the bird, the slower the action, and the more the body moves up and down. The smaller the bird, the faster the action, and the less impact there is on body movement.

When planning a 3D model of a bird, it is important to know the size, personality, and nature of the bird. The larger, more elegant birds, like eagles, have longer, smoother wing movements than the jerky, small movements of a sparrow. Small birds flit around the sky, while large birds move more smoothly.

California condors, like the ancient gliding birds, must have the right combination of air currents and rising air (or a steep drop-off) just to get off the ground. They then extend their 10-foot-span wings out and use updrafts and thermal activity to keep aloft. The disadvantage of this dependence on the wind is obvious, in times of hunger or danger, it could be disastrous.

Bird Beaks

A bird's beak or bill is an indication of the kind of environment in which the bird lives. The beak is a protrusion of the skull covered with a material similar to fingernails. It is very hard and an important tool for nest building, protection, eating, and attracting mates. (Ooooh, what a nice bill you have!)

Fishing birds, like the blue heron, have long necks and long bills so that they can reach quite far down into the water and grab unwary fish. Nature has provided them with a design that works well for their environment and needs. One of the oddest bills is the pelican's. (Its beak, according to Ogden Nash, can hold more than its belly can!) Although in cartoons the pelican is often portrayed as carrying fish in its bill, in reality, it only uses its bill to scoop fish and water from the surface as it dives down to catch food. Then the pelican crushes the bottom of its bill against its chest to force out the water and turns its bill up to swallow the fish head-first. See Figure 3.21.

Seed-eating birds have short, thick bills for cracking hard shells, as shown in Figure 3.22. Many natural adaptations have produced curious beak shapes. For example, the upper bill of the cross-bill crosses over the bottom bill, like when you cross your fingers. It eats pine nuts and needs this nutcracker action to open the layers of the hard cone.

Diving and other waterbirds have broad bills, enabling them to scoop up vegetation on the bottom of ponds.

Like the animals I discussed earlier, the nature of a bird's foodstuff and whether it's a predator or prey help determine the shape of a bird—and a bird's bill. As with any other serious 3D project, study your subject matter before you begin.

Figure 3.21

A pelican's beak is perfect for its lifestyle. It can scoop up fish and water with its bill, squeeze the water out by pressing the bill to its chest, and then, dinner's served!

Figure 3.22

Seed-eating birds have short, thick bills for cracking hard shells.

Bird Feet

Bird feet differ, too, and show a specific purpose. Most birds have three toes in the front and one in the back. However, evolution has provided some with specialized structures to meet the needs of their lifestyles. Woodpeckers, for example, have two toes in the front and two toes in the back, letting them climb up and cling to tree trunks while they are seeking grubs in the wood. See Figure 3.23 for a comparison of bird feet.

Birds that travel in mudflats and wet sand, like the sandpiper, either have webbing between their toes or very long toes to get the support they need on wet, mushy ground. Ducks and diving birds have webbed feet to aid in swimming.

Predatory birds such as owls and raptors, which pick up living mice and rodents for food, have very strong feet with hooked talons that let them hang on to their prey. By contrast, birds who live on carrion have weaker feet with dull claws suitable only for tearing apart such refuse.

Most small flying birds have weak feet, as they rarely land on ground. They perch instead on tree limbs and wires and can fly quickly away with a little push. Their feet are better designed for gripping twigs than for sitting on flat surfaces.

The personality of your 3D bird depends on its nature—light or heavy, slow and clumsy, fast and anxious...you get the picture. Again, the best source of information is your own eyes, so get those binoculars.

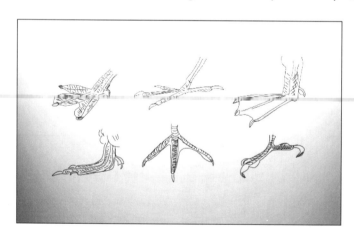

Figure 3.23

Bird feet have adapted through evolution for different bird lifestyles.

It's a Miscellaneous Life

I have included some miscellaneous animals in this section. Although less complicated than the species mentioned earler, they all have specific traits that should be noted here.

Fish, from Sea to Shining Sea

From the air to the water, fish have been around for millions and millions of years. Humans have aped their design in the designs for submarines, torpedoes, and airplane fuselages. In creating your own 3D fish, you must pay close attention not only to their shape, but also to their locomotion.

For all of you *old-timers* out there, you probably remember the 1987 3D short *Stanley and Stella in Breaking the Ice* from Symbolics, as shown in Figure 3.24. Stanley was a bird flying high above an ice barrier that let him fly with all his birdy friends, but kept him from his fish love, Stella, swimming under the ice below. It was a true-love story about star-crossed lovers battling all odds to be together. Makes a nice story, huh? Unfortunately for our purposes here, the technology did not exist then to make Stanley and Stella realistic. They were, well, symbolic more than realistic.

Most fish have rather primitive shapes—elongated, spindle-shaped bodies that don't appear to have much definition. It would be easy to end up with a Stella on your computer. The truth is that fish have a very

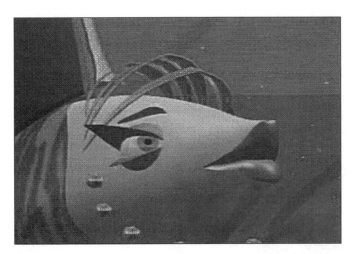

Figure 3.24

Stanley and Stella, the lovesick pair, were an odd coupling by Symbolics in 1987.

muscular trunk with a highly muscular tail that lets them move through the water very rapidly. In land vertebrates, this locomotion is achieved through limb movement, but in fish, the fins that represent the limbs are small and are chiefly used for balance and steering. See Figure 3.25.

Generally, the pectoral fins are more important in steering than the pelvic. The pectorals are the larger of the two pair and have a more developed skeleton.

A fish's tail, together with its undulating body movement, produces its locomotion. However, in all fish, waves of contracting muscle travel up and down the body, first on one side, then on the other, and finally through the tail. This gives the fish that wriggling effect, as waves of contracting muscles pass backward along the body and push against the water, thus propelling it forward. See Figure 3.26.

Another distinctive fishy trait is its eyes. There may be folds of skin around the margins of the orbit of the eyes, but that's all the eyelids a fish has. This produces that familiar round, staring eye. (It's interesting to note that there is a *four-eyed* fish which lives in the tropics. This fish has two separate retinas and two separate corneas in each eye so that when floating on the surface, it can see both above and below the water simultaneously.)

Snakes

The muscular body of the snake is so flexible that it can slither along the ground, or it coil into a spring-type shape then use its muscle to strike its target. See Figure 3.27 The snake's head is simply an extension of its body.

In the reptilian world, the staring eye without an eyelid is the stylistic choice of

3D Models provided by Viewpoint Datalabs International, Inc.

Figure 3.25

These fins are the dorsal, caudal, and anal fins lying on the midline of the body. The pectoral and pelvic fins are paired structures and can be related to our arms and legs.

3D Models provided by Viewpoint Datalabs International, Inc.

Figure 3.26

The waves of contracting muscles passing along the body to the tail cause an undulating motion.

Figure 3.27

The non-limb body of the snake is so flexible and muscular it slithers along the ground in an S-path.

all hip lizards and snakes. In the cartoon world, many snakes, like Kaa in Disney's animated *Jungle Book*, have eyelids added to make them more expressive and less sinister-looking. (Try conveying a frown without either eyebrows or eyelids!) However, in snakes and some lizards, a second superficial eye-covering of transparent tissue lies in front of the cornea, which gives them a blankly staring appearance.

The forked tongue darts in and out of a snake's mouth at irregular intervals. The olfactory organs of the snake are on its tongue, and no realistic 3D snake model would be complete without some tongue action. The mouth itself is silky white and may includes fangs in some varieties. The fangs are unlike teeth, as they are curved inward and contain venom that drips or is squirted out with a bite to stun or kill its victims.

Reptiles

Reptile ancestors came out of the sea. However, modern reptiles are basically land animals, even though there are some who live in wet areas and some who have even reverted to their watery past. Although a wide variety of animals are included in this genus, a few things are constant in the reptilian world. First, the reptile, unlike its amphibian ancestors, can't keep a constant body temperature. Their behavior is, therefore, greatly affected by this fact. You rarely find lizards in the far north, for example, and they are even rare in much of the temperate zones.

Like their fish ancestors, the ancient amphibians were covered with an armor of bony scales. However, modern amphibians have lost their scales and have a soft, moist glandular skin. The reptiles, however, are deficient in these glands, and with open air and sunlight, their skin turns hard and dry. Their bodies are covered with horny scales, and although the bony armor of ancient times is gone, bony scales or plates have redeveloped in some reptiles.

Although reptile limbs appear to have few similarities to the fins of a fish, in reality they do. With the exception of limbless snakes and some lizards, modern reptile limbs are sturdy and well developed, as shown in Figure 3.28. The limb of a reptile has three major segments. In both front and hind limbs, as in the pectoral and pelvic fins in a fish, the first segment projects out from the body and moves forward and backward in the horizontal plane. The second segment lifts the body off the ground; its movement is vertical, and together with the first segment, it can produce progression forward in its movement. The last segment is the foot, consisting of a wrist or ankle and toes. Reptiles generally have five toes front and back with many toe joints. From the thumb-side working toward the outside, each successive toe will have 2,3,4,5,3 (or 4) joints.

The movement of the reptilian leg joints is as follows:

- On the front leg, the radius and ulna (comprising the second segment of the leg) rotate freely about the humerus (the first segment). On the rear leg, the joint between the tibia and fibula (again the second segment) and the femur (the first segment) is usually a simple, untwistable hinge joint.

- Wrist articulations are usually hinge-like. However, while a mammal's foot is essentially a hinge, in reptiles and early amphibians, the foot can also be rotated on the lower segment.

Finally, as a sort of reptilian postscript, both a reptile's neck and tail are generally quite well developed, although perhaps not *buff* in the modern sense.

Insects

Insects are not really animals, but I've included them here because they're closer to animals than to humans. Insects have no bones, of course; their entire structure is supported by a tough outer shell (not unlike an M&M). Insects have three body segments, the head, thorax, and abdomen, and can be distinguished from other arthropods, like spiders, by the fact that they have only six legs, one pair on each segment. Most insects also have two pair of wings attached to the second and third segments, as shown in Figure 3.29. Both wings and bodies can vary in size and shape depending on the type of insect.

Most insects also have a pair of antennae and three pairs of primitive jaw-like mouth parts. This may be either a true biting jaw or modified to form sucking mouth parts.

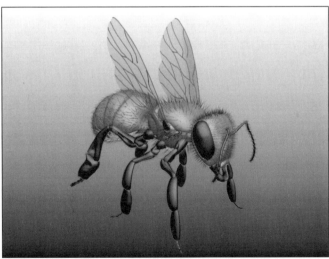

3D Models provided by Viewpoint Datalabs International, Inc.

Figure 3.29

Insects are represented here by one of the furrier bees.

Spiders

Arachnophobia! Creepy, crawly spiders. Yuck! They strike revulsion in the hearts of the best of us. Ever since I saw *The Incredible Shrinking Man* when I was five, a big tarantula spider has been one of the staples of a really good horror flick for me. The tarantula in *Home Alone* was funny, but still...could you really blame Daniel Stern for trying to beat it to death on Joe Pesci's chest? Even in *Jumanji*, the big black spiders that came out of the game were scary—I mean, I *knew* they were 3D, but it didn't help.

Spiders differ from insects in that they have but two body segments and eight legs rather than six, as shown in Figure 3.30. The first segment is the cephalothorax. It's where the six (yes, six) pair of appendages are located. The first pair is the jaws, containing the poison glands. The second pair is the *palps*, leg-like in the female, but shorter and bulbous in the male. The palps appear to be used like feelers. The remaining four pair are the walking legs. The eyes are on the top of the cephalothorax, toward the front. Most spiders have eight simple eyes.

The second segment of a spider is the abdomen. At the underside of the rear of the abdomen is the anus and just in front of that within the abdomen are the silk glands. These glands feed silk through the spinnerets, a group of flexible tubes that lead to the outside of the body. The silk, of course, is used by the spider to make its webs.

Spiders come pre-equipped with a reputation that make them effective 3D models. To create a *great* 3D model, first examine the structure of a real-life spider. You needn't go far afield and look at the real thing; there are plenty of examples on videotape. (Remember: *Arachnophobia!*) But if you are adventuresome, go to the pet store; at least there the spiders are behind glass.

Attitude

Attitude is sometimes described as character, personality, or expression. It's what makes an individual animal unique. It is very important when modeling a 3D animal to demonstrate attitude so that the animal has a distinct identity. Certainly

Figure 3.30

The spider is a creepy crawly with two body segments and eight legs.

there is less diversity in facial features between two lions than between two humans, and that may seem to make it difficult to create attitude in your creatures. In fact, one female black widow spider looks pretty much like any other female of the species. And one polar bear looks pretty much like most other polar bears.

But the one thing that can separate your 3D animal from the next guy's is *attitude*. It doesn't mean that you have to put a leather jacket or a rainbow-dyed mane on your next lion—unless you really want to. It doesn't even have to be funny. Attitude means that the animal must have actions and reactions to which we all can relate.

Let's begin with the head. The general tilt of the head, the placement of the ears, and the look in the eyes can demonstrate emotions that are immediately apparent to us. They signal us that the animal is happy, sad, angry, or alert.

The ears, if your animal has any, are an especially important part of your model. They will help you tell a story and give the audience a clue about your animal's personality. The neighbor's cat has its ears laid back flat against its head. Is it happy to see you and your yappy little dog? I don't think so! It's trying to tell you something. Your dog has its head tilted and its ears pricked up. That

should tell you immediately that something has gotten its attention.

Animal eyes also give you clues. Although an animal's eyes don't change shape as much as a human's, when they move, they can still be very expressive. Some animals, like reptiles or insects, don't have eyes that are naturally expressive. If you want to put some character in that 3D model, it helps to humanize it somewhat. What Disney did for Kaa, you can do for your character, too—that is, unless your model must be completely realistic. In that case, you'd better find another avenue for instilling personality into that insect.

From the Siamese in *Lady and the Tramp* to Sylvester in Looney Toons, cats have been favorite animation subjects, and for good reason. A cat's eyes are very expressive and change shape radically as its emotions change. They can be half-closed to show contentment or wide open to show fear or curiosity. Sometimes the eyes are mere slits—put that with those flattened ears, and watch out, that's one mad kitty!

A dog can be moderately expressive with its eyes and brows, but usually its expressions are conveyed with the tilt of its head, ears, tail, and that expressive dog mouth.

TIP

Don't forget to add blinks to your animal eyes. Just like with human 3D characters, they make the animal seem alive. If a 3D model stops moving and remains motionless, even for a short time, the illusion will fail. A blink can get you through a motionless moment and continue the illusion of reality.

Never have a lifeless tail. It has to have some movement. Never leave the tail resting on the ground for no reason. Even my cat's tail has a twitching tip when she's ready to pounce on her prey (usually a ball of string). Remember, the tail is attached to the rest of the body. It moves and reacts together with the body as a whole.

Don't overlook the function of a cat's tail in maintaining its balance. It's key to the cat's ability to land on its feet.

The horse, although it can show some expression with its brow, ears, and head position, seems to have just two eye expressions, calm and "The barn's on fire!"

A pig has a rather limited range of eye expressions (Porky notwithstanding). However, pigs have such small eyes that it's hard to say if their look is one of satisfaction or just plain sleepy.

The next features to look at in your 3D animals are tails. Does it have a perky, upswung tail? Or does it have a dejected tail that drags behind? Whatever type of tail your animal has naturally, it can do much to show the mood of your animal. The tail is a good place to add a little exaggeration for that extra dose of winning personality.

The neck is an often overlooked area of the body when it comes to attitude. In reality, the neck can show attitude or expression in many situations. The neck can be arched to show hostility or stretched out to indicate anger. But neck movement is used most often to complete the whole picture. A beautiful horse with a prancing step can have an arched neck and give the appearance of haughtiness. A dog on a leash can have its neck stretched f-a-r out to show its eagerness. So before you start that 3D model, plan, plan, plan.

An animal's hair or fur can also show its personality. If your dog is scraggly and unkempt, this could mean that the dog's sick, irritable, or simply old. Usually this look is good for male types. Soft, silky fur is usually a feminine trait. It shows a well-cared-for animal. As soon as the hair shaders catch up with animators' need for authentic computer-generated hair, this will be an area that will bear fruit.

Studying an animal's movement and reproducing it move by move will give you

If your 3D model is a movie "good guy," it is more likely than not, he will be depicted as small, cute, and nonviolent. (Stallone-type heroes are a different category.) It doesn't really matter if that's the way your animal would react or look in real life; it makes the audience identify with and root for the hero. The villain, on the other hand, is usually large, dark, and bossy. Many times, the villain has sharp angles (exceeding 45 degrees) in its face and body. This enhances the look of evil.

The compression and expansion in an animal's legs typically occur at either or both ends. It can be seen in the shoulders and haunches and in the paws and toes.

a natural-looking animal. But if you want to show life, your imagination will have to fill in the blanks. That extra lift in the foot, or the knees that knock together in fear, give the animal character. Muybridge's pictures might show you form and function, but they can't show that extra something that brings your model to life.

If your 3D animal character is destined to be an actor in a game, animated film, or movie, you will have to deal with a pre-defined personality that originates elsewhere. But if you, as an animator, can come up with a "bit of business," as they say in comedy, that helps to define or illuminate the animated character and is almost always welcomed by the director.

If an animal is to take on human characteristics, remember that the facial structures of an animal are different from those of a human. For most animals, the eyes don't change shape and the cheeks don't bulge, as ours do. Some animals are so slim and muscular that their muscular compression and extension can be very deceiving.

In this chapter, we have only skimmed the surface of animal structure and motion. Take the information here and get out those walking boots. Some of these animals will be harder to observe than others. Just remember, your eyes are the best teacher.

Next Chapter...

In the next chapter we will be playing God, my personal favorite pastime. We'll explore the imaginary structure of everything from aliens to Draco the dragon from the Universal movie *Dragonheart*. I'll also discuss dinosaurs, not because they're mythical creatures, but just because they're extinct. Because there is ample information regarding dinosaur anatomy available, you might be wondering why they're in the next chapter. The truth is that scientific battles rage constantly about whether they were warm-blooded or cold-blooded, active or slothful—in short, we really aren't sure how they moved or even what their true skin configuration was; it's a make-it-up-as-we-go kind of process. So get ready, it will be fun.

Chapter 4

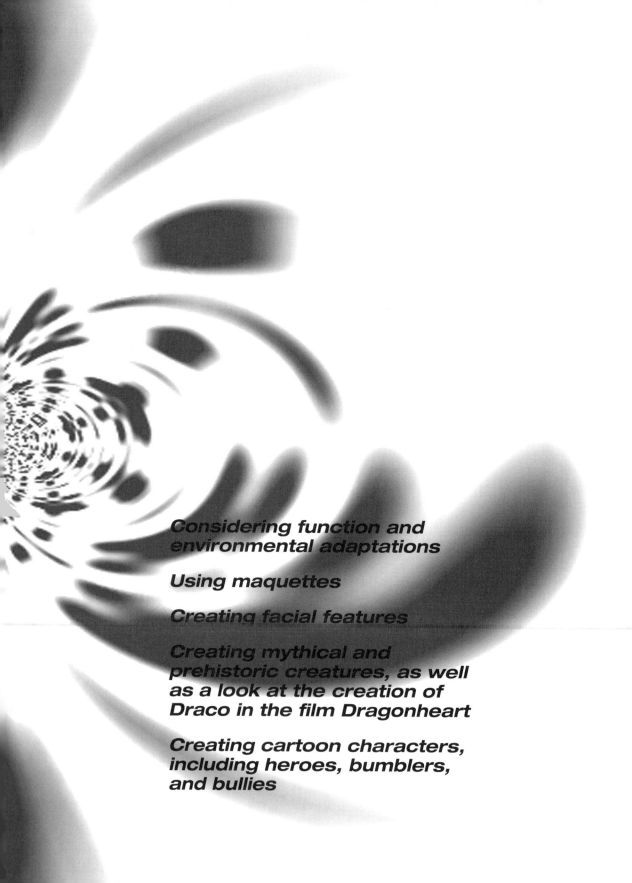

Considering function and environmental adaptations

Using maquettes

Creating facial features

Creating mythical and prehistoric creatures, as well as a look at the creation of Draco in the film Dragonheart

Creating cartoon characters, including heroes, bumblers, and bullies

Fantasyland

In this chapter, we escape from the restrictions of true-life subjects. Now it's time to apply the knowledge you gained from the last three chapters about real living things and learn how to create your own unique creatures. Maybe aliens with huge spaceships are your specialty...or dragons flying through the sky breathing fire. Maybe your dream is to give life to animals extinct for millions of years or just to the next host on Turner Broadcasting's Cartoon Network. With 3D characters, there's no limit to the possibilities. The first type we'll explore is aliens—those quirky extraterrestrials that keep popping up in popular culture from Jules Verne to ET to Star Trek.

The Genesis of a Fantasy Figure

In the beginning, the only thing you need is an idea. Dream up the kind of creature you want. Should it be large and bulky like an apatosaurus, or small and ethereal like a fairy? Scary or silly? Realistic or cartoony? If you need some ideas, go back and look at old *Star Trek* and *Star Trek: The Next Generation* episodes. Take out your laser disc copies of the Star Wars trilogy (if you have the CVA versions, you can freeze-frame during the Cantina sequence on Mos Eisley and find dozens of ideas). Spend a Saturday watching the morning cartoons with your kids. Mix and match. You never know what you'll think up if you just let your mind run free.

Once you've done all the video and TV browsing you can stand, start drawing a sketch. Yes, on paper. Even if your sketching muscles are a little weak, getting the basics on paper will help you as you build your creature. Describe in words all of the features you want in your creature. This helps sometimes if you don't *really* have a structure in mind. When you see it all on paper, it might all come together more easily. It might also spark your creativity to add still more facets as you try to incorporate all of the "Top Ten" features in one body.

The Needs of an Alien

Remember, your creature needn't look human; in fact, it doesn't even have to have eyes on its head—or maybe it has many heads and many eyes. But you should consider the following:

- Each creature must have some way to *detect and interact* with its environment, using the senses of vision, hearing, smell, touch, and/or taste, or any others you devise. In conjunction with the next two needs, these sensory organs make it possible for a creature to locate energy and a mate or mates (if sexual reproduction is necessary to the species), avoid physical dangers, and secure its physical space.

- All creatures must consume some type of *energy* to sustain life, be it plant, animal, energy from the sun, or 10W-30 motor oil. And there probably should be some orifice through which to ingest the energy,

as well as bodily structures designed to move the energy to the orifice. How would we eat without mouths, arms, and hands? Intravenous feeding just isn't very interesting.

- All creatures probably need some means and orifice for excreting *waste*, although this function is most often politely overlooked in animation. When dreaming up a creature, however, consider how your creature might accomplish this function and how it might affect its environment when it does. This might also give you a sense of the overall structure of the creature. Consider also whether two or more bodily functions can be accomplished with the same physical structure; the possibilities for comic relief are many.

- The norm for our earth-based biological mobile creatures is to *reproduce* sexually, although an alien may use any means you can conceive. Consider, though, when designing your creature how many of the human structural features are designed to enhance and ensure reproduction and perpetuation of the species. Maybe your aliens go gaga over big ears; it doesn't matter whether it's consistent with our own experience as long as it's consistent with your aliens' experience.

- All creatures need some form of *support*. Whether they use legs, pseudopods, cilia, thought balloons, or some form of support no one has ever imagined, creatures require some means to withstand the force of gravity. Even snakes spread their weight over their entire length (or most of it, anyway). When you design the size and structure of the supporting members, consider the mass of the supported body, head, or whatever, and the environment in which the creature lives. If it is a high-gravity world, even a low-mass creature requires substantial supports.

- All creatures are either *mobile or immobile*, and you can choose which you want (or maybe some of your creatures can zip around the others who are planted firmly on the soil). If your creature is to be mobile, you must provide some means for the creature to move around: walk, crawl, levitate, ooze, fly, whatever. Once you've chosen a means of movement, study any earth creatures who use that same means of transportation for clues on how to achieve it convincingly. By the way, levitation is the easiest means of transportation in 3D, because nothing has to move to make it possible, but I hereby declare that using levitation is cheating.

- To make your creatures more interesting to others, make them able to *communicate* with others in some way. It can be by audible speech achieved through a moving mouth, an orifice that opens to allow sound produced within to escape, or any other way you can conceive. Telepathy, like levitation, is the easiest to achieve in 3D, since nothing has to be animated; however, like levitation, I hereby declare that telepathy is also cheating! Remember, if your creatures are intended to be a part

of a world viewed by laypersons, you'll have to translate the creatures' communications in some way to involve the viewers with the action. Otherwise, it's like watching a Swedish movie with no subtitles—you can only guess what's going on, and if it's a Bergman film, you can't even do that half the time.

- Finally, second only to a creature's biological needs are its *social* needs. You should ensure that your creatures have the means to form social contacts with others of their species. They might or might not use the organs of communication, depending on your vision. But if your creatures interact by entwining tentacles, unless you're a very skillful 3D animator, you'll have to translate this activity for your viewers. And think of the difficulty of animating entwining tentacles in the first place.

If your creature has a plausible means of addressing all of these needs, then viewers won't automatically discredit your creature because it "doesn't act right."

Body Design

The body design is the first basic shape to decide on for your creature.

If you want the creature to fly, a bird's aerodynamic body is useful. If you want a more reptilian-type flier, the body muscle and wing shape will be important to keep the creature in the air.

Swimmers are another class in which to consider body shape. The tapered shape of a fish lets the animal move through the

Figure 4.1

A mermaid has the tapered body of a fish and a large tail for locomotion.

water with less resistance. See Figure 4.1. Even mermaids have the tapered body of a fish with an enormous tail. (See Chapter 3 for details.)

Land creatures have less need for a tapered form. They can walk on two, four, or as many legs as you want.

Maybe you'd like your creature to have more than one head—or no head at all; these are all decisions you have to make.

Facial Features

Even if your creature has two noses where a human's ears are or only one eye, you'll still need to follow a few rules of thumb to make your character credible to the viewer. Much of a character's personality is conveyed through its facial features, so modeling and animating them is crucial to the success of your animation. Because

eyes are considered the "windows to the soul," we'll start with them first.

Eyes

Eyes are an important part of your creature, whether it's a human, a cat, or a dancing frog. Choosing the proper eye movement for your type of creature is important. Of course, in a fantasy figure, you can have any type of eye you want. Just because its body is reptilian doesn't mean the eyes have to be reptilian as well. In fact, if the creature's an alien, it will look much more eerie if they're not.

Here are a few tips to remember when animating eyes (refer to Eye Movement in Chapter 5):

- The eyes should never remain still, unless your character is dead and just doesn't know it yet. Usually the focus of the eyes is constantly changing, so the pupils are in constant flux as the eyes shift and blink.

- Eyeballs are nearly always round, but there are some striking departures from this. Tube eyes (owl eyes), for example, are deep and narrow to gather in a great deal of light, so that its owner can hunt in dim light.

- Compared to the animal's mass, eyes are relatively small in large animals and large in small animals.

- Eyes are typically placed on the side of the head for those who take flight or need to watch for predators.

- Predators' eyes are typically placed on the front of the head to provide binocular vision for tracking moving prey.

- Eyelids always follow the shape of the eye.

- Reptiles, snakes, and similar creatures have solid-black, round, staring eyes. They have no visible eyelids.

- Pupils are usually transversely oval, except for cats, who have vertical pupils.

- Insect eyes are generally large, round, bulgy, and composed of many smaller eyes. They are called *compound eyes.*

See Figure 4.2 for examples of different types of eyes.

Mouths and Mouth Parts

The mouth, or mouths, on your creature certainly needn't look like ours. Different species have mouths and mouth parts that you might find more interesting and more appropriate to your creature. For example:

- Insects usually have three pair of primitive jaw-like mouth parts. The mouth parts of a grasshopper, for example, in-

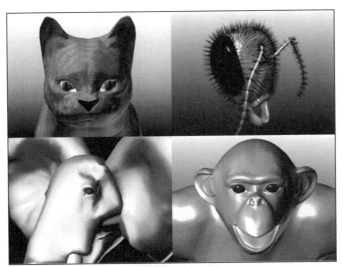

3D Models provided by Viewpoint Datalabs International, Inc.

Figure 4.2

A variety of eye types show different characteristics.

clude the upper lip; immediately under that are two *mandibles,* or heavy chewing jaws. Under the mandibles are two *maxillae,* each bearing a jointed *palp* (like a feeler). Between the basal parts of the maxillae lies the pear-shaped *hypoglossus.* The divided lower lip also has a pair of palps. The palps are sensory, while the remaining parts are used for food manipulation and chewing. Insect mouth parts may be used in biting or for sucking. See Figure 4.3.

- Birds have a variety of beak shapes, depending on their function. (See Chapter 3 for details.)

- Snakes have soft mouths that can open quite large to accommodate the ingestion of prey. Their fangs angle backward to hold their prey and keep it from escaping. Venom drips from its fangs into its prey. See Figure 4.4.

- Most fish have round, open mouths, although, again, mouth shape is

determined by the function. Some even have a sucker-like mouth for eating off the bottoms and sides of their environment.

Making Maquettes

Many of the premier special-effects houses like ILM and Pacific Data Images (PDI) typically begin body design by making one or more maquettes, or small statues of the fantasy figures they will be modeling in the computer later. Sometimes the tactile feel of actually moving the clay around to form your creature can be very rewarding and productive. Besides, you can't sit at a computer all the time!

If you want to try making a maquette, I recommend that you use an oil-based synthetic clay, like Super Sculpey. It's easy to manipulate and can be baked in a low-temperature (home) oven for convenience. Many times, sculptors use wire armatures as a skeleton inside a model to give it form and standardize the size. Armatures can

3D Models provided by Viewpoint Datalabs International, Inc.

Figure 4.3

The mouth parts of a typical insect.

Figure 4.4

A snake's mouth and fangs are unique.

also be jointed to give a natural bend at the joints.

By making these figures you will be able to see all those little extra touches that are so easy to add in clay and so difficult to control in a 3D version. For this reason, many of the elaborate 3D movie creatures, such as Draco in *Dragonheart*, are first sculpted in clay and then digitized into the computer as a 3D model for further manipulation. This process can be expensive, but it can give you impressive results if you are better with clay.

Dragons—and Draco in Particular

What if a dragon is more to your liking? With a 3D creature such as this, consider carefully the style of dragon you want. (Oops—back to planning!) A dragon can be an elusive giant that breathes fire and eats virgins like in *Dragonslayer*, or it can be a long, slender, colorful Chinese dragon often depicted on Chinese silk robes. See Figure 4.5 for a look at a great dragon.

Turning now to *Dragonheart*, the *tourdeforce* swords-and-dragon movie recently in theaters, let's look at what went into making the costarring dragon, Draco, seem so real. It's almost a textbook example of what goes into producing state-of-the-art animation with today's technology.

Draco was first designed as a highly detailed clay maquette by Academy Award Winner Phil Tippett, and then digitized by ILM. The goal was to produce a

Although most animation houses send their maquettes out of house to digitizing specialists, it's now possible to add an inexpensive digitizer to a 3D Studio MAX system. For less than $5,000, you can add a digitizing system to a typical 3D Studio MAX installation and save hours of expensive 3D modeling time.

Another alternative is the technique of photogrammetry, which creates 3D models directly from digitized images. Through the courtesy of CompInt, we are including an evaluation version of Photo4D that lets you experiment with this technique yourself.

realistic, 18-foot tall, winged dragon as a 3D model.

The next step was back to basic storyboards. (See "Storyboards" in Chapter 5.) These storyboards laid out the basic actions and let the CGI artists prepare low-cost animation tests so that the dragon's movements could be previewed. The

storyboards also helped the director frame the shots and anticipate composition problems with the background film image.

The Name Is Draco, James Draco

Problems didn't really arise in the process until Sean Connery was chosen to be the voice of Draco. Making a dragon look and move in a lifelike manner was a difficult

Figure 4.5

This dragon is a wonderful creation by Cyrus Lum, Director of Advanced Technology at Iguana Systems. OK, it was modeled and animated with Alias, not MAX, but it's still a great dragon!

enough task, making it speak like a human was more difficult, but making it wrap its dragon's mouth around Connery's Scottish brogue was a whole new level of difficulty. Motion capture would have been an option had the dragon's mouth resembled ours, but since it didn't, other options had to be explored. Ultimately, facial animation and lip-syncing techniques were developed by the crew at ILM, and Draco ended up speaking with Connery's distinct facial mannerisms. Completing the animation required a year of hard work by a large team of animators and filmmakers.

The 3D model of Draco was so dense that the software couldn't handle the massive amounts of data required to change the expressions on the dragon's face. Finally, the wizards at ILM developed software that let them move small portions of Draco's face at a time to allow for facial expression and muscle twitches.

One of the keys to the illusion that the dragon is really speaking is the movement of Draco's tongue; it moves perfectly as Connery/Draco speaks. The appearance of a wet, saliva-dripping tongue as it talked added a touch of realism that is so often forgotten in other animations.

Dragon Flight

Handling weight and gravity properly also played a big role in the lifelike appearance of Draco. The original creative vision had been to create a dragon made of light, yet still a terrestrial. Seemingly contradictorily, when the dragon walked, the ground should shake under its feet, but it should still take off and fly with little effort.

The animators didn't want the dragon to float, so they developed software for flying sequences that allowed the body of the dragon to remain alive and active as it flew, with its dramatic wing beats making its body shake. Draco uses its legs to turn and its tail as both a rudder and brake. The final result was a dragon who actually appeared to be using its massive wings and body muscles to propel itself through the air. Secondary motion was also used on the dragon's wings to add follow-through and extra weight to the skin.

Final Touches

The final touches that lend a look of perfection to Draco are: the great texture mapping of the skin, wings and mouth, teeth and claws, and the wonderful eyes. Those eyes! If you watch the eye animation, you'll notice that the pupils contract and dilate with the light and that the eyelids move and the eyes blink appropriately to really give a realistic appearance.

Others in the Creature World

Draco is a great example of dramatic modeling in 3D. However, there are other types of creatures besides dragons. Even some dinosaurs flew, complete with reptilian skin and bat-like wings. But what about more gentle souls like fairies? Remember the fairy with the beautiful transparent CGI wings in Willow? She's a great example of how fairy wings should look. To animate wings like hers in CGI, first examine how hummingbird wings work. (See Chapter 5.)

Jim Cameron's *The Abyss* pioneered the use of CGI with the graceful winged aliens who lived in the abyss. These creatures had more rubbery qualities to their bodies, with beautiful transparent winged appendages and skin. And of course, who could forget the water creature? The creatures in this movie are proof that if you can conceive it and execute it properly, you can convince the viewer it's possible.

Ghosts and Goblins

Ghosts and goblins are other fantasy creatures you might want to investigate. The best part about a ghost is that it can be anything from a human figure with it's opacity turned way down to a blob of mist that floats through the air. Anything is possible.

For pointers on ghost animation, review the movie *Casper*, another ILM project. Four ghosts spoke and interacted with other actors in that film, and at least one was onscreen for most of the picture. Special facial and lip-sync animation tools were created for the movie, but it was not nearly as complicated as that used to make Draco talk.

Disney's new animated motion picture of *The Hunchback of Notre Dame* includes some great gargoyles in its cast. These devil-like creatures that sit on the sides

of buildings were said to keep evil away. (I'll show you how to create a gargoyle with Character Studio in the second half of this book.)

Jurassic in Your Computer

Even though we have fossil skeletons and tons of data that help us understand how dinosaurs *probably* looked, moved, ate, and lived, I've added them to this chapter because we still really can't be absolutely sure. If you are in the mood to make a sequel to *Jurassic Park*, there's a wealth of paleontological data available; a quick trip out onto the Web will produce all you could hope for and more. (See the Resources appendix for more information.)

Remember that endowing a mythical or prehistoric creature with certain traits of present-day animals can impart realism to your creation. For instance, when ILM (again) was working on the dinosaur motion for the really *big* lizards in *Jurassic Park,* they used motion capture to record the movements of elephants. Since it was familiar to us, we accepted it as a likely simulation.

As always, *know your creature.* Was it an herbivore or carnivore? What areas did it live in? Get answers to these questions before you start to push pixels around.

Don't forget that when you are animating ghosts or any other creature with flowing robes or fabric, add secondary motion to give it that final "kick." (See Chapter 5 for details on secondary motion.)

Movement for Reality-Based Creatures

The data on your list and in your sketches will give you a good start toward determining your creature's basic movements. Each movement must at least *seem* logical. The basic rule to follow here is that a creature needs a smooth and unhindered movement that looks natural to its species, whatever that is.

PDI created a wonderful species of humanoid aliens for the Universal Studios movie *The Arrival*. Not only were they wonderfully modeled, but the skin texture mapping and the movement of the head flaps covering the brain were remarkable. It wasn't until they pushed their knee joints backward and started walking that the effect was weakened for me. I'm sure that the concept was to differentiate the aliens from the run-of-the-mill, I've-seen-them-in-every-space-movie aliens. However, to me, the movement seemed unnatural to the body structure, appearing jerky and looking as though the creatures required great effort to move. It's probably not how a species would evolve naturally.

So, as you're planning your creatures, remember to find a movement that is appropriate for the type of body structure of your creature.

Cartoons in 3D

Cartoons in 3D should be very similar to cartoons in 2D: the same rules apply. The difference, of course, is that the 2D artist has much more control over the fluid movement of the character. In 3D, we are working with a simulation of a solid creature. Our effects will include that solid structure in every frame, which deters us from some typical cartoon special effects such as including just a part of the character in some frames. (I first noticed this when I went through the Disney movie *Who Framed Roger Rabbit?* frame by frame, but it's a classic cartooning technique that has been used for decades. Once I noticed it, I saw it everywhere!)

Cartoon Characters

When creating 3D cartoon characters, remember that a cartoon is usually peopled by stock "types," that is; a hero, a villain, a bully, and maybe a cute little pet. Each type of character has a classic form that has been developed by generations of cartoonists. To "sell" the idea that one of your 3D creatures is heroic, villainous, or cute, borrow the appropriate form from the cel animators who have preconditioned us to accept the appearance of each type.

Follow these suggestions, and when your long, angular 3D villain appears in the scene, viewers will immediately understand that *he is the villain*. It will make your job as an animator that much easier.

Cute Creatures

If cute is what you need, your creature should have the same attributes as a baby. (See Chapter 1.) Generally, the cute character has an oversized head with large eyes. Its body is chubby and round. See Figure 4.6.

3D Models provided by Viewpoint Datalabs International, Inc.

Figure 4.6

A cute creature usually has the attributes of a baby.

Heroes

The male hero creature is shown many times in the Superman image, triangular in body shape with a square chin. He should be very handsome, of course, in a cartoon sort of way. See Figure 4.7.

Villains and Other Bad Guys

To create a character who looks like a villain, use a more angular appearance. Think of Jafar in Disney's *Aladdin* or the evil queen in *Sleeping Beauty*. A villain's eyebrows are usually turned up at a 45-degree

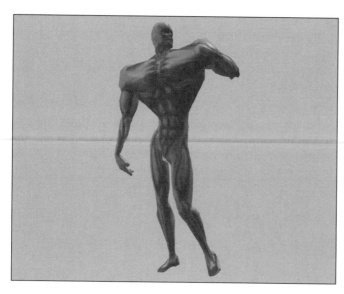

Figure 4.7

A heroic creature typically follows the Superman image.

Figure 4.8

Villains and bad guys.

angle. The eyes are narrow. The face may also be angled to a pointy chin. See Figure 4.8.

Cartoon villains can also be animals, anything from a rat (Professor Ratigan from the movie *The Great Mouse Detective*) to a tiger (Shere Khan from the movie *Jungle Book*). Obviously, a fuzzy bunny is never going to *look* like a villain, *Watership Down* notwithstanding.

The bully is another bad guy, but instead of a long, angular face, he usually has a small head on a large muscular or rotund body. Disney's giant in the classic cartoon *The Brave Little Tailor* is a typical cartoon bully. And who can leave bullies without mentioning Popeye's nemesis, Bluto?

Goofy Creatures

The goofy creature is the bumbler, the uncoordinated fool. This type of charac-

ter is usually tall with large feet. His facial features are exaggerated in a long face and neck. See Figure 4.9.

Cartoon Expressions

Cartoon expressions must be shown on the whole body, not just the face.

Compared to realistic character animation, a 3D cartoon character is much more rubbery. When the face changes, the whole head must move to show the change. For example, in a frown, the head can begin with a stretch and then squash down until it appears almost folded to produce the classic cartoon effect. Following are rules to think about as you animate your 3D cartoon character:

- Look for actions that *you* wish *you* could do.

Figure 4.9

This uncoordinated goof has all the classic features.

- Give your character something to react to.

- Make your expressive movement larger than life.

- Slow the action down as you change an expression. It's better to make the change at the end or after a move is completed. This allows time for the audience to see it.

- Be careful not to cover your expressions with body movements, such as waving arms, or with secondary movement, such as clothes flapping.

- Never make your character look up to frown, unless you mean it to be sinister.

- Don't make facial features so large that they cover up expressions. For example, a large nose could hide a smile.

- Show the right expression for the action.

- It's the *change* of expression that shows that the character is thinking. It's the *thinking* that gives the illusion of life, and it's the *life* that gives the meaning of expression.

Eyes for Cartoon Figures

Remember that if the pupil in a cartoon eye is very small, it produces a dazed, weak, unconvincing look to the expression; if the pupil is very large, it shows interest and awareness. See Figure 4.10.

If the pupil touches the rim of the eyeball, the character appears forceful, but if there is white all the way around it, it makes the expression appear vague.

Eye movement in cartoons is the same as in real life; it moves in arcs rather than straight lines. Otherwise, the eye looks like it's simply sliding from one side of the eye socket to the other. See Figure 4.11.

Character Animation with 3D Studio MAX

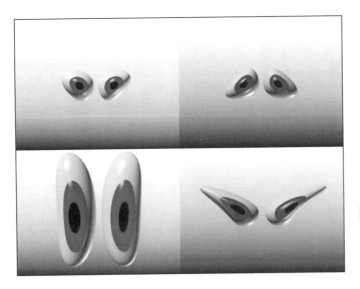

Figure 4.10

Eyes convey different emotions readily.

If the pupil is moving up and down on one side of the eyeball, it's more convincing if the eyeball itself stretches slightly in the area where the pupil is touching it. See Figure 4.12.

In cartooning, eyes looking up are more appealing. From the days of the Renaissance painters, eyes looking up (toward heaven) have denoted innocence and purity.

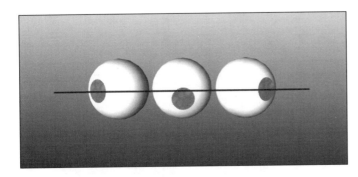

Figure 4.11

The eye moves in arcs in a cartoon eye, as well as in real life.

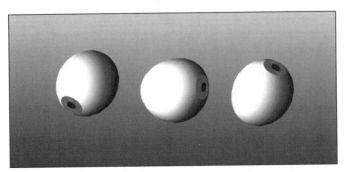

Figure 4.12

When the pupil moves up and down on the side of an eye, the eye shape should change as well.

Use squash and stretch on cartoon eyes just as on the rest of the body.

If you want your 3D cartoon characters to look like robots, fix their eyes in a blank stare. On the other hand, if you want exuberance and life to show in your characters, the eyes must remain moving. Dancing eyes show a lot of movement that can range from wide-eyed excitement to crinkled in laughter.

Some cartoon eyes can be made simply as circles expanding from the same point, as shown in Figures 4.13a and 4.13b.

The sclera (whites) of villains' eyes sometimes aren't white. Making the entire eye a single color can lend a sinister look.

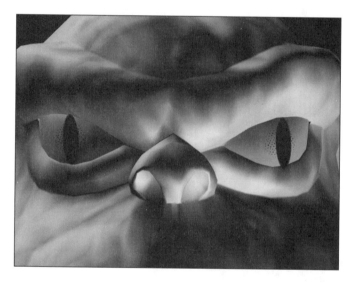

a.

Figure 4.13

An example of cartoon eyes.

b.

Even eye blinks can help tell the story in a cartoon. Blinking can mean a character is dazed, confused, or just sleepy. The fluttery blink of someone just waking up is achieved by staggering the blinks. Only the whites of the eye appear instead of the pupil until the eye gradually opens.

Next Chapter...

In this chapter, we've covered everything from dragons to bullies. In the next chapter, I'll analyze movement, how it should look, and how to get it. It's the final ingredient before we begin animating our 3D creatures in Character Studio.

Chapter 5

Storyboarding and staging

*Animating emotion through
facial expressions*

*Animating, walking, running,
laughing, and picking up
objects*

*Understanding timing and
subtleties in body language*

*Adding anticipatory and
follow-through movements
for enhanced realism*

*Using overlapping action and
secondary motion*

Animating animals and insects

Motion capture overview

The Nature of Motion

In the previous four chapters, learning body anatomy and structure was our main objective. Although body construction is an important part of character modeling, I'm going to let you in on a little secret; movement is the *real* star. Your model might be absolutely perfect, but without believable movement, it will always look like a model. In fact, if the movements are right, even a desk lamp can look alive! Enhancing your animation with those little subtle movements that make your model seem real is what character animation is all about. It's what makes your 3D character look real, gives it, well, character and personality...makes it come to life. That's what this chapter is all about: how to create realistic movement and, thus, realistic characters.

Animating Human Movement: The Process

Even though you might not be aware of it, precise body movement has become an important part of your life experience. From the time you were born, you have been watching people move and build up an unconscious vocabulary of human movement. This knowledge would seldom occur to you until you see an animated character that doesn't move quite right—that's when you delve into your vocabulary and compare the movement with what you know should be true. If they don't match, you know that what you are seeing is synthetic and unacceptable.

Making a lifelike model is relatively simple compared to the task of giving it believable movement. The best solution, of course, would be to use models that move in every way like their real-life counterparts. Good luck! The muscles and tissues of a living thing are organic and alive. It is important to understand that the whole body is not only connected by moving joints, it also has a soft moveable layer of muscle and tissue over a hard surface, the skeleton. This construction not only lets the body move, turn, twist, and bend, it also creates a whole range of subtle surface movements. Without these, living creatures (or models of them) would move like robots.

A simple head movement, for example, affects many areas of the body in terms of both position and balance. Try turning your head and looking over your shoulder. Unless you are very limber (or oddly constructed), you will not be able to turn your head sufficiently without also twisting your torso and dipping your shoulder. Stand up and bend your head down to your chest; feel how your body shifts to compensate for the change in your center of gravity. It's these types of subtle changes that are most often missing in 3D character animation. We see a character turn his head like Robby the Robot, completely around the vertical neck axis with no other motion.

For this reason, it is very difficult to re-create believable human movement without the help of motion capture. The best we can hope for otherwise is *lifelike* movement. This is the challenge facing an animator charged with the task of creating realistic animation. And it can be an overwhelming task.

Planning

Whether you are animating a single 3D model or a sceneful, planning is the important first step. Unless you're just building your demo reel for future employment, you probably will start each animation job with an assignment. If you're lucky, you might even be able to participate in the planning and design of the elements you'll be animating. Since 3D animation is still so new and relatively limited in its capabilities, an animation producer would be wise to involve the artists in the planning process.

Wherever the initial idea comes from, the next step is usually an iterative process of design sketches, story refinement, more sketches, more rewriting, and so on until there is some final agreement between the producer, artists, and client/boss regarding the shape and scope of the project.

The next step is usually a more complete visual depiction of the story line and the animation sequences that will make up the final production. This is the storyboard.

Storyboards

Storyboards are used by modelers, animators, and producers to lay out the actions and viewing angles graphically before actually animating the scene. A portion of a typical storyboard is shown in Figures 5.1. The use of storyboards lets the team plan motion in advance, making it easier for everyone to visualize the entire project before actual animation begins. It also provides a milestone and a deliverable that can be useful for gauging progress and securing approvals. Finally, storyboards provide a visual source for creating a shot list, the master document that lists and gives particulars for all shots that will be part of the production.

Changing and polishing action on a storyboard is much more efficient than waiting until after a sequence is near complete and then having someone decide that instead of the character bending left at frame 100, it should jump like a rabbit at frame 250.

Lines of Action

The *line of action* is an imaginary line showing the angle and direction of the character's body as it moves through an action sequence. The line of action can be as simple as a line drawn on your storyboard (or even using a china marker on your computer screen, although I don't recommend this) that shows the flow of movement that the body follows as you move your character into the correct position. See Figure 5.2.

Planning the lines of action helps you produce more dynamic, more effective animations. The line of angle concept is an old standby in 2D animation but not often applied in 3D. Using lines of action, you can help your characters convey emotion and personality.

Character Construction

The next step for you as an animator is to construct or secure from other sources all of the 3D characters, props, and sets necessary to complete the assigned sequences. In some animation shops, these tasks are split among several staff members. Where several 3D artists are working on a single production, it is more efficient and practical for all to share a common set of models, maps, backgrounds, and materials. This also ensures consistency of form and color from shot to shot.

Some productions, such as movie 3D stunt doubles (like those produced for *Batman Forever* by Pacific Data Images, Inc.) require that the modeler produce exact 3D replicas of real actors. This is best accomplished by 3D scanning, if the actor and costume are available. In general, any production that requires the combination of several media, such as 3D animation together with live video or film, requires some of the most exacting modeling to ensure a seamless final production.

If the modeler and animator are not the same person, the modeler must receive input from the animator to ensure that the 3D characters are constructed to allow the desired movements. Simple actions viewed from a distance might require only simple

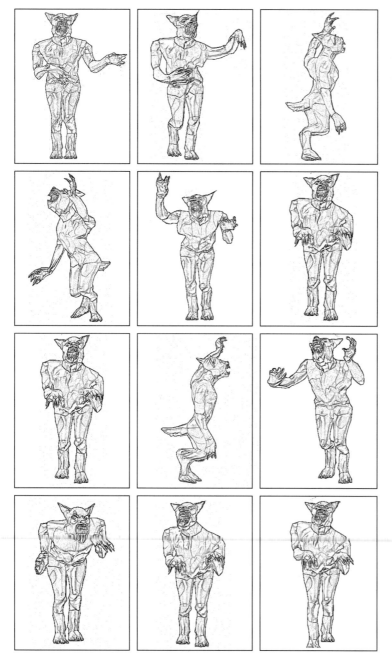

Figure 5.1

A storyboard gives everyone a better understanding of how an animation sequence should look before building models and setting

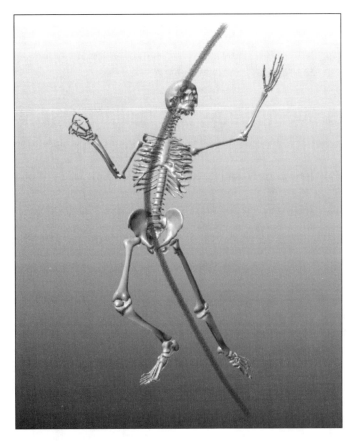

Figure 5.2

When animating an action movement, a line of action will serve as a guideline.

models, but close-ups typically require more complex, definitive models. Often, several versions can be prepared with different degrees of complexity for these uses.

Model construction is also determined in part by the actions the characters are required to perform. Will a character run madly across the screen or tip-toe through sleeping guard dogs? Will she walk into heavy winds or throw an ax? The smoothness and effectiveness of the animation of the character will depend in part upon the animators having complex enough models to re-create realistic motion. Skimp here and no amount of money during animation will make up for it.

Appeal

Your characters must *appeal* to the viewer. Appeal doesn't necessarily mean little cutesy, fluffy bunnies, but it does mean that your characters must have what the viewer wants to see. Whether it's a pleasing look, charm, personality, communication, or simplicity, appeal is what draws your viewer's eye and holds it. Clumsy, awkward designs and movements have low appeal. The viewer, after all, wants to be entertained.

Think of the characters that appeal to you. The toys in *Toy Story* were appealing because they represented toys we all had as kids, come to life. They were likable characters facing an unlikable foe, Sid, next door. The tension between the principal characters added to the excitement, and the lifelike movement made the concept believable.

When animating your 3D characters, try to avoid stiff, wooden actions. This usually occurs when both arms or legs are in the same position doing the same thing. Even one side of the face should never mirror the other. Try to vary each side of all parts of the body to make it appear more natural.

Staging

Staging is something that often seems to be forgotten in 3D animation. If you want to build 3D models for sale or just to pass time on a Saturday afternoon, staging is unnecessary. However, if you are telling a story or showing personality, staging can be very important. In general, staging has been described by John Lasseter as "...the presentation of an idea so that it is completely and unmistakably clear."

Staging can mean making a character's personality absolutely unmistakable, creating a facial expression that can be readily seen by the audience, or conveying a mood that can affect the viewers. Staging can include the backgrounds, lighting, effects, movement, camera angles, and all other aspects that contribute to the final appearance of the work.

In staging the action in your scene, lead your viewer's eyes to the place in the scene where an idea or action is occurring. It's also important to present only one action to the viewer at a time. If too much action occurs in a scene at once, it causes the viewer to try to divide his or her attention. The result is confusion and an unclear message.

Staging arises from the story, graphic design concepts, mood, and capability of the animators and software producing the work. Compare the bright, comfortable lighting and props in Andy's bedroom in *Toy Story* with the dark, sinister appearance of Sid's bedroom next door.

Staging is just as important in the creation of 3D video games as in motion pictures. Although the popularity of 3D characters in video games has soared, many times problems arise when animators combine 3D and 2D animation. Sitting side-by-side, 2D and 3D have distinctly different looks. (Many traditional 2D cel animators have criticized 3D animation for this very reason.) Some animators have solved this appearance problem by reducing their glossy, high-resolution 3D imagery to a low-resolution, low-color format. Compare the high-resolution 3D image, Figure 5.3a, with the reduced-format image in Figure 5.3b.

This was the solution adopted by Lucasarts Entertainment in their graphics adventure game *Full Throttle*. The animation of the geometric shapes of the vehicles were easier to produce in 3D, but the character animation was more effectively done in 2D. To mesh the two, the artists rendered the 3D geometry at the low resolution of the game, using a severely limited palette and producing a more traditional 2D look.

Figure 5.3

139

Chapter 5: The Nature of Motion

Image a. is a typical 3D rendering, while image b. has been rendered at low resolution with a reduced palette to simulate 2D paintwork.

a.

b.

3D Models provided by Viewpoint Datalabs International, Inc.

In motion pictures, other problems appear. Typically, lighting is a big problem when combining 3D animation with film. This was apparent in Universal Studios film *Jumanji*. As good as ILM's animal modeling and animation were—and they were generally excellent—some of the exterior 3D segments seemed to have lower color saturation than the accompanying live action. Film lighting is much more intense than generally used in CGI, and this must be taken into account to produce a consistent look.

Another problem occurs when the action of the character or other object of interest does not contrast sufficiently with the background action. We always focus on the silent hero standing strong in the midst of the chaos swirling around him or running through the silent children's ward at night.

Backgrounds are essential to complete an animation and tie it into the story line. However, there should be nothing behind the characters that detract from the foreground action. Too much color or distract-ing patterns in the background can conflict with the characters and make the scene very confusing. The background tends to detract from the character if it's too busy or lifelike, as seen in Figures 5.4a and 5.4b.

In film this is accomplished by setting the focal length of the lens to blur the back-ground while the foreground is sharp. 3D animation software has always rendered everything within camera view with the same degree of sharpness. This not only

a.

3D Models provided by Viewpoint Datalabs International, Inc.

Figure 5.4

The background is overwhelming the foreground character in Figure 5.4a. In Figure 5.4b you can see how the character is brought out as the main focus by muting the background.

3D Models provided by Viewpoint Datalabs International, Inc.

b.

does not match film, it also doesn't match our own experience. (Try staring at this book in the foreground and then look over the book edge without refocusing your eyes. The wall beyond should be blurry.) However, even desktop animation systems are now gaining the capability of blurring the backgrounds. For example, Digimation's LenZFX MAX lets you set the effective depth of field in 3D Studio MAX scenes to simulate traditional depth of field blurring. (See the Resources appendix for details on how to obtain this product.)

The rule of thumb is this: The eye will be attracted to movement in a still scene and to the still object in a busy scene.

Another way to control visual distraction is to simplify the objects in the background, as shown in Figure 5.5. This technique has been used in many of Disney's more elaborate animated films. Disney animators are trained to use backgrounds to focus attention on foreground action.

To control background distraction in 3D, select the background images or the sets and props carefully and use custom lighting to light the foreground more brightly.

Also, apply background fogging, dimming, or blurring, depending on which is available in your software.

Animating the Head and Face

As humans, we focus on the face and head for communication of all kinds. We receive information not only from spoken words, but also from facial expressions, the eyes,

3D Models provided by Viewpoint Datalabs International, Inc.

Figure 5.5

A carefully designed background can be used to frame the central figures in your scene.

Character Animation with 3D Studio MAX

TIP *Remember that even though the background should be controlled carefully, you still need a distinct solid plane for your character's feet. A fuzzy surface might cover up a multitude of animation sins, but it can also make your star look like he's standing on a cloud.*

and even the head posture. Learning how to animate the head and face effectively is extremely important for a 3D animator, as there is little in the way of commercial software that provides a substitute.

Eyes in Motion

It's said that the eyes are the window to the soul and, indeed, the eyes are the first thing we notice on a person (although some feminists argue that men look elsewhere first). The best way to learn about eye movement is through observation, observation, and more observation. As I've cautioned in previous chapters, try to be discreet. If you're shy about staring at others—or live in New York where it's frowned upon—try using a mirror in a room by yourself to examine your own facial movements.

Notice that the eyes move and blink constantly. Even as we sleep, our eyes continue to move. Eye movements show expression and give the impression of life; in fact, *any* eye movement is better than a straight-ahead, static stare. (Yes, Aunt Gertrude's been dead awhile, but we like to prop her up for special occasions.)

Peek at people on the street. Watch them as they change their focus to something new, and you'll notice that their eyes turn first in anticipation of the head moving. This action isn't dramatic, but it is consistent. Add even a slight eye motion to your 3D characters to give them a much more realistic appearance. Remember, the eyes always lead the head motion, and if the head motion is rapid, the eyes close, as mentioned above.

CHARACTER ANIMATION RULES

1. Nothing alive ever turns or moves in perfectly straight lines.

2. Everything moves in arcs: eyes, limbs, bodies—everything.

3. There are no perfectly flat surfaces on bodies. Every surface is curved and rounded.

Consider a simple quick turn of the head. As the turn starts, the eyes start the turn, then close, and the head tilts down slightly. As the head reaches the desired end position, the head tilts back up again and the eyes reopen. See Figures 5.6a through e.

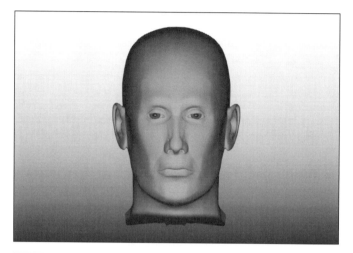

a.

Figure 5.6

When a head turns, it never moves in straight lines. The head moves in an arc as the eyes close and open again.

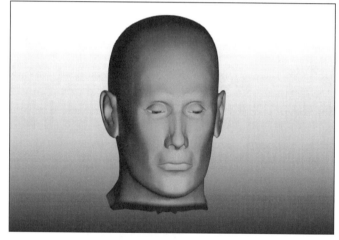

b.

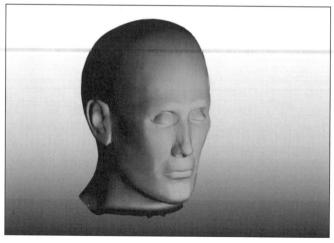

c.

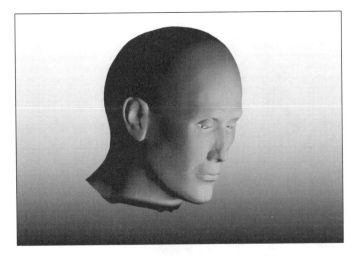

d.

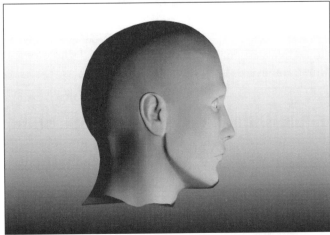

e.

Sideways

Even a simple-appearing sideways glance is actually a very complex motion. More changes occur in the eye than simply moving the iris from one side of the eye opening to the other. The shape of the eyelid itself alters according to the position of the iris. The rule of thumb is that the high point of the arch in the upper lid is always above the iris. The lower lid, however, changes very little. The result is that the eye shape changes as it moves to the side.

Downward

Looking down also involves special attention. Unless the eyes are closing, the pupil is always visible in the opening. This is accomplished by bowing the lower lid, producing a crease under the lower lid. The further down you look, the sharper the bow becomes and the deeper the crease gets. See Figure 5.7.

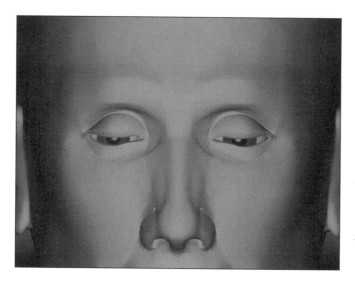

Figure 5.7

A downward gaze is accomplished by bowing the bottom lid so the pupil can still be observed through the opening.

Upward

The upward gaze is another complicated movement. It is one of the few eye movements in which you can see white under the iris. In the first stage of raising the gaze, the upper eyelid retracts, almost disappearing. The upper arch of the eye gets steeper. As the iris rises further, the angle of the upper arch steepens further as well. At this point, the pupil has moved slightly above the midline of the eye's corners. The lower lid straightens. The eye is raised to its limit once the lid has opened as far as possible. Above this point, the pupil will be covered. See Figure 5.8.

Figure 5.8

An example of an upward gaze.

TIP *Make sure that the pupils are always visible in the opening between the lids, or your 3D character will look like Sleepy of the Seven Dwarves.*

Wide Eyes

Extra-wide eyes are usually easy to spot. A person with their eyes opened *extra* wide gives the appearance of being either frightened or surprised. The angle of the top lid becomes higher than normal and more of the white is visible in all sections of the eye. See Figure 5.9.

The steepest angle of the eyelid arch is about 45 degrees at the center of the eyelid for either the wide-eyed or upward gaze. The main difference between the wide-eyed and the upward gazes is in the shape of the bottom lid. In the upward gaze, the bottom lid straightens out, while in the wide-eye look, it doesn't.

Smiling Eyes

Those wonderful smiling eyes are really squinting eyes combined with bulging cheeks! The smiling eye is controlled by the muscle surrounding the eye called the *orbicularis oculi*, or the squinting muscle. It is an oval muscle that encircles the eye and covers the area of a good-sized eye patch. Part of the *orbicularis oculi* runs through the thin skin of the eyelids. The outer portion of the muscle attaches to the skull, while the free end attaches to the cheeks.

There are two parts of the *orbicularis oculi*, upper and lower, that work semi-independently. When the lower portion contracts, the eyes squint and the cheeks bulge, which, as you recall, is the key action in a smile. Notice that the lower lid is almost a straight line and laugh lines appear from the outer eye corner. See Figure 5.10.

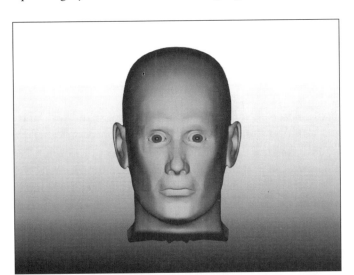

Figure 5.9

The extra-wide eye can look similar to the upward gaze. The difference comes from the shape of the bottom lid.

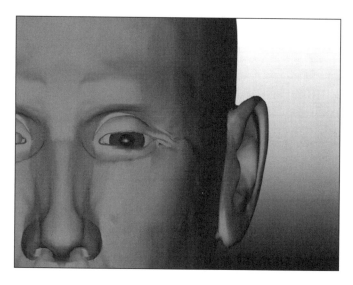

Figure 5.10

A smiling eye has a squinting motion with bulging cheeks.

Before the eye can truly *look* alive, it must be focused *on* something or someone.

- If you have a scene with more than one 3D character, make sure that they are interacting with one another, unless the story line calls for one to ignore or be ignorant of the other.

- If a 3D character is looking at an object, make sure that the eyes are in fact focused on that object.

- If there is nothing for a 3D character to look at, you might consider focusing his attention on you.

In short, give your character life! After all, a real person seldom just stares blankly into space, except during a final exam or in a reverie of love.

See Chapter 1 for more on eye focus.

Facial Expressions

Facial expressions are formed by such minute changes in the human face that it's no wonder human emotion is so hard to portray correctly in 3D. The recognition of expression is so ingrained in us that we recognize a change instantly, even from long distances. In fact, the recognition of facial expression is so instinctive researchers have found that even patients with severe brain damage who cannot recognize their own faces in a mirror can recognize changes in expression. It's no wonder then that a facial expression done incorrectly on a 3D character is so obvious.

Facial expression is almost an involuntary muscle reaction. It appears on our faces instantly in response to our emotions. For thousands of years, the fundamental human emotions have remained the same. A baby born thousands of years ago cried in the same way that babies cry today. It is simply a natural instinctive response to show fear, joy, sadness, surprise, disgust, and anger.

Although it is easy to recognize these expressions, creating them in 3D can be a monumental task. The facial animation program developed and used by Pixar in Disney's *Toy Story* used mathematical equations to calculate underlayments to emulate facial muscles. This made it easier to make a 3D face smile consistently time after time. Of course, you have to remember that it's toys we're talking about here. Even their human-type faces still don't have the complexities of a *real* human face. Buzz Lightyear and Woody are cute, OK? But we'd never mistake them for Tim Allen or Tom Hanks!

The closest to real-life facial expression on a 3D character I've seen to date is Draco, the 3D dragon brought to life by ILM in *Dragonheart*. Even though Draco doesn't have a human face, the human expression and subtle facial movements achieved by ILM make you believe that he is truly Sean Connery in drag(on). As I said in Chapter 1, the making of Draco was not an easy job, and more than a dozen animators worked on him for over a year to get the dragon's mouth to move believably and with Sean Connery's facial mannerisms to boot.

Obviously, I can't explain everything there is to know about facial expression in this chapter. Major research efforts are underway at a number of universities studying these very problems (see the Resources appendix for a list of their web sites). However, I will cover muscle movements in the face for all the basic emotions. If you require more information, a good anatomy text such as *Gray's Anatomy* or software like *A.D.A.M. Comprehensive* can be helpful.

There are six basic expressions that can be varied or combined to form all other expressions. Different emotions may make use of the same muscle movements, but in varying degrees. Some looks are complex expressions that combine two or more facial movements, as shown in Figure 5.11. The six expressions are, however, a start for modeling any 3D face. When body language is added to a facial expression, a number of different emotions can be conveyed.

Sadness

Almost all of the adult facial expressions are related somehow to our original expression at birth, the baby's cry. Sadness is the most closely related expression to the cry, but the same muscle contractions can be found in the other expressions. Other emotions can be a more subdued form of sadness such as grief or distress.

The muscle movement for the bottom half of the sad face is created by a combination of the outward pull of the muscles around the lower mouth and the upward pull of muscles around the upper mouth. This gives the mouth a wide, squared-off look. The mouth is pulled back tightly against the teeth, and the lower teeth in the extreme corners of the mouth may show. The muscles above the mouth create a nose-to-mouth fold. The lower lip is tight, so

Figure 5.11

A smiling face can be combined with other facial expressions to show sly, eager, and a happy/sad combination.

the muscle that usually pushes up the middle of the lips and rounds the chin just bows the lower lip upward in the middle. This gives the effect that the corners of the mouth are turned down, while in reality, the middle of the bottom lip is just pushed up, as shown in Figure 5.12. The expression shown is an exaggerated form of sadness; other sad faces can be attained by subduing the muscle movement.

The top part of the sad face is formed by the squeezing together of the eyes. This happens when large quantities of air are expelled from the lungs and great pressure is put on blood vessels in the eyes. Squeezing the eyes shut takes part of the pressure from the eyes, making them more comfortable. This act of squeezing the eyes shut is seen in crying, sneezing, coughing, and laughing. The harder you cry, the tighter

Figure 5.12

The muscle movement in a cry can be seen by the direction of the arrows.

your eyes squeeze together. In fact, it is difficult to cry, laugh, sneeze, or cough with your eyes open. Try it—you'll be amazed how difficult it is!

When crying, the brows are lowered, especially on the inner end close to the eye, and some vertical wrinkling appears between. However, the forehead remains smooth. Deep creases can appear from the inner-eye corner across the bridge of the nose, and wrinkles like crow's-feet appear at the outer corner of the eye. Cheeks are raised, tight, and rounded. This forms the *nasolabial* fold, which originates at the side of the nose and runs all the way down to the chin. It can be seen in Figure 5.12.

Anger

Anger can be shown in many ways, from screaming rage to tight-lipped glares. However, the basic rules apply to all the faces of anger. The expression of anger centers around the eyes. The eyes widen with anger, and the wider they are, the angrier we look.

The eyebrows, however, are what produce an appearance of rage or a glaring stare. The lower and tighter together the brows are pulled, the more anger is expressed. The brows can appear to be just above the eye or pulled down lower than the top lid in the expression of rage. In a glare, the eyes are opened wider, making the brow come up somewhat. It is not necessary for the whites to show above the iris for the expression of anger, although at least three-fourths of the iris must show to be effective. The top eyelid line appears to run into the eyebrow.

Another aspect of an angry eye is a tightened lower lid. This seems to intensify and harden the gaze.

These three elements—lowered brow, widened eyes, and tightened lower lid, as shown in Figure 5.13—should give you a good start with an angry expression. However, they won't give you the total effect you might be looking for by themselves. The mouth will help you clarify the look you're after.

The mouth in anger is a bit more complicated than the eyes. If a shouting rage is what you're looking for, the open-mouth sneer is your answer. In this action, the upper lip is curled up and a little wrinkle appears above it. The lips are tightened and stretched, showing teeth The nose is totally reshaped; the side nostrils are lifted up and flared out, giving them a pointy look. The cheeks are pulled up and puffed, forming bags under the eyes. See Figure 5.14.

Tight-lipped anger can be seen with the mouth closed tightly. You know that look your mother always gave you when she was trying to restrain herself after you broke something? In this expression, the lips are pressed tightly together, almost forming a single line. The lower lip juts forward slightly, and bulges appear both above and below the lip. The ends of the mouth turn down, and the chin is tightened and pushed out, causing a bumpiness to the surface as the muscle contracts. See Figure 5.15.

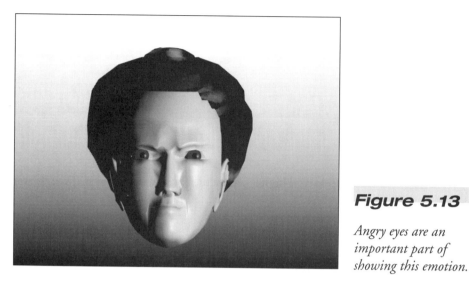

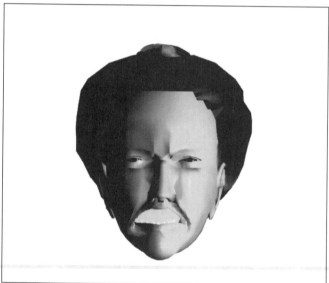

Joy

The smile is the second form of expression we humans learn in infancy. It transcends all cultures and is the one emotion, with laughter, that is most commonly appreciated and encouraged. Besides being a pleasant expression, it is also one of the least complicated to achieve. The ex-

pression is controlled by just two muscles, the *zygomatic major,* which pulls on the mouth, and the *obicularis oculi,* which narrows the eye. Even the faintest of smiles will trigger these two muscles.

The smile can be recognized by the narrowing of the eye with a bulge below. The

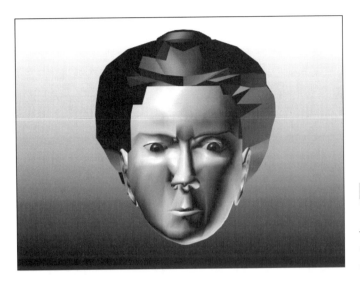

Figure 5.15

A tight-lipped mouth on an angry face shows some restraint.

more you smile, the more the eye squints. The lower lid bulges, shortens, and rises up on the eye, covering part of the iris. In a laugh, the eye is closed more from below, with the lower lid meeting the upper lid halfway, higher than when the eye is closed normally. This makes the lash line appear straight rather than curved, as it is when the eye is closed normally.

Crow's-feet wrinkles may appear from the outer eye corner, and laughter may even cause wrinkles to appear from the inner corner. The cheeks swell and tighten, forming an apple shape centered at the nostrils. Dimples may appear at the base of the ball shape of the cheeks. The more relaxed mouth stretches the skin up high on the teeth as it's pulled out and up. The chin drops down and back, forming folds between the chin and neck. In a laugh, the mouth is more stretched, thinning the lips, particularly the upper lip. There is no movement above the brow line, so the forehead stays relaxed and smooth. See Figure 5.16.

An overjoyed look can be achieved by dropping the jaw until the mouth appears longer than it is wide, and by raising the eyebrows to show folds horizontally above brows. This action will open the eyes somewhat by raising the upper lid.

Fear

Abject terror: the expression Saturday afternoon horror movies are made of. This emotion is the one we reserve for truly terrorizing, life-threatening moments. We use a more subdued variety of the fear expression in our everyday lives—you know, the one you use when you see one of those yucky spiders I talked about in Chapter 3.

In the expression of fear, the entire brow is lifted up and the eye is widened. The brows themselves are pulled inward as they are lifted up, and the mouth drops open, showing the bottom teeth. The easiest way to describe the shape of the mouth is as a capital D lying on its back, with the bottom lip straight across. The mouth drops open because generally when a person is

Figure 5.16

A smiling face; the arrows show the directions that the muscles are pulled.

afraid, he or she breathes harder. The eyes open as wide as possible, showing the whites; the wider they are opened, the more frightened the look. See Figure 5.17.

Disgust

Do you know that feeling you have when you see liver is on the menu for dinner tonight? Yuck! At least that's what I feel.

This emotion is purely a physical response to something we find stomach-turning.

Disgust can be shown by lowering the brows, squinting the eyes to produce a curved fold underneath the eye, and pulling up the sides of the nose to form wrinkles on either side. The nasolabial fold will deepen most alongside the nostrils,

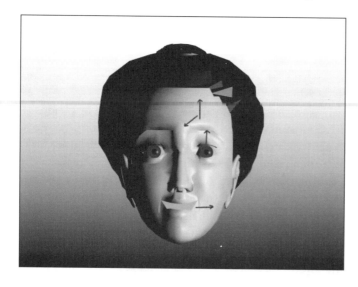

Figure 5.17

An expression of fear, with directional arrows showing the movements of the facial muscles.

and the upper lip will be squared off and pulled into the face. See Figure 5.18.

Surprise

Surprise is the most instantaneous of all emotions and also the most fleeting. As in anger and fear, the eyes in surprise give away the intensity of the emotion. The wider the eyes are open, the more sur-prised the look. No one can look sur-prised unless the eyes are opened wide. Generally, wide eyes, raised brows, and an open mouth give the surprised look. See Figure 5.19.

Variations of the surprised look occur if the surprise is a happy one. A happy sur-prise typically produces a mouth that takes

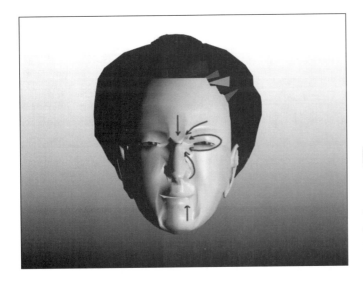

Figure 5.18

The expression of disgust, with directional arrows indicating the movement of facial muscles.

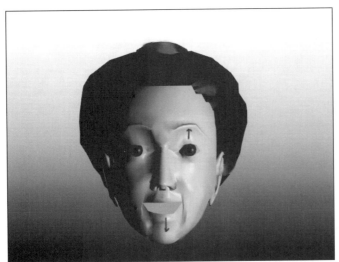

Figure 5.19

The surprised face and how the muscles are pulled to demonstrate it.

a shape halfway between a smile and the usual dropped-open mouth.

Animating the Body

Many times animators overlook the basic body movements that have a strong effect on the quality of character animation. Read the descriptions of the movements below and then watch people yourself. Become aware of your own body and how it moves in even the most mundane actions.

Walking

Even a simple walk involves the feet, ankles, and legs *plus* the arms, hands, hips, shoulders, back, and head. Anyone who has tried to animate a bipedal walk knows how difficult it is to get it to look just right. With Character Studio, you'll find that it is much simpler to do, as footstep-driven animation, inverse kinematics, and dynamics are used to achieve surprising realism. However, no automatic program-ming system can perfectly reproduce human motion.

Observation is still the key. Watch someone walking, standing, running. How do their feet move? Up and down like little pistons? Well, not on this planet!

Watch your own legs in a mirror as you walk. Your leg moves in a slight arc as the hips swivel and the feet are turned slightly outward. The ankles are not fused into a stiff position—they move as well, allowing the toes to move up and down in an arc as the foot is picked up and brought back down on the floor.

As you watch your feet in action, notice that they don't just rock from front to back on the ankle joint. They are flexible and rotate, swivel, and bend inwardly. Feet even have arches that act like shock absorbers as the body's weight comes down on them. Look at the footprint shown in Figure 5.20. Notice that you see the imprint of the toes, the ball of the foot, the

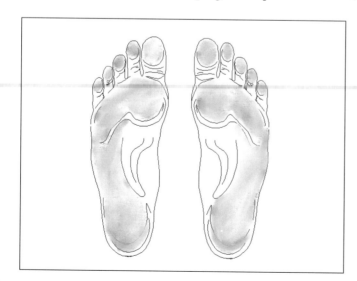

Figure 5.20

Footprints show how much of the foot we walk on and where the contact points are.

outer edge of the foot, and the heel. The arch usually does not make contact with the ground, except on a very soft surface.

Don't forget toes—they do more than make your feet look good in sandals. They add balance and, as the foot bends, so do the toes to propel the body forward.

When walking, one foot is always in contact with the ground to maintain balance. The body weight shifts from one foot to the other—even as the ground foot is coming up on its toes, the other foot's heel is coming down to balance and pull the body forward into the next step. Therefore, it can be said that walking is the loss of balance from one foot while recapturing it with the other. See Figures 5.21a through e.

Of course, there is more happening in a walk than just the feet moving back and forth. Part of maintaining equilibrium is a body shift that happens in the shoulders and hips. The shoulders rotate

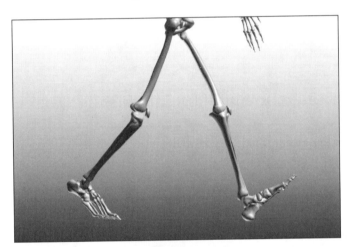

Figure 5.21

The foot follows a series of complex movements when you walk. See the variations in the following figures.

a.

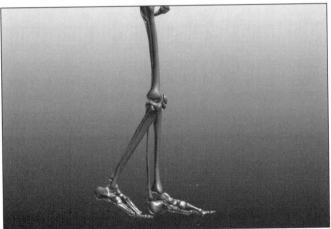

b.

3D Models provided by Viewpoint Datalabs International, Inc.

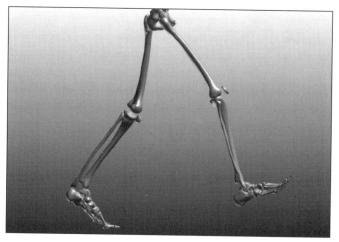

c.

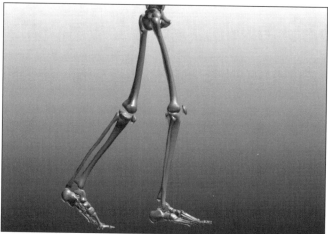

d.

e.

3D Models provided by Viewpoint Datalabs International, Inc.

Character Animation with 3D Studio MAX

around a vertical axis as the arms move back and forth; when the right shoulder is back, the left shoulder is forward, and vice versa. At the same time, the hips move in a counter-swing motion, with the left hip moving back and the right hip forward. This can be exaggerated in a swagger. See Figure 5.22.

Running

The same movements are used in running as in walking, but they are more exaggerated. Unlike walking, running covers more ground, and the feet are not always in contact with the surface. Watch a runner in slow motion. The feet swivel and move at the ankle as they run. As in the walk, they don't just shuffle back and forth.

Also, in a run, the body weight shifts up and down as well as forward. The shock absorbers of the body—the hips, knees, ankles, and feet—compress and expand with the weight.

A walker always has a foot on the ground to maintain balance, where as a runner is never in a balanced position. See Figure 5.23. The center of gravity is always in front of his or her support. Thus, to maintain balance, the runner must always bring that next foot down in front, or fall.

A runner's size helps determine how he or she runs. A heavy person has more weight to carry and runs in a more upright position and with less animation. Also, the fatter a person is, the more jiggling motion there is in the body fat. A thin runner extends his or her body in a more forward position, raising the legs higher and moving faster. A skinny person obviously has little or no body fat to jiggle. See Figures 5.24a and 5.24b.

The body also moves its arms for more power. Usually, the side of the body with the arm in a downward position is also the side with the leg in the forward position and vice versa.

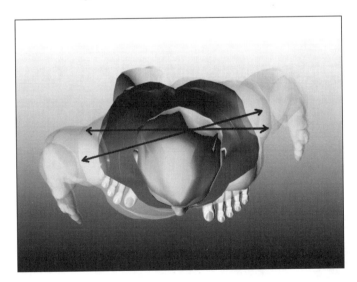

Figure 5.22

From the top view, a single swagger step illustrates the counter-swing movement between the shoulders and hips.

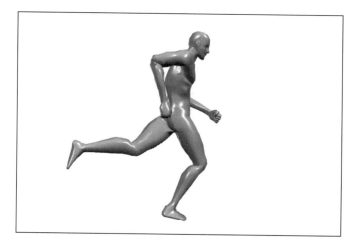

Figure 5.23

A runner is never in balance because the center of gravity is always in front.

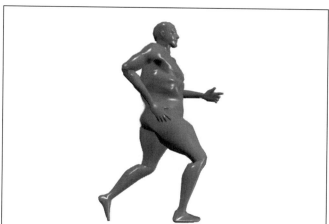

Figure 5.24

Note the difference between the running stances of a fat person and a thin one.

a.

b.

In the run, arms are usually bent to give more speed; a bent arm is a shorter lever and can be moved more quickly, causing a pumping action that gives more power to the run.

In my own observations, (yes, I watch too) the body starts moving the mass upward to take the next step. As it is doing so, weight is shifted from the weight-bearing leg, allowing those joints to decompress. The body lifts up while the foot is bending and pushing but is still in contact with the ground. The foot does not leave the ground until the upward motion is at its peak

As the center of gravity shifts to the other side, the foot hits the ground first at the heel, and while it rolls to a flat position and up again for the next step, it pulls the body forward. The downward body movement of the joints compressing follows this and gives the body a downward shift, but the foot is still planted on the ground position. The head moves and bobs, and the hair and clothing follow.

Always take into consideration *where* your character is walking or running. Here are a couple of things to keep in mind:

- If he's walking downhill, a slight backward lean with the arms more open is appropriate to brake his speed. As he goes downhill, he gains momentum, and his center of gravity is pushed further in front of him. This causes him to go faster. To compensate and slow his descent, he shortens his steps and straightens his legs a bit. See Figure 5.25.

- If he's walking uphill, then a forward lean with arms bent and moving back and forth gives him an added push. Remember, he must work harder to push his body up the path. His legs are bent more to give a grab-and-pull action. See Figure 5.26.

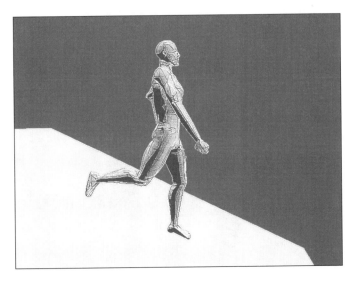

Figure 5.25

A person walking downhill has a slight backward lean.

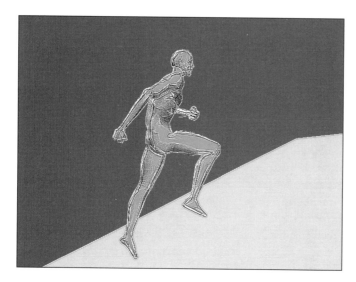

Figure 5.26

A person walking uphill has a more forward body lean.

- These actions are even more exaggerated in a runner.

Adding Personality

Any animated walk or run is going to be pretty dull unless you add personality. Get out your sunglasses again. This time, look not just at the basic movements of walking or running, but at the subtle difference between people as they go by. Do they take short little steps or stumble along in a daze? Do they swing their arms vigorously, or are they carrying their arms down by their sides? Do they limp, or are they pigeon-toed? After watching a few hundred people, you'll be convinced that even while the basic movement may be the same, there is no such thing as a "standard walk."

If you want to add personality to your character, try angling the knees out or in slightly. Exaggerate the bounce, hip rotation, or pelvic swing to produce a distinctive walk.

Laughter and Body Movement

Laughter is not just a facial expression. It's a good example of unconscious body movement. When a person laughs out loud—one of those great big belly laughs—he moves in an uncoordinated manner. The shoulders rise up as the head goes down, then the shoulders descend as the head goes back up. The rest of the body can do a variety of things, such as holding the belly as it jiggles up and down, slapping a knee, or falling on the floor. These actions are up to you. See Figures 5.27a through c.

Subtleties in Realistic Movement

Subtle facial and body movements are extremely important in adding life to a

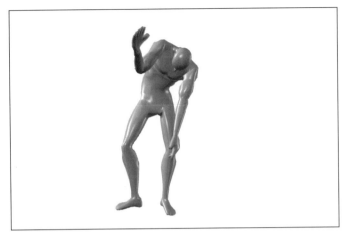

a

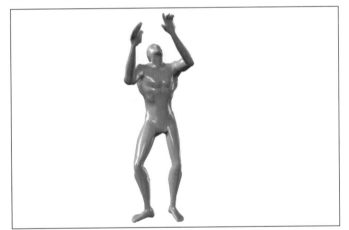

b.

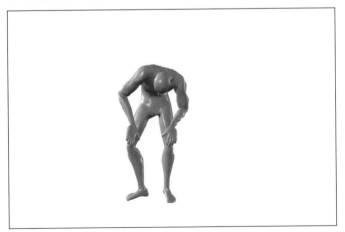

c.

Figure 5.27

Laughter is not just a facial expression, but a combination of body movements as well.

3D character. Some people call this body language.

tion and proper timing can help you convey emotion in your animations.

Body Language

Body language is what makes it possible to tell a person's mood from a distance. Is she happy, sad, depressed? You might not even be able to see her face, but the way she holds her body can answer many questions for you. Some samples of body attitude that we see every day include:

- The forward lunge of one who is angry.

- The shoulder slump when one is sad.

- The instinctive raising of hands to one's face to indicate horror.

- The hands clasped behind the back with head down and feet shuffling when one is shy.

These are things that a good animator notices and conveys in his or her character's movements. Even with the best facial expressions, sometimes the message is unclear without the extra information the body attitude gives you. Use of anticipa-

Anticipation

Action occurs in three parts: anticipation, the main movement, and the termination or follow-through of the action. Anticipation is the *preparation* for the motion and may even be a motion in the opposite direction to prepare for the motion. It is often forgotten when animating a figure in 3D, although it's standard fare in cartoon cel animation.

Anticipation can also be used to focus the viewer's eye on the right portion of the screen at the right time so an action won't be missed. A cartoon character who looks offstage a second before a bullet comes from that direction draws the viewer's eye to that side of the screen.

Anticipation varies according to the speed at which the main action occurs. If viewers are prepared by anticipation, the main action can occur very rapidly without losing them. If they have not been prepared by an anticipatory action, the main action might go by too fast for them to absorb it.

In such a case, the main action should be lengthened or the anticipation increased. If the main action is slower, anticipation can be minimized and the thought carried by the main action.

When showing weight in an animation, anticipation becomes very important. Try putting a heavy box in a truck bed or on a shelf. You probably won't use a single, smooth motion, unless the box is not really that heavy, or you really *are* Arnold You-Know-Who. Often it takes several small swings to build up enough momentum to lift the box. Those small initial movements before the big swing are anticipation movements.

Sometimes you might have to readjust your hold on the box to lift it to a height. This might entail additional anticipation as you stop, bring a knee up on which to rest the box momentarily, and move your hands to a different position. If you want to re-create this action in 3D, don't forget to add a more pronounced backward curve of the spine and bend to the knee.

Anticipation needn't mean a static pose; it can be a lesser movement that provides momentum for the action required. When moving a character from a sitting to a standing position, anticipation can make it much more realistic. For this move, try a little initial backward lean, with the head tilted down and the hands on the chair arms to assist, followed by forward motion up onto the feet, with the head moving up and looking straight out. See Figures 5.28a through f.

Follow-through

Just as anticipation prepares the viewer for an action, follow-through terminates the action realistically. Actions rarely come to a sudden stop naturally but are usually carried past the end points of effective action. For instance, when a pitcher throws a ball, the hand keeps moving in a follow-through after the ball has left the hand.

In most actions, all parts involved don't move at the same time. Some parts initiate the move and the others follow. For

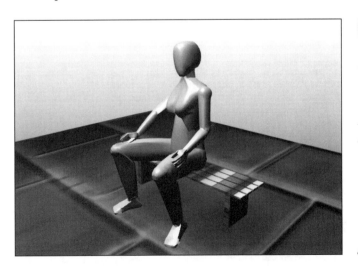

Figure 5.28

Moving from a sitting to a standing position usually requires anticipatory movements to prepare for the change.

a.

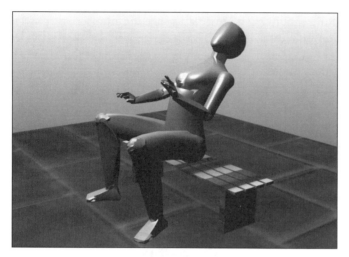

b.

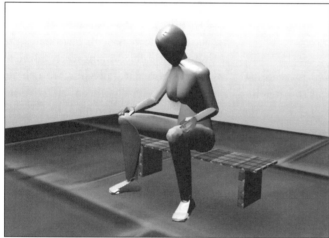

c.

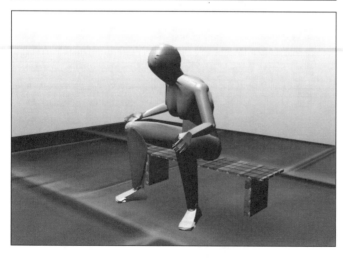

d.

Character Animation with 3D Studio MAX

e.

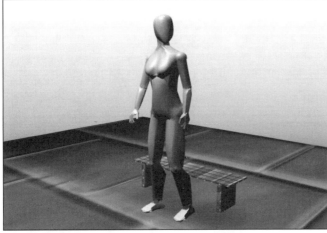

f.

example, most large body movements start in the hips. The hip action leads the leg. Then as the hip twists, the torso follows, followed by the shoulder, the arm, the wrist, and the fingers. However, in a hand gesture, the wrist leads the fingers.

Loose parts or appendages drag behind a leading part. Depending on their weight, when the leading part stops, the trailing appendages take longer to reverse the action and come to a complete stop themselves, possibly including some oscillating motion as they come to rest.

Exaggeration of these loose parts can be useful in cartooning; however, often slight variations are added to give a more natural appearance. This continuous motion is called *overlapping action.*

Overlapping Action

Overlapping actions can be very important to the flow of your animation. They provide continuity of action and simulate the real world, as described in the quote from Walt Disney.

Timing

Timing is an exceptionally important concept in animation. It lets the animator control the pacing to give more importance to some actions than others. Important actions can be slowed or even followed by a pause that lets the viewer absorb its significance before the next major action diverts his or her attention. No action should stop completely before the next one starts.

More than any other aspect of movement, timing defines the weight of an object. By manipulating timing alone, you can make two objects of the exact same size and structure appear to have sharply different weights. The heavier your character is, the more force is required to move it. Therefore, the actions of the large character will by necessity be slower, usually requiring more anticipation. However, once the character gets all that body mass moving forward, it takes more force to stop or change direction. Thus, the stopping action or follow-through takes longer as well.

It is not necessary for an animator to take a character to one point, complete that action completely, and then turn to the following action as if he had never given a thought until after completing the first action. When a character knows what he is going to do he doesn't have to stop before each individual action and think to do it. He has it planned in advance in his mind. For example, his mind thinks 'I'll close the door—lock it—then I'm going to undress and go to bed.' Well, you walk over to the door before the walk is finished you're reaching for the door—before the door is closed you reach for the key—before the door is locked you're turning away—while you walk away, you undo your tie—and before you reach the bureau, you have your tie off. In other words, before you know it you're undressed—and you've done it in one thought, 'I'm going to bed.'

Light objects have little resistance and therefore take much less effort to start and stop. A butterfly can be stopped by a very small force—even a slight breeze!

Remember that the way objects look in motion is related primarily to the number of frames given to a motion, not to the objects themselves. A giant doesn't behave like a giant if he's animated incorrectly.

The emotional state of a character can also be shown through careful timing. Think of poor Wile E. Coyote propelled off a cliff for the umpteenth time in an episode. He lingers in midair and we hold on his action until he realizes his plight. Then, with a look of resignation, he falls into the canyon below. Without the pause to show his changing emotions, we'd never have the chance to laugh at his plight.

The Effects of Weight and Gravity

Gravity pulls at every object on the planet and affects the way we walk, run—in fact, just about anything we do. In 3D model building, gravity isn't a major concern, except to ensure that the character is sized appropriately for the anticipated gravity. However, in animation, it becomes very important.

One of the most common problems in 3D character animation seems to be that characters appear to float above the ground. There seems to be little or no resistance as the character moves and comes in contact with the ground.

As I described in the sections on walking and running, compression and expansion occur as the weight of the body is shifted from one leg to the other. All the weight-bearing joints of the body (the hips, knees, and feet) give a little to compensate for the extra load caused by weight shifts. The result is that the body moves in a slight up-and-down motion in both a walk and a run.

More body movements occur than we are aware of. Think about how a 3D character would bend over and pick up a heavy box. What's the very first thing the character would do? Tilt its head down and look at the box. You'd be amazed how many animators would skip this first important step!

Next, the character would bend down—hopefully at the knees—and take hold of the box. Now, just lift? No, in order to keep in balance, the character's head must come back to compensate for the added weight as the box is lifted. As the character's back straightens to an upright position, the head returns to its normal position, but the spine bends backward and the knees also bend to compensate for the extra body weight. Generally, the more a body is carrying, the more it must shift to compensate for the weight. See Chapter 1 and, in particular, Figure 1.43 for details about a lifting motion.

Now consider how a character should move with our heavy box. As he starts out, he has more to move—the box as well as himself. This slows the motion down as he tries to maintain control of the box in motion. Depending on the weight of the box, he might need to slow down his foot movement as each lifts from its weight-bearing position. He might even need to pause with both feet on the ground to catch his balance.

Now let's suppose he moves the heavy box onto one hip. (This is a more common technique for women with children.) He must adjust his stance to compensate for the weight shift. On the side of the body carrying the extra weight, the hip comes up, the shoulder drops, and the body leans away from the weighted side. Also, the free arm may come out to add additional compensation for the weight, much like a tightrope walker using a long pole for balance.

With the hips and shoulders shifted, the walking position and stride are affected. It looks something like a limp, because one leg is higher than the other. If the weight is very heavy, the weighted leg might even move a little slower yet, making the limp even more pronounced. See Figure 5.29.

Whenever you want to animate a 3D character in an unusual way, try it out for yourself first. Hey, you might even get those heavy boxes put away from last spring! Paying attention to the world around you is still the best teacher.

Secondary Motion

Secondary motion can be described as the motion of passive elements in a scene that are driven by the movement of the main character. This might include a fat belly jiggling on a dancing hippo or the swing of, well, an unsupported and pendulous bustline as Aunt Bessie walks along the sidewalk. (If you've ever seen stand-up comedian Bob Nelson mimicking his grandmother, you'll understand this latter concept particularly well.) Those dog ears flapping in the wind as it runs? You guessed it: secondary motion. These movements make the animation look more realistic and lifelike. However, they have been largely ignored in some 3D animations primarily because achieving realistic primary motion has been so difficult that animators didn't bother with subtleties.

Since these passive movements are determined by the characters' actions and the

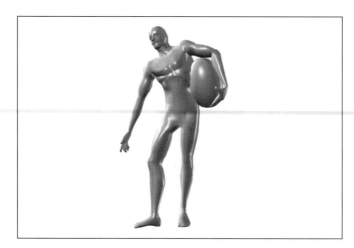

Figure 5.29

With a heavy weight carried to one side, the line of gravity shifts and the resultant walking gait is affected.

environment around them, the degree of interaction between the two movements depends on the action you need in your animation. A person jumping on a trampoline will have a much tighter connection to the secondary movement of the trampoline stretching as she lands on it. The action of the trampoline bouncing back will enable the character to leap higher into the air. On the other hand, when a person is running, the secondary motion will have little effect on the person. The movement of her clothes is a secondary motion, but the moving clothes have little effect on the way the character is moving. It is a case where a rigid body has an effect on secondary movement, but the secondary movement has no effect on the rigid body.

Once you decide what type of action you need, it's easier to determine how to add it to your animation. In the case of the runner, the flowing clothes can be added after the running body is created. A word of caution, however, animating the drape and movement of fabric is difficult without special software. And that's why so many 3D characters wear spandex. (In fact, animating a trampoline jumper is actually easier than animating loose clothing. By combining keyframing with controlled deformation, a realistic jump cycle can be achieved. I'll explain how to do this in the second half of the book.)

Secondary motion is always less important than the main action. If the secondary action becomes more interesting or dominates the action in any way, the staging is incorrect or the secondary motion is just not the right choice.

Sometimes even facial expressions are secondary motions when the body movements are the center of attention in conveying a story. In a situation like this, the change in facial expression must come before or after a move to make sure that the expression change can be seen by the viewer and is not lost in the frantic body movements.

Exaggeration

Exaggeration is an essential part of every cartoon. However, exaggeration does not have to mean the distortion of shapes or objects that make an action appear more violent or unrealistic. A scene has many parts: characters, action, lighting, color, sound, and emotions. Any of these parts can be exaggerated but should always be coordinated with the rest of the scene.

Remember mean widdle Sid in *Toy Story*? His character's looks and actions were exaggerated to show how mean he was. However, if his room had been as bright, cheery, and tidy as Andy's, he would have looked grossly out of place. His environment, the lighting—everything—was balanced to convey Sid's character and instill fear in Andy's toys.

However, when exaggerating a scene, be careful that you don't exaggerate *everything*. Your viewers need some point of reference to be able to compare exaggeration with the real world and make it believable. The Pixar folks contrasted Sid's sinister world with the normal, white-bread world of Andy and his family. Without Andy's world, Sid's world would seem the norm rather than the feared exception.

To exaggerate an action, you need only make believable actions larger, longer, or smaller. In other words, out of the normal range. Exaggerate a movement to accent it by making it go past the stopping point and then bringing it back to its correct position.

For cartoon-type exaggeration, the more exaggerated actions, emotions, and character features, the better. Make the head remain in place as the body falls, stretching the neck before snapping in back to the body. Flatten a body into a pancake shape after being run down by a car, and then have it pop back to its original shape. There are millions of movements that can be adapted to your character, but one sure-fire way of exaggerating a movement is a take or double-take.

Takes and Double-Takes

A take or double-take shows extra impact or sudden surprise. A take is simply an overreaction to an event. A double-take is something you've seen a million times: a character looks, looks away, and then snaps his head back to look again. In a double-take, you can have more fun with the reaction of your character. Any uncontrollable action in between takes makes it that much more effective. In either a take or a double-take, the action is usually stretched in the opposite direction before the planned move to add a bit more exaggeration to the action. See Figures 5.30a through h.

The take and double-take are fine for cartoon figures, but for a realistic 3D character, these techniques can make the character appear rubbery and unreal. To avoid this, you might use exaggerated staging or camera angles instead to create the look you want.

Sneaks

Sneaks are exaggerated walks that tell your audience a story. There are many variations on a sneak that can be changed from character to character or situation to situation. However, you can basically break the sneak into two categories, fast and slow.

The fast sneak is the one a character might use to tiptoe up to a friend to yell "Surprise!" The purpose, of course, is to move as surreptitiously and quickly as possible. The body is usually held in a hunched position to avoid observation, and the character moves on tiptoe. See Figure 5.31.

A slow sneak, on the other hand, is just as it says, a slower-paced sneak. When a character is trying to sneak quietly out of a situation without being noticed by his arch enemy, a slow sneak is the one to use. Unlike the fast sneak that keeps the body hunched over throughout the action, a slow sneak moves the body much more forward and back, but still keeps the character on his toes. See Figure 5.32.

Whichever sneak you use, try and incorporate some of your own movements into it. Give it some personality. And remember, the size and nature of your character will determine how it's going to move.

a.   b.

Figure 5.30

173

Chapter 5: The Nature of Motion

A double-take exaggerates the movement of your character.

c.   d.

 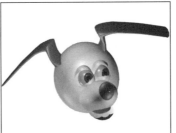

e.   f.

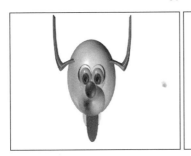 

g.   h.

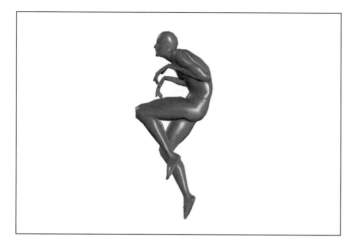

Figure 5.31

A fast sneak is usually in a hunched position and on tiptoe.

Figure 5.32

The slow sneak has a much more forward and backward motion to it.

Staggers

Stagger is a cartooning term used for vibrating objects. Whether it's a character or something else in your scene vibrating, a stagger is the displacement of one end of an object while the other end is held still. A typical example would be an arrow hitting a target; the shaft of the arrow would be displaced back and forth several times past the center line before coming to rest. See Figure 5.33.

Other uses for staggers are to show nervousness or fear in your character.

Wind and Weather

Another form of exaggeration is a character walking with the effects of weather. To show the resistance to wind in an animation, it's not necessary to use props. The basic stance of a person walking into a heavy wind is head down, leaning forward, with a protective hand on head, hat, or

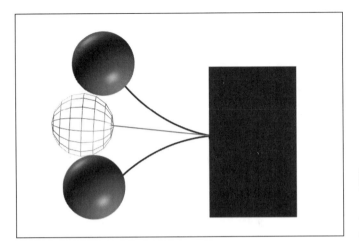

Figure 5.33

A stagger can be used to show vibration.

clothing. The stronger the wind, the further the lean. Movement would be slower than normal. See Figure 5.34.

Animal Movement

In Chapter 3, basic animal structure was covered. However, movement in animals is as different and unique as it is in humans. To understand the movement that is unique to the type of animal you are animating, watch a live-action film, go to the zoo, even watch your pet cat or dog at home. As you watch these animals move, notice that balance, timing, rhythm, and attitude play an important part in making that fox look like a fox and not a dog. It's the attitude and actions unique to the animal that make it recognizable. While you're at the zoo, be sure to notice how the animals react to each other, as well as to their environment.

Figure 5.34

Wind affects the stance and movement of your 3D character.

Four-legged Animals

Although these animals are all unique, they do have some basic characteristics in common. Essentially, a four-legged walk can be described as similar to the human gait. As the weight is shifted, the hip tilts and the weight is redistributed onto the weight-bearing leg. The walk itself for a four-legged animal is called a cross-legged gait, because the right forefoot is followed by the left hind foot and vice versa. See Figure 5.35. Get down on your hands and knees and see what works. The cross-legged action is the only natural way to progress and keep you in balance. When this natural gait is broken, the animal immediately loses the appearance of coordination.

Animals seldom walk very far in the same gait. They speed up, slow down, change their leg patterns, and concentrate mainly on where they are going. While a human has three main gaits (walking, running, and skipping), a four-legged animal can have up to six or seven gaits, because the more legs an animal has, the more gaits it can achieve. However, all four-legged animals don't necessarily have the same gaits. For example, horses and camels can pace, but camels don't trot. The trot moves as the cross-legged gait above. Pacing follows a similar pattern; however, the front and hind sets of legs move as same-side pairs. See Figure 5.36.

Just as human arms and legs don't move back and forth in a stiff pattern, animal limbs don't move in a set pattern, either. Movement occurs because the muscles are contracting and pulling on the bones, pivoting the joints. They move at varying speeds, moving more rapidly toward the middle of their swing and slowing down as they come to the point of reversing the action.

Figure 5.35

A cross-legged gait is typical of four-legged animals.

Figure 5.36

The pace shows how the legs move in a horse.

Another thing to consider when animating an animal's gait is where the muscles are attached to the bone. In humans, muscles are attached close to the joints so that even if your elbow is bent, you can still flex and extend your hand. In running animals such as horses and dogs, the muscles and tendons are arranged so that motions of one joint are influenced by motions of another joint on the same limb. A horse cannot extend its hind foot if the knee is flexed, or vice versa.

Animals with thick limbs and wide joints, such as the thighs and shoulders on a horse, have restricted movement at these joints. For example, a dog's hind thighs generally move 90 degrees, while a human's move almost 180 degrees at the hip.

For animals with multiple joints in a limb, added acceleration and increased range of motion to the limb is a plus. The great length of the hand and foot bones of horses and other hooved animals is what allows them to have a very high terminal foot velocity.

When looking at an animal in motion, you might have difficulty understanding where the compression and expansion occurs in the four-legged animal action. Figure 3.6 detailed a cat's springing movement, showing where the compression and expansion appeared in the cat leg. See Chapter 3. The action primarily occurs in the haunch (or hip) and the toes.

Expect fast animals to have long, slim limbs, and slow but powerful animals to have short, stocky limbs.

When planning an animated gait and stance, consider the animal's purpose in moving. Is it going for a stroll or hunting food? Or is it being hunted itself? There should be some reason why the animal is moving. This gives you a place to start when determining the animal's gait.

Another item to keep in mind is the size and weight of the animal you are animating. A large, thunderous elephant is going to have a different gait than a cat!

While it is possible to teach animals other gaits, it is basically unnatural. However, there are exceptions to the rule, and some animals have gaits that don't come under this cross-legged action. The giraffe, for example, has to move each front foot out of the way as it swings the back foot forward, because its legs cover so much distance in a stride.

Look at your pet cat or dog. Not only do you see the main movement, such as Ruby loping across the room to be petted, many secondary movements make up the whole expressive package that makes Ruby special. When Ruby walks across the room, she wags her tail, her head bobs up and down, her ears flap, her eyes blink and look around, the loose skin on her belly bounces, and that tongue of hers is hanging out and flapping again. But wait, that's not all: Ruby also has a skin twitch; it seems that the new flea powder just isn't

doing its job. It's these many secondary motions that give that very important true-to-life look. Remember the skin movement in *Jurassic Park's* dinosaur as he breathed in and out? These spectacular secondary motions helped make the dinosaur characters look real.

If you find it difficult to animate a character with all the secondary motions at once, don't worry, everyone has this problem. Try layering your animations. Complete the main-action animation for your character, then go back and look at it. What secondary movements does your character need? Does it appear alive? Do its eyes move? If you see a need, animate it, then repeat until you are satisfied with the results.

Insects

Insects have two primary types of motion, wing motion and leg motion. For slow-flying insects, like butterflies, the wings flap about their root axes, presenting little problem to the animator. Some insects produce an irritating high-pitched whine when they fly because they must beat their wings so quickly to suspend their relatively high body weight. Mosquitoes are the classic example of this type of insect. In order to present a lifelike appearance with a 3D mosquito, you might need to use motion blur, or, as in *Jumanji*, increase the number of wings beating to, say, four or five wings to give a proper illusion of wing blur.

TIP *Remember that every movement has a path of action and will follow through to the end. So if that dog's tail is wagging, it must complete its action to the end.*

The same type of wing can be used on everything from a hummingbird to Tinkerbell.

Insect leg motion is similar to the cross-legged gait of the four-legged animals, except that there are more legs to animate. Experiment to see what looks best with your character. Usually the legs move in sequence: the first one moves, followed by the second, and so on. On the other side, the same movement is happening, except starting one leg back. If you look closely at the giant spiders in *Jumanji*, however, they don't seem to move their back legs much at all. They're almost dragging them as they go. Yet there is so much to look at, you don't even notice.

Flocking

The flocking movement of birds and other creatures has been of interest to animators for years. The herd of wildebeests in *The Lion King* was an amazing triumph of 3D flocking. In *Jurassic Park*, the herd of fleeing gallimimus was great. Now, how about that flock of birds you wanted to animate?

When more than one animal is going to be moving in a scene, there is always a temptation to animate the same action over and over. However, the flocking movement can be more exciting if the individual animals are moving in different paths, pulling away from each other and then coming back in, moving ahead and then falling back as though a rubber band were holding them together.

In the movie *Jumanji*, a flocking sequence was created for the bats that swarmed around the character Sarah's head. Three wing-flapping cycles were created, and the bats were distributed on predetermined paths. The paths were then animated around Sarah's head, and the wing-flapping cycle for each bat was added.

To create a flock in CGI, you usually must use special software that both allows for individual variation and follows a controlled path. For some purposes, a capable particle system can substitute for flocking.

Fantasy Animal Movement

Finally! You have free rein in this area. Making dragons, fairies, and dinosaurs move is up to you and your imagination. Look at the animals we've talked about, look at real-world creatures that are similar to your creatures, and let your imagination do the rest. Just remember to take into consideration the size and weight of your creature. Are you doing cartoon or real-life animation? What type of personality does your character have? These are things you must determine for yourself. Be creative.

Illusion is the most important thing. If that means your perfectly modeled bug all of a sudden must have four wings instead of two to achieve the desired effect, go for it. It's the finished animation that's important.

If you want to make your fantasy animal walk like a human, remember what I said in Chapter 1; it will look more believable if it's dressed like a human.

Motion Capture

In the beginning, there was animation. The people saw the animation and said, "Hey, that's cool." And it was good. Then the people said, "But we want realistic action." So they begat rotoscoping to copy live action frame-by-frame onto animated cels. And the people saw that *it* was good— but time-consuming. Finally, on the morning of the fourth day, the people said, "Hey, how can we get that look of a living, breathing person without unbelievably tedious and painstaking work?" And behold, motion capture was born. And the people said, "Bitchin', dude!"

Applications

Motion capture is described as the science of analyzing the movements of the body in motion. It was first used in to help professional athletes perfect their performances. Initially, the results were output to videotape, but this allowed only a single viewing angle. Today, with the use of computers and 3D models, the action can be viewed from any angle.

The wizards at ILM used motion capture of elephants to reproduce persuasive saurian movement in *Jurassic Park*. Taking it to the extreme, a French production company has claimed to be planning a remake of Jules Verne's *20,000 Leagues Under the Sea* with the most extensive use of motion capture to date. All actors in the movie will be fitted with motion capture suits, providing movement data to synthetic actors in computer-generated sets.

One of the most popular uses of motion capture is in the video game industry. To stay current, game companies are using motion capture to provide movement data for fighting games and sports simulations.

The medical imaging industry is making its first steps toward remote surgery by fitting surgeons and residents with refined motion capture rigs that let them practice surgery on a synthetic body. So far, not a patient has been lost.

Oh, and don't forget Moxie, the 3D host on the Cartoon Network. Moxie was created using a combination of motion capture and traditional drawn animation. Colossal Pictures, the people behind Moxie, used proprietary software called Alive! that allowed them to add cartoon animation to the sequence as it was being captured. For example, Moxie always faces the camera, and his funny little secondary movements, such as ear wiggling and finger curling, are added automatically by the software.

Alive!, like other good performance software, allows parts of the character (eyes, brows, mouth, arms, legs, etc.) to be moved directly by joystick, by sound from the microphone, by data captured with mechanical or optical devices placed on anything moving (not necessarily human), by motion data encoders attached to cameras, or even by a mouse, trackball, or foot pedal. To add even more complexity to the action, these software packages can also provide characters with time-based motion that automatically makes their eyes blink or their noses twitch.

Techniques

The two most common methods of motion capture today work on the same basic principle. Actors wear either sensors or light reflectors strategically placed on their bodies, and perform predetermined actions. These motions are detected either by video cameras placed in an array around the actors or via magnetic sensors. Three-dimensional data from each sensor is then fed to a computer that integrates and records it, and then applies it to a 3D model.

In optical capture, each actor is fitted with reflective markers. An array of cameras track and record the markers in the XY positions. The software converts the multiple arrays of 2D XY coordinates from all cameras and then converts them to XYZ positions for every marker. All of this takes place in real time.

One disadvantage to this technique is that the movement is only seen in 2D by each camera. The first problem is marker dropout. This occurs when a reflective marker is invisible to the cameras because it is being overlaid by another body part. To overcome this, motion capture software companies have created software that use sophisticated algorithms to make a "best guess" at where the marker is in the motion animation. A second problem with optical motion capture is the potential for light interference in the studios when tracking reflectors.

Magnetic capture requires a centrally located transmitter and a set of receivers attached to the actors by wires. This system outputs the coordinates directly into the computer in three dimensions. The motion can then be attached to a 3D model to simulate real-life movement.

The disadvantage of this system is the long trailing wires that attach the sensors on the actor's body to the main unit. This hampers their ease and level of movement that can be captured in a single action. The action can't be too fast or the system won't be able to handle the information fast enough. All metallic surfaces must be removed from the actors' costumes to avoid confusing the system. Finally, there can only be a minimal number of sensors, which means the results are sometimes misleading.

A third method of motion capture uses optical capture, but instead of live video, images from a video tape are used to provide the motion data. If you'd like to see what this type of software can do, Photo4D by CompInt has provided a fully functional evaluation version of their software for Windows 95 and Windows NT users. It's on the CD-ROM.

Facial Motion Capture

Another form of motion capture that has been making some news recently is facial animation motion capture. Using this technique, animators can more closely mimic human facial expressions. The equipment uses a single fixed camera or a miniature camera mounted on a helmet. Up to thirty-two reflectors are applied at crucial locations on an actor's face, then the camera captures and feeds the images to the computer, where they're analyzed. The resultant facial animation data can then be applied to a 3D model through anima-

tion software such as Autodesk 3D Studio Release 4, Softimage, or Alias/Wavefront.

In all of these systems, spatial information is registered at a rate of anywhere from 15 to more than 100 times per second. Because of the high speed of data recording, every nuance of movement can be incorporated into the 3D character's movement, making it smooth and flawless.

Next Chapter...

In this chapter, I covered the magic of movement. Whether you're animating the movement of your 3D character by hand or using a motion capture file, the important thing to know is how the action *should* look. In the next chapter, we'll begin our exploration of Kinetix Character Studio. We'll take a look at both Biped and Physique and see how they fit in the 3D Studio MAX system—and also how they work together.

Part Two

Chapter **6**

MAX, Meet Character Studio

In the first five chapters, we covered basic human anatomy and animal anatomy, both real and imaginary, and movement. In this chapter, we'll take a look at the system requirements for Kinetix Character Studio, how to install it, and the capabilities of Biped and Physique, its two component parts.

3D Studio MAX

Kinetix 3D Studio MAX is the successor to four releases of Autodesk 3D Studio, the most widely used DOS-based 3D modeling and animation programs in the world. (In case you don't know, Kinetix is a subsidiary of Autodesk that includes what used to be called the Multimedia Business Unit.)

3D Studio has been widely used by professional animators and artists for more than five years since its initial development by the Yost Group under contract to Autodesk. One of the reasons for the more recent success of 3D Studio has been its open architecture that has allowed third parties to write "plug-in" applications that extend the functionality of the base program. 3D Studio MAX continues and even extends that philosophy; much of its core functionality is contained in plug-ins that can be replaced or supplanted without the user even being aware that he or she is using add-on technology.

187

Through careful design of the Applications Programming Interface (API), the Yost Group has made MAX an extensible, powerful program that can be expanded or modified as the user's needs expand or change. Character Studio was the first commercial plug-in to be announced for MAX, and has been followed by a wealth of other software that add lens effects, advanced particle systems, jiggle, wobble, and collision detection, and multilegged IK. And even more are on the way.

One of the advantages of this type of development system is that not only can users extend the functionality of MAX almost at will, but plug-in developers can take advantage of the built-in user interface API to produce tools with a familiar and comfortable look and feel. Character Studio is a classic instance of this. It is composed of two separate plug-ins written by different outside programming teams and published by Kinetix. Its components drop into the pre-existing MAX directory structure and add sophisticated character animation and skinning without replacing or modifying any of the MAX core components.

Prerequisites

Before jumping into Character Studio, make sure of the following:

- Your system is adequate for the additional requirements imposed by Character Studio. See the section below entitled "System Requirements" for details.

- You have installed Character Studio properly. See the section entitled "Installation and Authorization" for details.

- You have completed the set of tutorials that accompany MAX and read through both volumes of the User's Guide. Really! MAX is such a complex program that you should make yourself familiar as much as possible with all of its intricacies. Keep both volumes of the User's Guide handy for reference while working with Character Studio.

- You should be thoroughly familiar with the MAX operating environment and user interface. See the section entitled "Required Knowledge" for details.

System Requirements

System requirements for Character Studio are essentially the same as for MAX. If you are able to run MAX without paging to disk during rendering, you should be able to install and run Character Studio without problems. However, because of the additional computational requirements of Character Studio, I recommend the following.

CPU

Although MAX and Character Studio run acceptably on a sub-100-MHz Pentium-powered system, the more power you can lay your hands on, the better. Thanks to the good graces of Intergraph, I have been running MAX on a dual 200-MHz Pentium Pro TDZ-400 system; it's plenty fast enough to do everything Character

TIP *Make sure that 3D Studio MAX is installed correctly before attempting to install Character Studio.*

Studio needs. I've also tried Character Studio on a 120-MHz Pentium system and found that except for mesh and rendered animation playback, it was fine.

Memory

Although Kinetix suggests only 32 MB of RAM for MAX, Character Studio adds so much to the system demands that Kinetix recommends 64 MB minimum. The Intergraph system I mentioned above has 128 MB of RAM; it seldom pages to disk, no matter what I've been doing. The Pentium system I described above has 40 MB of RAM and quite frankly is inadequate to do any production-level work in MAX, much less in Character Studio (a few bitmaps of any size and I'm paging).

Graphics Display Card

MAX uses a software Z-buffer as the default rendering system. A GLint display card won't aid MAX or Character Studio because the Kinetix products were designed around an alternate rendering system called Heidi. I strongly advise adding a Heidi-compatible graphics card with enough RAM to use double buffering in your system.

Graphics Configuration

Although you can run MAX (and thus Character Studio) in any color depth above 8-bit, I strongly recommend that you not attempt to use high color or true color in the interface, as it will only slow down your system performance without adding much to the utility except in the Material Editor. With a RAM-heavy Heidi display card (at least 8 MB and preferably 12 MB or more), you can run MAX in true-color mode with reasonable performance.

Installation and Authorization

To install Character Studio, insert the CD-ROM into your drive and open it in either the File Manager (Windows NT 3.51) or Explorer (Windows 4.0). In the root directory of the CD-ROM is the Setup program; double-click on it to start installation. Kinetix uses the Install-Shield installation system, so installation is a breeze, but I do recommend that you install all of the files on your hard disk, including all sample files. You can always delete them later if you find that you need the room.

Directory Structure

The Character Studio installation system installs the Biped and Physique plug-ins in the **plugins** directory in the MAX root directory. All sample and script files are installed in a directory named **cstudio**, also in the MAX root directory. Within this directory are the subdirectories as shown in Table 6.1.

Authorization

After installing Character Studio, you won't notice anything different about MAX, except for two things: a Biped button appears on the Create | Systems panel and Physique appears in the More Modifiers list in the Modify panel.

When you first click on the Biped button in the Create|Systems panel or attempt to add the Physique modifier to a mesh, the authorization dialog box appears. Recall that MAX uses a hardware lock to protect against piracy; MAX and all protected plug-ins are written to poll the hardware key and generate a unique application ID for each hardware lock.

Call the telephone number listed and give the technician your application ID; you will receive in turn an authorization code that will let you run Character Studio.

Required Knowledge

Before using Character Studio, you should be able to do the following:

• Create, transform, and modify objects using the standard MAX tools.

• Select objects by clicking or dragging in viewports.

• Select objects using the Select by Name dialog box.

• Control and change the views in the viewports.

• Change your viewport configuration.

• Use Track View to view and edit animation tracks.

Table 6.1

The Character Studio installation program creates this directory structure in addition to copying the program files themselves into the **plug-ins** directory.

Directory	Contents
scenes	.max scene files
scenes\images	still and .avl animated image files *
scenes\lowres	.max scene files with low polygon count human figures
scenes\charactr	.max scene files with higher polygon counts, includes alien, raptor, etc.

NOTE: To reclaim more than 20 MB of disk space, you can delete this directory after studying the sample images and animations.

Make the authorization call while sitting in front of your computer with the authorization dialog box in front of you. When you receive the authorization code, type it in immediately and make sure it works. This saves possible repeated phone calls from miscopied or misheard numbers. Finally, write down the authorization code on the inside cover of the Character Studio User's Guide so that you will always have it available when you need it. (Do the same for your MAX authorization code.)

If you can do these things, you should be able to work with Character Studio successfully.

Character Studio

Character Studio combines two components into a single package: Biped is a skeleton creation tool and animator, while Physique is an object modifier that controls deformation of a mesh object. Because they are different in nature, you find them in different places in MAX. Biped is in the Systems portion of the Create panel, while Physique is found in the More Modifiers dialog box in the Modify panel.

Biped does two things: it creates a fully linked, hierarchical, bipedal skeleton that can be used as "bones" for a mesh skin, and it has a built-in inverse kinematics engine controlled by footsteps that you create. This second part of Biped also applies real-world physics to its calculations, letting you create moonwalks or realistic jumps. Biped also lets you attach and detach objects from the hierarchy selectively. You can easily create a realistic pitcher or quarterback and throw a ball under complete control.

Biped also gives you an IK lab for moving and keyframing particular actions. The built-in automatic IK can only create one kind of solution to a particular set of motions for any creature. It can't do exaggeration or automatically create anticipation or subtle timing; what it does is provide an easy facility in which to use both forward and inverse kinematics to add the subtleties the program lacks. Once you have created the basic walking, running, jumping, or climbing motion, you can then edit the basic motion to create the exact kind of movements you want.

Physique seems simple at first, but an amazing amount of sophisticated (and painstaking) control is built into the program. Not only can you use Physique to attach a mesh skin to an underlying skeleton so that the mesh deforms when the skeleton moves, you can also control what parts of the skin are deformed in any movement. You can also add the look of tendons and muscles under the skin with proper bulges and stretches. Physique can also be used with other hierarchy-based programs such as Digimation's Bones Pro MAX.

Biped

At first glance, Biped looks simple. To create a skeleton, all you do is click on the Biped button in the Create|Systems panel and then drag an outline upward from the ground plane in any viewport. Biped creates a two-legged skeleton, complete with two arms, two legs, and a complete set of up to five fingers and toes. See Figure 6.1. While still in the Create mode, you can rename the root Biped object to make it easier to remember and also edit the Biped's create parameters. Biped skeletons are composed of simple geometric shapes that can be displayed in wireframe, shaded mode, or as links, forming a stick figure.

Biped can create almost any kind of two-legged human or creature. You can edit the proportions of the skeletal parts, add a tail that swings (like a good tail should), and change the number of component parts in the legs, arms, spine, neck, fingers, or toes to meet almost any need. The one thing you can't do is create a quadruped; that's not the name of the program, and that's not what it does. Normal MAX transformation tools are used to shape Biped skeletons; with them, you can quickly create a variety of unique postures, proportions, and physical attributes. This is especially useful for characters that are old, fat, or have other distinct characteristics.

Biped skeletons are linked automatically when created with a center of mass object as the parent. Automatic linking can save you literally hours of linking a skeleton hierarchically and adjusting the joint parameters of each joint by hand. Believe me, I know—it took the better part of a day to link and adjust the Viewpoint skeleton used for illustrations in the earlier chap-

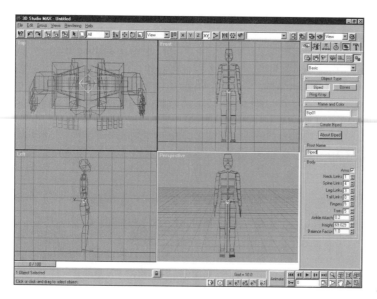

Figure 6.1

Biped lets you create quick hierarchically linked bipedal (two-legged) skeletons and control the physical form of each.

ters. A set of up to twenty-two dummy objects are also created at the same time the Biped is created as end effectors for the automatic IK.

Footstep-Driven Animation

Biped uses both inverse and forward kinematics for movement. Basic walk, run, and jump movements are controlled by a series of nonrendered footsteps that appear in the viewports rather like *gizmos* used in MAX for other animation and modeling tasks. Footsteps are shown on the screen as green and blue (right and left) footprint outlines. If you took dance classes in the eighth grade, this concept should be familiar to you. Arthur Murray, eat your heart out!

There are two ways to create character animation in Biped. You can place each footstep manually, or you can specify a series of footsteps of a single type to be generated automatically. See Figure 6.2. Whichever method you choose, you can then edit the position of each footstep and customize it for your particular needs. Once each footstep is in place, one button-click causes Biped to create a series of multitrack default keyframes to produce an editable "sketch" of the character's motion that doesn't violate the constraints established by the footsteps.

The use of footsteps lets you interactively compose the timing and placement of each step and create walking, running, jumping, or any other arbitrary movements such as dancing, climbing stairs, and so on.

Physically-Based Interpolation

You can also raise or lower the center of gravity of the biped character, depending on the type of movement or body type you require. The character then can move, rotate, and balance around its changed center

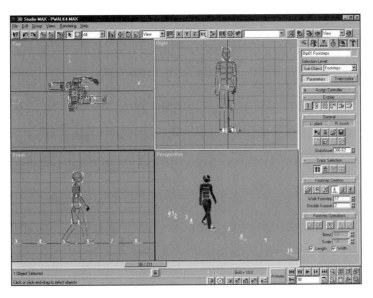

Figure 6.2

Basic Biped animation is controlled by a series of footsteps that can be generated automatically or one at a time by the animator.

of gravity to give a more natural appearance. Biped automatically lets the character walk and maintain the biomechanical relationship between the ankles, leg, and pelvis. Biped also lets a character automatically bank into turns as a function of its speed and path.

Biped interpolates the vertical keyframes using classical Newtonian principles and takes gravity into account, so a character won't just float off into the air if it steps off a ladder—unless you want it to do so. If your character isn't earthbound, however, you can turn off the motion dynamics for intervals that you specify, allowing a character to fly, swim, or cycle.

Motion Splicing

A Biped motion or position can be copied from frame to frame, or can be mirrored from one side of the body to the other. Therefore, when a repetition or mirroring of a movement such as a jump or a dance step is required, a simple built-in clipboard lets you splice motions together by copying and pasting or inserting sequences of footsteps. Pasting a sequence repeatedly produces a seamless motion cycle and is very effective for such motions as dance steps.

Motion Mapping

A Biped motion file can be saved and used on other 3D models. This lets you save the expressive quality of the motion while still maintaining each character's unique physical characteristics. Biped can automatically account for any differences in the size of a Biped character by adapting the placement of footsteps

according to the overall size of the legs and pelvis. This comes in handy if a motion created for a small-scale creature is being applied to a 3D model of the 50-Foot Woman. Luckily, Biped also adjusts the gravity to the scale of the character's height, so our 50-foot woman will keep her feet on the ground.

Motion Over Uneven Terrain

If making characters move naturally over bumpy surfaces is a problem you face, Biped will generate walking motions that move over uneven terrain by varying the heights and orientation of the footsteps. The footsteps can be adjusted either when initially placed in the animation or at a later time. This lets a character climb up ladders, jump off cliffs, or walk over bumpy ground.

In Biped, a character's foot will automatically and accurately collide and roll over each footstep location in a natural way, pivoting between the heel, sole, and potential contact points of the toes or claws. This is an important aspect of making a character's walk look real.

Using Biped in Character Animation

As I discussed in previous chapters, the task of animating a person or bipedal animal with realistic action has been almost overwhelming up to this point. Character Studio is the first modeling and animation program for MAX that allows the freedom to make our 3D characters move the way they should.

Footstep-driven animation takes the tedious manual labor out of traditional animation. Because Biped produces a set of default patterns for footsteps, it lets you adjust the larger movements of the character's behavior, dynamics, and timing quickly and easily. The little expressive details can then be animated to give the look of natural movement. Once Biped has laid out the basic sketch of your character's motion, you can change and refine the footstep design by using the Biped tools to edit both animation keys and footsteps.

What makes Biped so special to the character animator is that it bases the in-between positions on the assumption that you are animating a two-legged figure rather than on an arbitrary number of linked objects. Biped's *physically based keyframe interpolation* produces realistic foot touchdown and liftoff movements that can't be matched by spline-based animation systems. Splines produce smooth movements, but they can also produce unnatural-looking actions, especially in this area.

When a character walks, Biped follows the basic mechanics of walking movement. If the character runs, jumps, or hops, Biped uses the dynamics of gravity to attain a genuine sense of weight and gracefulness.

The ability to have continuity of speed at liftoff as well as touchdown is due to its application of the vertical dynamics of gravity. Also, note that while the biped figure is in the air, the center of its body mass moves in a horizontal plane at a constant speed along a straight line, just as it should.

Although Biped is called a footprint-driven animation system, basically it's still a keyframe-based system. What that means is that while Biped tries to interpolate the keys using physically based principles, it does not force you to stay in physically feasible positions. The only restriction placed by Biped is that if the model is airborne, its vertical height is determined by the magnitude of its gravity parameter.

Physique

Physique is a modifier plug-in that connects 3D meshes to Bipeds (or other bone systems). Once you have the animation down in Biped, you can apply a mesh body to the Biped skeleton and make it follow the animation you designed. Physique provides the character with a custom skin surface that bends, moves, stretches, wrinkles, or bulges as the motions require. See Figure 6.3.

TIP *The footsteps are connected to the rest of the body framework. If you adjust the footsteps, the posture of the associated leg and body keys will adapt. Editing footstep timing and duration causes these same leg and body keys to adapt as well. If a key is deleted or modified, Biped will adapt its timing and placement to the surrounding footstep pattern.*

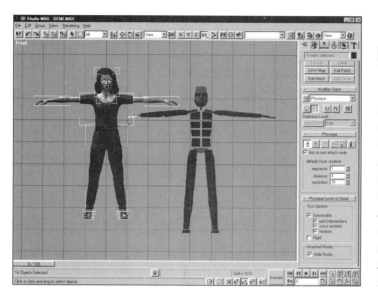

Figure 6.3

The mesh on the left is ready to be linked to the Biped on the right. Normally, you place the skeleton within the mesh to make alignment easier, but it has been removed here to show the relationship.

Tendons and Bulges

Just as your arm or leg has a structure of bone, tendon, and muscle to allow movement and give the appendage shape, Physique works in much the same way to give the character realistic skin and muscle movement with precise control over creases, wrinkles, and bulges around joints. See Figure 6.4. (Physique doesn't provide the motive power, just the shape and the *appearance* of muscles.)

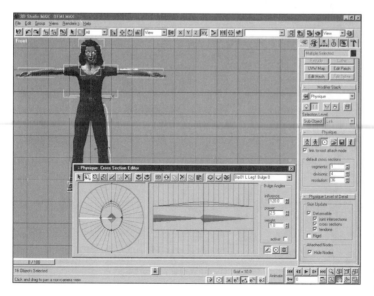

Figure 6.4

The Physique Cross Section Editor lets you specify the look of the skin at each joint and adjust the bulges as desired for different joint angles.

Tendons in Physique work across skeletal joints much the same way ours do, to smooth and shape the skin as it moves. These are very helpful for neck areas, shoulders, and pelvis, where compound curves are evident and additional control is needed to deform the skin properly.

The real nitty-gritty of Physique comes when you fine-tune the skin behavior as it moves in relationship to the underlying skeleton. This is accomplished initially by Physique automatically, but every mesh seems to need some adjustment (see Figure 6.5). You can select the skin vertices to be affected by the movement of a particular joint manually, link by link. This lets you smooth the shoulder joint as the arm moves or crease the skin correctly inside the arm as the elbow bends.

Physique has the ability to create and store any number of three-dimensional contour groups, called *bulge angles*. These bulge angles are applied to any part of the model so that when a preset body or joint angle is reached, the stored contours appear. This function precisely controls the degree of blending across multiple bulge angles so that a bulge can either be localized or applied throughout the entire range of motion of a limb. In effect, this controls the muscle to let it appear gradually as the model moves or all at once, like Popeye flexing after eating a can of spinach.

Physique allows personalization of your characters and makes them come to life. It can be used with two-legged humans, four-legged animals, inanimate objects, or anything in between.

Creating Skin

Physique skin can be a geometric shape, a patch object, a spline, or even a text shape.

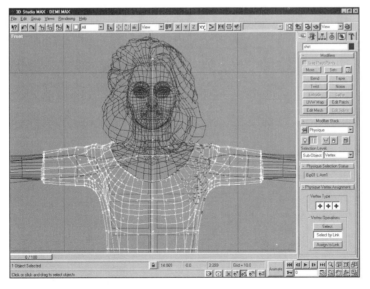

Figure 6.5

Physique initially assigns a set of vertices, in the area of each link, to be affected by movements in the link (one readjustment is required), vertex by vertex, link by link. It's a shortcoming of Physique and an opportunity for fine control.

You can use a prebuilt mesh object or set of objects, a mesh object with modifiers already applied, or a mesh created from a compound object such as a boolean. You can even create a Physique skin out of several disconnected objects, such as a clothed model or a jointed mesh model. For example, the mesh figure shown in Figures 6.3 through 6.5 is actually a set of component pieces.

I'll get into the actual steps required to "skin" a Biped in Chapter 8, but the basic steps are first to adjust your mesh skin so that it is in a neutral position (called a *reference pose* in the Character Studio User's Guide); then, create a Biped that is the same height as your mesh and use MAX transformations to adjust the Biped to fit properly within the mesh; next, select the entire mesh and apply a Physique modifier; and finally, link the modified mesh to the skeleton.

Next Chapter...

In the next chapter, I'll show you how to create a basic Biped and adjust it for various types of figures, bipedal animals, and so on. I'll then show you how to animate it in a variety of situations. This will be a fun chapter, so don't put the book down *now!*

Chapter 7

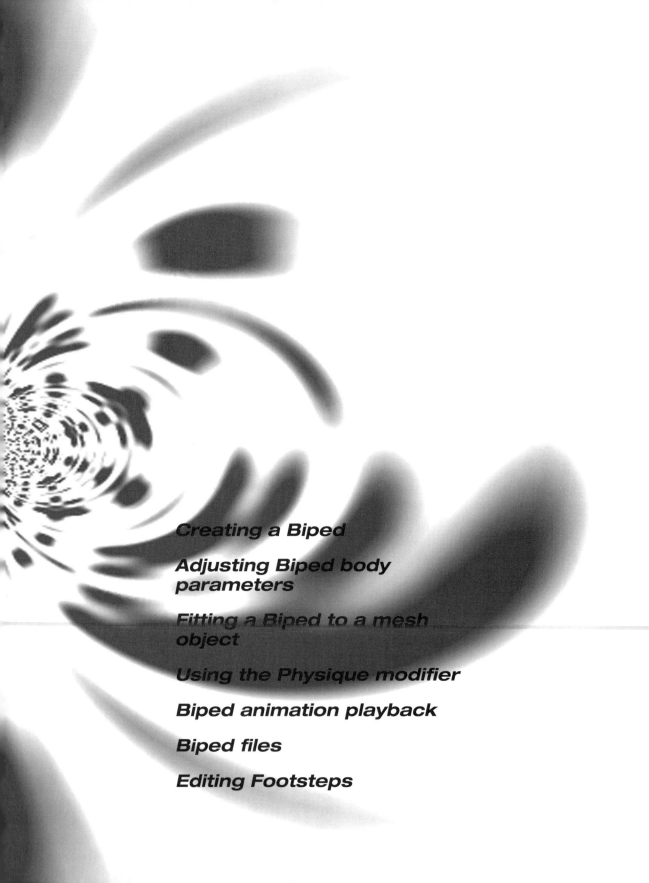

Biped 101

In this chapter, you'll learn the basics of Biped: how to create a Biped skeleton and how to make it move. The first tutorial is a Quick Start that takes you through the complete process of creating a Biped, attaching it to a simple mesh character with Physique, and making it dance. In the following tutorials, I'll take you through the steps required to master and control Character Studio.

I strongly recommend that you complete the tutorials in order, as each builds on the one before. If you decide to skip one or more tutorials, I have included the appropriate starting file for each subsequent tutorial on the CD-ROM in the *tutorial\chap7* directory.

Icons

MAX is full of new icons for new functions, and Character Studio is no different. To help you pick out the right button in this new, icon-oriented interface, these icons are displayed in Appendix A for your reference.

Keyboard Shortcuts

MAX includes a large number of keyboard shortcuts to help you work quickly. I've found these to be a great help, and whenever they are available, I include references to them in these tutorials to help you get used to using them.

You can customize the keyboard shortcuts—and review the current assignments—by selecting Preferences from the File menu and then choosing the Keyboard tab. Unfortunately, MAX doesn't let you assign keyboard shortcuts to plug-ins like Biped or Physique, so you can't create shortcuts for their functions. Maybe next release....

Tutorial Files

Files needed for the tutorials are on the CD-ROM in the *tutorial* directory. Within that directory are a series of subdirectories identified by chapter number, such as *chap7*, *chap8*, and so on. You can load each file directly into MAX from the CD-ROM or copy the entire *tutorial* directory onto your hard disk as a subdirectory of the MAX root directory. Then, if you choose, when you have completed the tutorials, you can delete the entire *tutorial* directory to regain the hard disk space used by the files.

Starting and Resetting MAX

In each tutorial, I begin with the assumption that you have started MAX and that it is operating properly. If you have been working in MAX before starting a tutorial, be sure to reset MAX to its default state before beginning the tutorial; otherwise, your results might vary from what you'll see in this book. To reset MAX, choose Reset from the File menu and confirm that you want to reset the program.

Quick Start Tutorial

The Character Studio plug-in lets you take a premade mesh object and animate it with an automatically constructed, hierarchically linked skeleton created in Biped. This skeleton can be adjusted for gravity, posture, size, structure, and so on to give you very lifelike movement. The mesh object does not have to be hierarchically linked before being attached to a Biped; in fact, you don't even have to use a single mesh object—you can use Biped to control a set of separate objects that together make up a character figure.

Since I know that most of you probably don't have much patience when it comes to learning a new program—I sure don't!—I've designed a Quick Start project you can do just to get your feet wet. In this first tutorial, I won't go into a great deal of depth on program functions, but I'll try to help you understand some of the nuances of using Character Studio, particularly those aspects that are not covered well in the User's Guide that comes with the product.

In this first Quick Start tutorial, you'll attach a Biped to a simple car mesh and then modify it with Physique so it can dance like those cars and gas pumps in the Shell Oil commercials.

Character Animation with 3D Studio MAX

Load a Mesh File

In this section, we'll open a mesh file and prepare it for use with Biped.

1. Choose Open from the File menu (or press Ctrl-O).
2. Load *tut7_1.max* from the *\tutorial \chap7* directory on your CD-ROM.

A sports convertible (resembling a Mazda Miata) mesh appears standing on its rear bumper in the middle of the MAX universe. If you examine the Summary Info (Alt-F, F) for this file, you'll see that it has a surprisingly low face count for its completeness; only 13,475 faces. This makes it a pretty good candidate for use with Physique, although more faces would allow it to bend more smoothly.

3. Click in the Front viewport, then press W to maximize it to full screen. Drag a selection box around the entire car to select all of its components. Name this selection set "Mesh All" in the Named Selection Sets field in the 3D Studio MAX toolbar. (This makes working with Biped much easier, believe me.)

4. Go to the Display command panel (see Figure 7.1).
5. Click on Freeze Selected in the Freeze by Selection rollout.

The car mesh turns dark gray. It's now frozen into position so that you'll be able to move and adjust the Biped figure without accidentally disturbing your mesh (see Figure 7.2). To speed up the process of freezing selected objects, you can assign the command to Shift-Ctrl-F in the Keyboard Preferences dialog box.

Create a Biped

In this section, we'll create a Biped to control our car.

1. Click on the **Systems** icon in the Create command panel; click the **Biped** button. The Name and Color and the Create Biped rollouts appear.

Note: If the Biped button does not appear in the Create Systems Object Type rollout, you might need to reinstall Character Studio.

2. In the Front viewport, drag the cursor from the bottom center of your

TIP *Before you create a Biped to control your set of mesh objects, make sure that each has a sufficient number of faces to allow smooth animation. What is sufficient? It depends on the shape of the object, its position in the figure, the distance of the figure from the viewer, and the extent of the animation. This is something that you can only learn from experience with MAX and Character Studio. If you find that a mesh needs more faces after modifying it with Physique, the only solution is to remove the Physique modifier, apply an Edit Mesh modifier to the offending objects to tessellate them, and then reapply Physique.*

Figure 7.1

Display panel showing the Freeze by Selection rollout.

car mesh to the top of the mesh. A blue bounding box appears as you drag the cursor. When you have reached the top of the mesh, release the button and a Biped figure appears. See Figure 7.3.

You've created your first Biped!

3. Examine the Body parameters in the Create Biped rollout. The numbers you see are the default values. As a default, each Biped is created with

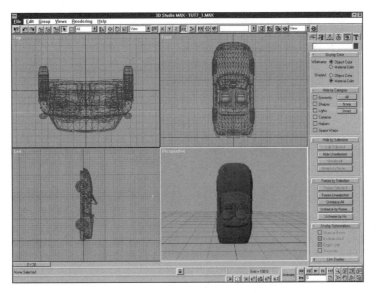

Figure 7.2

Screen with car mesh frozen.

two arms, two legs, no tail, and a full complement of five fingers and toes on each appendage. To vary this structure, it's easiest to change it in the Create panel when you create the Biped.

If you want to change the root name of the parts of your Biped hierarchy, you must do it before leaving the Create panel; otherwise, you're stuck with the name assigned by Biped. Bipeds are created using the root "Bip," followed by a two-digit number representing the order of creation. If you are going to have several Bipeds in a scene, it's best to give them more meaningful names than "Bip01" or "Bip02." You must change the name in the Root Name field in the Create Biped rollout; changing their name in the usual MAX name field only changes the name of the Center of Gravity object.

4. Click on the Arms checkbox to deselect it, since our convertible will be the Venus de Milo of Miatas— that is, armless as well as topless! Set the number of toes to 1—you can't reduce this number any further. The changes are automatically reflected in the viewports. See Figure 7.4.

5. Drag a selection box around the entire Biped to select all components, then name this selection set "Biped All" in the Named Selection Sets field.

6. Select the Center of Mass object and create a named selection set of this object called "Center of Mass."

7. Click on Zoom Extents All and W to return to four viewports.

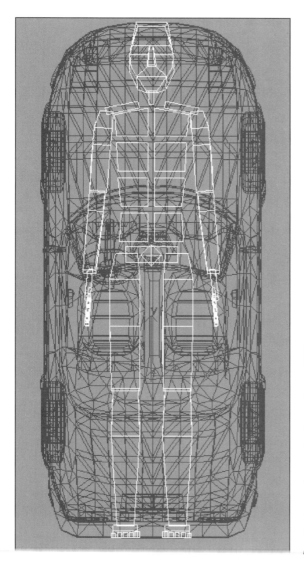

Figure 7.3

Biped figure aligned with the car mesh. Note: If the Authorization dialog box appears when you click on the Biped button in the Object Type rollout, you must contact Kinetix for an authorization number before using Biped. See the Character Studio User's Guide and Chapter 6 in this book for details.

Adjusting the Biped to Fit Your Mesh

Each Biped is created in a default standing position with arms down at its sides. To attach a Biped to your mesh you must first adjust the Biped to fit the size and posture of your particular model. With some creatures, like velociraptors or ducks, a great deal of adjustment may be necessary; however, to fit the Biped to our sports car, little adjustment is required.

Immediately after creating a Biped, the center of mass object (the absolute parent of the Biped hierarchy) is selected. If you

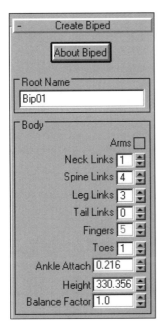

Figure 7.4

The Body parameters portion of the Create Biped rollout.

have deselected it in some way, press H to bring up the Select Objects dialog box, and select the Bip01 object.

Another quick way to select the center of mass object is to click on the **Center of Mass** button (also sometimes referred to as the **Center of Gravity** button) in the Track Selection rollout of the Biped panel. You reach the Biped panel by selecting any Biped object and then moving to the Motion panel.

Adjusting the Center of Mass

We'll start by adjusting the position of the Center of Mass. The Center of Mass is the tetrahedron in the pelvis area of the default Biped. The Center of Mass object is the parent of the entire hierarchically linked Biped and can be adjusted for gravity, posture, and stance in a resting position.

1. With the Bip01 object selected, go to the Motion panel.

The Biped panel appears (see Figure 7.5).

2. Press the **Figure** mode button in the General rollout.

The button turns yellow to indicate that **Figure** mode is active.

You can move the Biped in any viewport to line it up with the mesh. It's best to position the Biped in the center of the mesh you will be animating.

3. Press the **Rubber-band** mode button to the right of the Figure mode button in the General rollout. The **Rubber-band** button lets you move the Center of Mass object without moving the rest of the Biped.

Figure 7.5

The Biped panel appears in the Motion panel when any Biped object is selected.

4. Using the usual MAX Select and Move tool in the Front viewport, move the Center of Mass object down along the Z-axis to just above the rear tires. See Figure 7.6.

Adjusting the Biped Height

The head of your Biped must be slightly taller than the car mesh to ensure that Physique can link all of the mesh's vertices to the Biped. Otherwise, vertices will displace into 3D space unpredictably as the rest of the mesh is moved by the Biped.

1. Select the Biped Neck.
2. Using nonuniform scale transform, scale the neck along the X-axis until

Character Animation with 3D Studio MAX

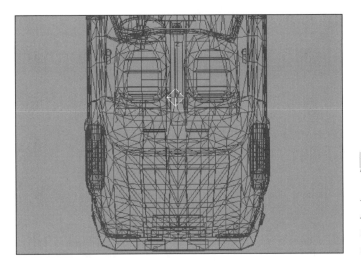

Figure 7.6

Placing the Center of Mass down in the car makes the "leg" motion more effective.

the top of the head is slightly higher than the mesh. See Figure 7.7.

That's all the Biped adjustment you need to do for this project—it's definitely one of the easier ones. Later, we'll spend more time customizing a Biped to fit a mesh.

Modifying Your Mesh with Physique

Now that the Biped is aligned with your mesh, Physique must be applied to the mesh to make the Biped and mesh move as one. Physique enables the mesh to bend and move smoothly in any direction the Biped can move.

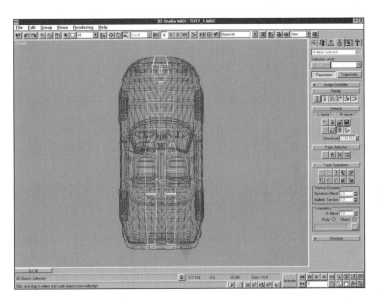

Figure 7.7

The Biped head must protrude slightly through the front bumper.

1. Go to the Display command panel and unfreeze all in the Freeze by Selection rollout.

The mesh objects unfreeze and return to their original object colors.

2. Make sure that the **Figure** mode button in the Motion panel is still on.
3. Select Mesh from the Selection Set to select all of the mesh objects.
4. Go to the Modify panel and click on More in the Modifiers rollout.

*Note: If you are going to be using Physique a lot in your work, you can assign it to a button. Click on the **Configure** button sets icon to the right of the **Sets** button in the Modifiers rollout.*

5. Click on Physique. Then click on OK. Physique now appears in the modifier stack and the Physique rollout appears (Figure 7.8).

Note: If Physique does not appear in the Modifiers list, you might need to reinstall or reauthorize Character Studio.

6. Click on the **Attach to Node** button in the Physique rollout.

The **Attach to Node** button turns green to indicate that it is active. **Attach to Node** is used to tell Physique which Biped it should use to link vertices.

7. Activate the Front viewport, then press W to enlarge it to full screen.
8. Press Alt-Z to activate Zoom Region, then drag a window around the pelvis area. You need to be able to pick out the orange line of the Biped pelvis object through the cloud of white selected mesh objects.

Note: Do not attach Physique to the Center of Mass object; it must be applied to the Biped pelvis. The Center of Mass object moves around in relation to the rest of the Biped and can produce unpredictable results.

9. Move the cursor over the line that defines the pelvis object, and click on the pelvis when the cursor changes shape to resemble the **Attach to Node** icon (Figure 7.9).

Character Animation with 3D Studio MAX

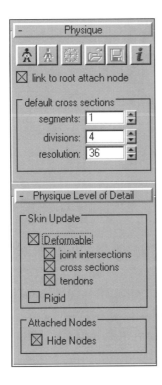

Figure 7.8

The Physique rollout.

*Note: When **Attach to Node** mode is active, the cursor can take two shapes:*

 when Physique cannot be attached or;

 when Physique can be attached.

After a few moments, a set of orange links appear that follow the Biped and pass through the mesh objects. This indicates that the Biped is now linked to the mesh through Physique. If the links seem to be incorrect, you must remove the Physique modifier from all of the mesh objects, make sure that the Biped is aligned as shown in Figure 7.7, and then reapply and relink Physique.

Animating Your Mesh

The Biped and mesh object are now connected and ready to animate.

1. Press W to restore four viewports, select Center of Mass from the named selection sets, then go to the Motion panel.

2. Deactivate Figure mode by clicking on the **Figure** mode button in the General rollout.

3. Click on the **Load File** button in the General rollout.

The Open File selector appears, set to load *bip* files. These files store keyframe settings,

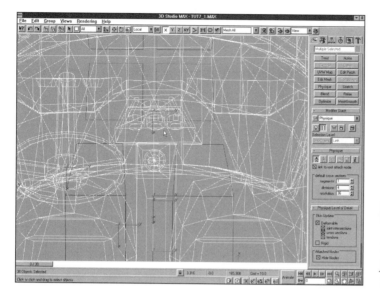

Figure 7.9

The cursor over the pelvis shows where to attach Physique.

Biped scale, and the gravity value, but do not include Biped figure information.

4. Open *dance.bip.* The mesh automatically moves to the position at the first frame of the animation.

5. Click on the **Biped Playback** button in the General rollout. A stick figure

of your Biped appears and dances to the footsteps in the file (see Figure 7.10).

Note: You can play your Biped animation in three ways. First, although Biped playback displays only a stick figure of the Biped links, it can do it in realtime. Second, you

Figure 7.10

The Biped playback stick figure is a quick method of seeing a real-time preview of your animation.

Character Animation with 3D Studio MAX

can also use the Playback controls in the Viewport Controls region of the screen to play back the animation of the mesh. Because of the difficulty in updating the screen at 30 frames per second, this method of playback usually skips frames to attempt to maintain the selected playback frame rate. However, if you've turned off Real Time Playback in the Time Configuration dialog box, MAX will display every frame, but typically not in real-time. This third method is the only way to see every frame of the mesh animation.

6. Maximize the Perspective viewport and click on Extents All. If the figure and its footsteps are not all in the window, readjust the view with the Field-of-View, Pan, and Arc Rotate controls until you can see everything. (You can press Shift-Z to zoom out quickly.)

7. Select Biped All in the named selection sets, then press Shift-H to hide the selected objects. (This avoids a side trip to the Display panel.)

8. Click on the **Play Animation** button in the Viewport Controls and observe the dancing car. If you want, you can render an *avi* file of your dancing car animation. I've included a file on the CD-ROM called *tut7-1.avi* if you'd like to see how one version looks.

And you thought that you had to work for R/Greenberg to make cars dance, didn't you.

9. Click on the Figure Mode button to return the Biped to its setup position.

10. Now click on the Save File button in the General rollout. This brings up the Save File dialog box to save figure files using the extension *.fig*. Save this file as *sports.fig*. Later, you can load this *fig* file to conform a Biped to meshes with similar stances and proportions.

Tutorial for Basic Biped

In the above tutorial, we took a quick look at how Biped and Physique work together, and we created a striking dancing car animation with very little work. Now we'll take a more in-depth look at Biped. In this tutorial, you will create a basic Biped, adjust the structure, and use the footstep animation tools.

About Biped

The Biped is hierarchically linked automatically for you when it is created, with a Center of Mass object in the Pelvis as the parent object. When the Biped is created, the Center of Mass object is automatically selected, not the entire Biped skeleton.

The skeleton is created with Links and Nodes. It is important to remember that

Links behave like bones, while Nodes behave like flexible joints. You will notice that the default Biped is human form. This is because Biped is geared to a two-legged figure. (For four legged creatures, see Chapters 11 and 12.) However, that does not mean that humans are the only figures you can use with Biped. As you saw in the first tutorial, any creature or thing using two-legged movement can be used with Biped.

The Biped acts as an armature for your body, not unlike the ones used with clay models we discussed in Chapter 4. Armatures—and Bipeds—give form to models and allow natural movement. However, remember that the Biped itself cannot be altered to make the basic skeleton into a finished skinned figure on its own. *Physique* is used to apply a skin or mesh over a Biped to give you a finished product. It's handy to render a Biped animation as a quick motion study, however.

About the Center of Mass Object

The tetrahedron in the pelvis is the Center of Mass or Center of Gravity object. It is identified in the selection list as Bip01 for the first Biped in a scene, Bip02 for the second, and so on, unless you rename the root name when you create a Biped (see the tip under Step 3 in the section, "Create a Biped").

In Biped, you can change the position of the Center of Mass and thus change where the Center of Gravity is located in your 3D model. If you lower the Center of Gravity, the body's stance and posture

will change, making it appear as if it's bottom-heavy. If you raise the Center of Gravity, the body will appear to have less weight. The Center of Gravity should be moved back into the pelvis for bodies that are curved forward to compensate for the weight shift. For bodies that you want to move with a backward slant, the Center of Gravity should be placed forward in the pelvis. However, be careful not to move the Center of Gravity too far forward in the pelvis or you will get unnatural movement.

The Center of Mass Shadow

Whenever a Biped is displayed, you will notice a dot on the ground plane between its feet. This is the shadow of the figure's Center of Mass. As the Biped moves, the shadow moves along with it. Use this shadow to align your Biped movement with other objects in a scene. See Figure 7.11.

The Balance Factor

The Balance Factor can be difficult to understand unless you see an example.

1. Load *halfactr.max* from the *tutorial \chap7* directory on your CD-ROM.

In this scene there are two Bipeds, one blue, one green, seen from the side as they do backflips from a high position. The blue Biped has a balance factor of 0.0; the green Biped has a balance factor of 2.0, the maximum. In all other respects (except Y position), the two are identical. See Figure 7.12.

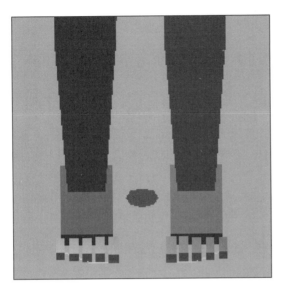

Figure 7.11

The Center of Mass shadow helps you align the Biped to other objects in your scene.

2. Play the animation using the View port playback control with Real Time turned off.

As you watch the two Bipeds flip, note the relative positions of each as they go through their routine. You'll notice that, in general, the blue Biped is much more fluid in its movements and assumes much more natural positions than the green. Tuck this bit of information away in the back of your mind as you work with Biped.

Creating a Basic Biped

In this tutorial, we'll create a Biped and experiment with its parameters a bit.

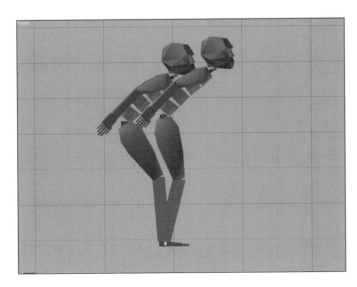

Figure 7.12

These two Bipeds differ only in Balance Factor. The blue Biped, standing more erect in this image, has a Balance factor of 0.0, while the green Biped has the maximum value of 2.0.

The Body Parameters section lets you instantly change the shape of your Biped. The Arms checkbox lets you control whether your Biped has arms and the spinners let you control the number of links for each of the named links. The higher the number of neck, spine, leg, or tail links, the more flexibility the part has. You can set the number of fingers from 0 to 5 and the number of toes from 1 to 5; you must have at least one toe on each foot.

Ankle Attach controls where the foot is attached to the lower leg. The smaller the number, the further back the feet will be attached. If you choose 0.0, the rear edge of the foot is attached to the lower leg. The highest setting is 1.0; at this setting, the toes are attached to the leg. (I haven't figured out yet what walks like this, but it might be good for alien creatures.) The default setting is 0.2.

Height is set when you create a Biped. However, you can change the height manually, using the spinner or entering a value in the height field.

Balance Factor affects the Biped's movement rather than its appearance. The Balance Factor lets you adjust the distribution of weight in your Biped without moving the Center of Mass object. At a setting of 1.0, the Biped is balanced and has an even distribution of body weight. As you increase the Balance Factor value, the weight distribution moves toward the head, allowing it to compensate for a leaning spine. Decreasing the value narrows the Biped's weight distribution to an area surrounding the Center of Mass object. This limits the Biped's balance to a smaller area as the body shifts.

You can adjust the Body Parameters in two places: before you leave the Create panel after creating a Biped, or in the Structure rollout in the Motion panel as long as Figure Mode is on.

Biped is intelligent in that it adapts automatically to whatever structure you assign. For example, you can create a dancing car, and then move the dance steps over to a duck, a dinosaur, or a human. Biped adapts to each structure.

1. Just as you did in the Quick Start, click on the **Systems** button in the Create Command panel and select Biped.
2. Maximize the Perspective viewport and press S to activate the Snap toggle.
3. Place the cursor at approximately 0,0,0 in the Perspective viewport and drag the bounding box up until the height spinner in the Create Biped Rollout reads 70 units. Release the mouse button and the Biped appears.
4. Go to the Body Parameters in the Create Biped rollout.

Note: You can access Body Parameters whenever you create a Biped, or in the Motion Panel Structure rollout when Figure Mode is activated. You can change the structure of the body at any time during creation or animation of a Biped up until Physique is applied. After Physique is applied, the Biped can no longer be altered.

For a discussion of Body Parameters, see the sidebar of the same name.

5. Adjust the spinners in the Body Parameters to show four tail links, four fingers, and four toes. Your Biped changes immediately to reflect the changes. See Figure 7.13.

When creating a Biped, adjust it to match the kind of creature you are animating. You can have up to five spine links and five neck links to give you the freedom to cre-

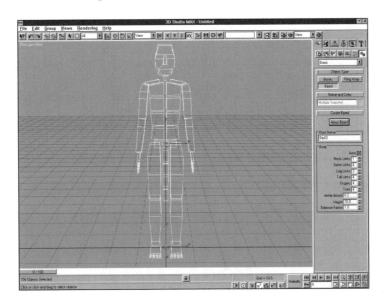

Figure 7.13

The Biped display changes immediately to adjustments in the body parameters.

ate ungainly storks and long-necked aliens. At the same time, you can add a fourth link to the legs to conform their structure better to a typical saurian. The key here is to have the mesh in mind before creating the Biped.

Adjusting a Basic Biped

In this short tutorial, we'll modify our Biped to give it "dinosaur arms."

1. Activate and maximize the Front viewport.
2. Go to the Motion panel.

The Biped rollouts appear (Figure 7.14). Note that if a Biped component was not selected, only the **Parameters** and **Trajectories Biped** buttons would appear.

Note: You can select an entire Biped by pressing H to bring up the Select dialog box, entering Bip* in the entry field at the top, and then pressing Enter. However, by doing this you might inadvertently select the

Bip footsteps as well. If the footsteps are selected along with the Biped, the Biped controls will not appear in the Motion command panel. Deselect this item and you should have no trouble.

3. Click on Figure Mode.
   The **Figure** Mode button turns yellow to indicate it is activated.
4. Press H to bring up the Select dialog box, and select the Bip01 R Arm1 object. This is the right upperarm object.
5. Click on the **Symmetrical Tracks** button in the Track Selection rollout and lock the selection set by pressing the spacebar.

Note: Before doing any transforms, always lock the selection set. Note that in MAX version 1.1, you can now reassign selection set locking to another key combination.

Both upper arms are now selected.

6. Nonuniform scale both upper arms to 50 percent along the X-axis to shorten the arms.

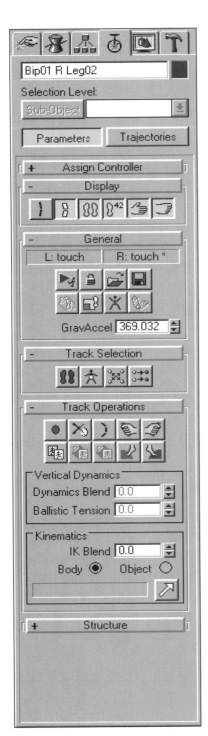

Figure 7.14

The Biped Motion command panel.

The Figure Mode button is one of those things that you must keep track of as you work with your Biped. If you don't, things can happen that are confusing and frustrating—really frustrating! Remember, any time you change a Biped, and this includes moving, scaling, rotating, changing body parameters in the Motion panel, or linking to a mesh using Physique, the Figure Mode must be on.

Figure mode lets you edit your Biped. When Figure Mode is activated, the Biped returns to its last Figure Mode position and location, usually the "setup" position. If you have made no adjustments to it at all, this position will be just as it was when it was "born." If you have made any adjustments, loaded a bip file, or made any changes with Figure Mode off, the Biped returns to its last Figure Mode position.

*When Figure mode is turned off again, the Biped reverts to its animated position. So it is extremely important to remember that while the **Figure** mode button is on, you cannot load or play back an animation. You can, however, load or save a .fig file that stores figure parameters.*

*When Figure mode is active, the **Footstep Tracks**, **Biped Playback**, and **Set Key** and **Delete Key** buttons are all disabled.*

You can have as many Bipeds in Figure mode at the same time as you want. To show the state of each individual Biped, just select it and turn on Figure Mode.

7   Unlock the selection set by pressing the spacebar, then press the Page Down key to move to the next lower link(s) in the hierarchy. In this case, the Bip01 R Arm2 and Bip01 L Arm2 objects are selected.

Note: *Use the Page Up and Page Down keys to move through the hierarchy of a Biped (or any other hierarchy in MAX). However, if* *you move down the hierarchy from an object with multiple descendants, such as the Pelvis, you will select not only the thighs, but also the lowest spine link.*

8.   Repeat Step 6 on the lower arms.

Your Biped now is almost ready to be used as a dinosaur.

Remember that you can select the axis constraint by pressing F9 for the X-axis, F10 for the Y-axis, F11 for the Z-axis, and F12 for the combination axes. Press F12 repeatedly to select the combination you need. You can also add Cycle through Scale Modes to a custom set of MAX keyboard shortcuts in the Keyboard Preferences dialog box.

Saving and Loading Biped Files

Once you have created the Biped you want to use in your animation, you can save it as a Figure file. This lets you use the same figure over and over for different meshes without having to readjust it each time. Remember that a figure file saves the figure characteristics only, not the animation.

Saving a Figure File

1. With Figure Mode still active, click on the Save File icon in the General rollout.

The Save File dialog box appears.

2. Type in **Tut2** in the Name field and click OK. The file will be saved with a *fig* extension.

Loading a Figure File

1. With Figure Mode still active, click on the **Load File** button in the General rollout.

The Load File dialog box appears.

2. Select *General.fig* file and click OK. The Biped adjusts to conform to the parameters in the figure file. (In this case, the parameters conform to the General from Viewpoint Datalabs, Inc., as modified for this book. I'll

refer to him as "the General" from now on. The Biped is fingerless because the General mesh has gloved hands held as fists.)

Note: As long as Figure Mode is active, any footsteps attached to a Biped remain scaled to the previous figure parameters. When you turn Figure Mode off, the footsteps are rescaled to match the new figure parameters. In this way, Biped adapts an existing animation to different figure characteristics.

Remember, loading a new figure file *replaces* the parameters of the active Biped. If you want to retain the parameters, save it before loading the new file. We will be using this new figure file for our next tutorial.

Loading a Motion File

Motion files store the footstep and key values, but not the figure parameters. Here's how to load and use a motion, or *bip*, file.

1. Turn Figure Mode off.

Because we haven't animated the Biped, he remains in his basic setup position.

2. Load *Basic.bip* file by clicking on the Open File icon.

The Biped automatically moves to the position of the first footstep of a basic walking animation. The footsteps that control the Biped walking motion are visible in the viewport; blue footsteps for left steps and green footsteps for right. See Figure 7.15.

3. Click on the **Biped Playback** button in the General rollout to see a stick figure animation of the General walking. Or you can click on the **Play Animation** button in the Viewport controls to see the full Biped in action. Your Biped will walk across the screen, placing each foot on a footprint.

Editing Footsteps

Footsteps are the basic control medium of Biped. Using a combination of forward and inverse kinematics, Biped attempts to create animation keys that place a foot in each

footstep. If the Biped components won't reach from footstep to footstep, Biped adds a pretty natural-looking jumping or hopping motion. In this tutorial, we'll add some fillips to our existing walking animation to test Biped's animation powers.

Adding to an Existing Animation

First, let's add a jumping motion to the end of the existing animation.

1. Click on the Go to Start button in the Viewport controls. The Biped returns to the first frame starting position of the walking animation.

2. Click on Footstep Track in the Track Selection rollout.

The Footstep Creation and Footstep Operation rollouts appear (Figure 7.16).

3. Click on the **Jump** button in the Footstep Creation rollout.

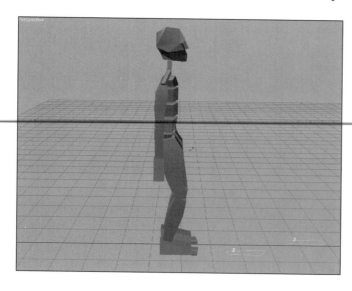

Figure 7.15

The General at the start of the basic walk.

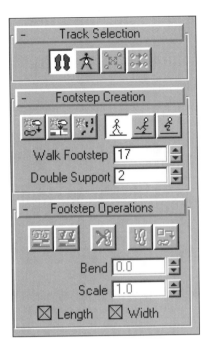

Figure 7.16

The Footstep Creation and Footstep Operation rollouts.

There are three buttons in the Footstep Creation rollout that determine the gait of newly created footsteps: **Walk**, **Run**, and **Jump**. What differentiates one from the other are the number of frames that each foot is on the ground, the number of frames that both are on the ground at the same time, and the number of frames that the Biped is unsupported, or airborne. Table 7.1 lists these default values.

4. Click on the **Create Multiple Footsteps** button in the Footstep Creation rollout.

The Create Multiple Footsteps dialog box appears (Figure 7.17).

5. In the Create Multiple Footsteps dialog box, leave all of the values at their defaults and then click on OK.

Table 7.1

Default gait values in frames.

	Walking	Running	Jumping
One foot on ground	17	11	—
Both feet on ground/ two feet down	2	—	9
Airborne	—	4	11

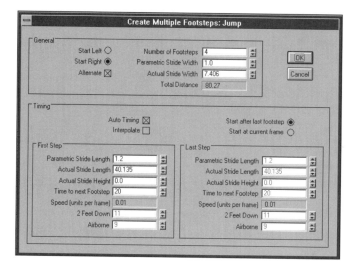

Figure 7.17

Create Multiple Footsteps dialog box set for two two-foot jumps.

Biped generates four new footsteps, consisting of two, double-foot jumps added onto the end of the current animation. However, if you try to play the animation to see the new jumps, you'll find that the General stops after the first set of steps and ignores the new steps. This is because Biped doesn't generate new movement keys until told to do so.

Note: When Biped creates footsteps, it places them according to the parameters you specify, but it does not create new keys for the component parts. In order to create the keys that perform the actual animation, you must manually tell Biped to create the keys.

6. Click on the **Create Keys for Inactive Footsteps** button. This generates

keys for the new footsteps and blends the new footsteps in with the existing.

Now when you replay your animation, the Biped does its two jumps.

7. If you'd like to experiment a bit, first select Hold from the Edit menu so that you can return to this point, then press Alt-Backspace twice to undo your last footstep creation and try different parameters. Try deactivating the Alternate checkbox in the Create Multiple Footsteps dialog box; the general hops on one foot. Make sure that you click on the **Create Keys for Inactive Footsteps** button each time you generate new

You can load either of two kinds of motion files in the Motion Load File dialog box: bip files are binary motion files that contain both footstep and key values, while stp files are ASCII text files that contain only footstep parameters. Footstep files are useful if you want to generate Biped motion manually or create a program that generates it. You could even program a spreadsheet to generate a footstep file!

Character Animation with 3D Studio MAX

footsteps. When you're done experimenting, select Fetch from the Edit menu and proceed with the next section.

Adding Individual Footsteps

Now let's add a little twist to the animation by adding individual footsteps manually at the end of the animation.

1.   Maximize the Top viewport and press Shift-Z to zoom out to create a little working room.
2.   Make sure the **Footstep Track** button in the Track Selection rollout is still active.
3.   Click on the **Run** button in the Footstep Creation rollout.

This time, we'll create some running steps rather than jumps.

4.   Click on Create Footsteps (append) in the Footstep Creation rollout.

The **Create Footsteps (append)** button turns green to show that it is active.

5.   Using the cursor, place ten footsteps at the end of your animation footsteps. You may vary their placement to suit your fancy, but remember that the gait is set for running steps. You can get a little crazy, but try to stay close to the bounds of reality! See Figure 7.18 for one possible arrangement. (By the way, if you get too crazy, Biped will still try to compensate, but I won't guarantee the results!)
6.   Click on the **Create Keys for Inactive Footsteps** button.
7.   Press the F key to switch to the Front viewport, then watch your animation…. pretty cool, huh? Notice the difference between the walking and running gaits: in the running gait, both feet are off the ground for a couple of frames each step, even if the stride length is short. A short-strided running gait produces a jog.

Bending Footsteps

Walking, jumping, and running in a straight line are fine, but sometimes you

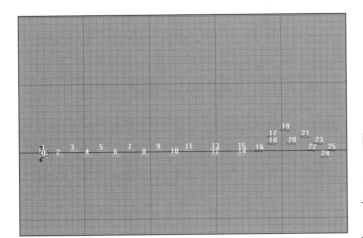

Figure 7.18

One possible placement for ten new footsteps appended after the jumps.

Notice that the footsteps are placed alternately: right, left, right, and so on. If you want your Biped's footsteps to be in sequence, such as right, right, right, for a hopping action, hold the Q key down on the keyboard as you place the footsteps.

just need to turn a corner. Here's how to turn a right-hand corner in Biped.

1. Press T to switch to a full-screen Top viewport and press Alt-Ctrl-Z to Zoom Extents All.
2. With the Footsteps Track still active, drag a selection box around footsteps 4 and 5.
3. In the Footstep Operations rollout, enter a value of 45 in the Bend field and press Enter.

Biped applies a 45-degree bend to each of the selected footsteps; all of the footsteps from 6 on are now heading to the side.

4. Play your animation.

Notice that your Biped leans to the inside of the turn as it goes around the corner.

Backward Movement

Here's one more little trick that Biped lets you do. In this tutorial, we'll teach the General how to retreat.

1. Reload *Basic.bip.*
2. Go to frame 211 and click on **Create Multiple Footsteps**.

The Create Multiple Footsteps dialog box appears.

3. In the First Step section of the box, change Parametric Stride length to -0.5.

4. Leave Actual Stride Height at 0 and Time Until Next Footstep at 15.
5. In the General section of the dialog box, change the number of footsteps to 20, then click on OK to create twenty footsteps. See Figure 7.19.
6. Click on **Create Keys for Inactive Footsteps**.
7. Play your animation.

The General is in respectful retreat. By changing the Parametric Stride Length to a negative value, you caused the Biped to back up.

Climbing Movement

Now we'll add an obstacle for the General to climb over—what else would be appropriate but a classic computer-animation teapot?

1. Reload *Basic.bip.*
2. Using File|Merge, merge in *tut7-pot.max.* When the Merge dialog box appears, select Teapot01 and click on OK.

A teapot appears right in the General's path to the right of the footsteps. If it's not visible, press Alt-Ctrl-Z to Zoom Extents.

3. With the Footsteps Track active, click on **Create Footsteps (append)**.
4. Press T to switch to the Top view, and press W if necessary to switch to full-screen.

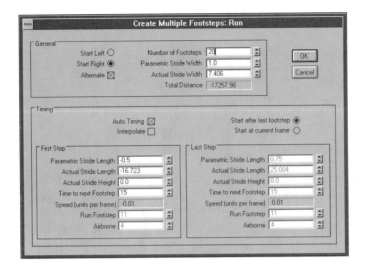

Figure 7.19

The Create Multiple Footstep dialog box set for twenty backward steps.

5. Press Alt-Z to activate Zoom Region and zoom in on the teapot area.

6. Place five footsteps atop the teapot, plus a sixth on the far side, as shown in Figure 7.20. If you misplace one, press Alt-Backspace to undo it and try again.

7. Press F to switch to the Front view.

Notice that your footsteps are at ground level, not on top of the teapot. Let's fix that.

8. Click on the Create Footsteps (append) button to deactivate it.

9. Click on footstep 12 to select it, then click on Select and Move, and press F11 to activate the Z-axis constraint.

10. Move footstep 12 up until it's on top of the teapot handle.

11. In turn, select and move footsteps 13 through 16 until they're roughly in position atop the teapot, as shown in Figure 7.21.

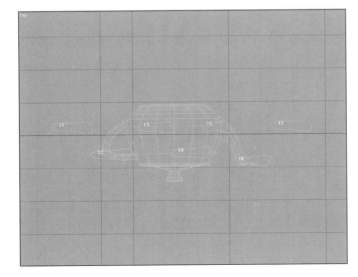

Figure 7.20

Follow this guide to place six footsteps along the teapot.

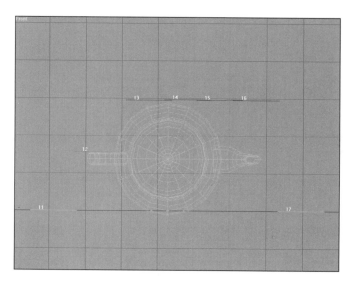

Figure 7.21

The footsteps in rough position on the teapot as shown in the Front view.

Unfortunately, the footsteps don't fit well on the rounded teapot. If we generate keys for these footsteps now, the General won't look natural. But we can fix this, too.

12. Select footstep 13, click on Select and Turn, then press F10 to activate the Y-axis constraint.
13. Rotate footstep 13 until it fits reasonably well on the curvature of the teapot. You might have to switch back and forth between Rotate and Move to position it properly.
14. Repeat Step 13 for footsteps 14 through 16 until the footsteps look like those shown in Figure 7.22.

15. Click on the Create Keys for Inactive Footsteps button.

Now play the animation and watch how Biped adjusts the angle of the foot for the position and angle of each footstep.

Next Chapter...

Now that you have a feel for how to use Biped, in the next chapter we'll take a look at some of the more advanced features, including dancing, flying, swimming, and throwing a ball. Now, *this* is fun!

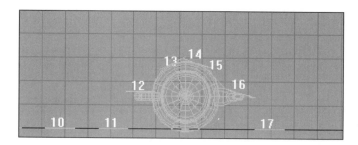

Figure 7.22

The four footsteps properly positioned on the teapot.

Chapter **8**

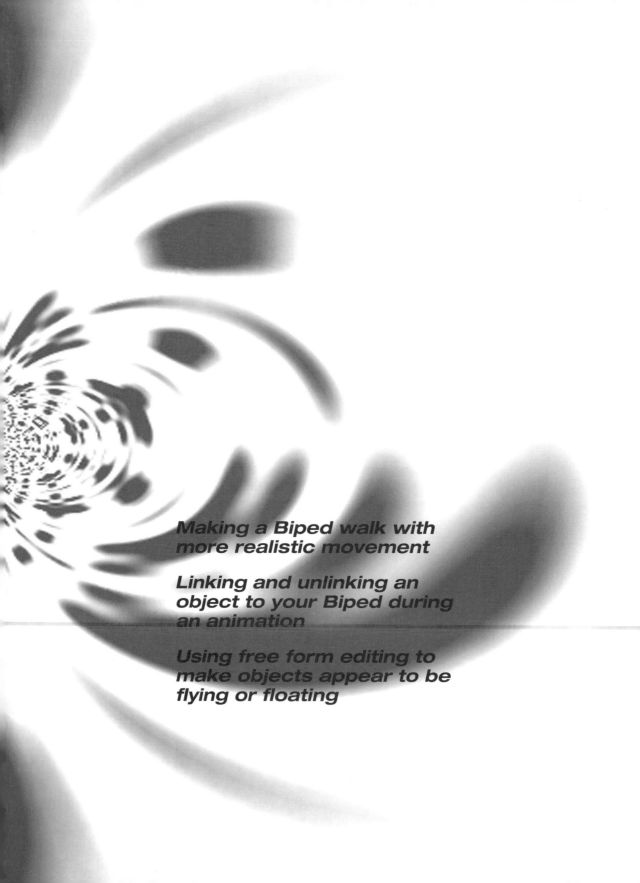

Making a Biped walk with more realistic movement

Linking and unlinking an object to your Biped during an animation

Using free form editing to make objects appear to be flying or floating

The Advanced Biped

In the first half of this book, we looked at what characteristics and movements give humans a life-like appearance. In Chapter 5, we saw the way a human moves as it walks in detail. In this chapter, we will use that information to make our Biped move more realistically as it walks and plays basketball.

Making a Basic Walk More Natural

A basic walk has little body movement.

1. Load Tut8_1.MAX. A basic biped appears with the default walking motion.

2. Click on the **Play Animation** button and watch the Biped walk. You can change the way the Biped moves, and at the same time, change the attitude and feel of your Biped. See Figure 8.1.

Giving Your Biped Spine More Movement as It Walks

As you saw, the default walk has very little motion. We want to put a little swivel on the spine to give him some more natural movement. Because the pelvis in Biped can't move independently in this axis, we will use the spine.

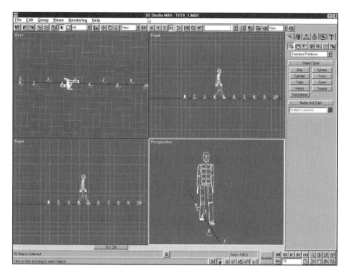

Figure 8.1

The basic walk.

1. In the Top viewport, select the Bip01 Spine object.
2. Click on the **Animate** and the **Key Mode** buttons.
3. Go to frame 25, and click on the **Bend Links** Mode in the Tracks rollout.
4. Rotate the spine around the X-axis to -15 degrees.
5. Go to frame 45. Rotate the spine object to 15 degrees around the X-axis.
6. Repeat Step 4 at frames 65, 105, 145, and 185.
7. Repeat Step 5 at frames 85, 125, 165, and 205.

Play the animation again, this time the Biped's hips swivel as it moves. You will note that the entire spine has a curving action because the **Bend Links Mode** affects the entire spine. See Figure 8.2.

Giving Your Biped More of a Swagger

If your animation is in need of a little attitude adjustment, you can give the look by giving it a little swagger as it walks.

1. Maximize the Top viewport and select Bip01Spine3.
2. Go to frame 25. With the **Animate** button and the **Bend Links Mode** still on, rotate it about the X-axis 30 degrees.

To change the position of any part of the Biped during an animation sequence, the Animate button does not need to be activated; however, you must be sure to click on the Set Key button.

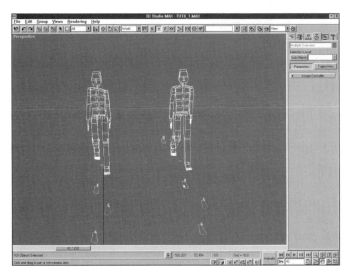

Figure 8.2

The Biped on the left has hips that swivel as it moves.

3. Go to frame 45 and rotate the object -30 degrees about the X-axis.
4. Click on the **Next Key** button in the Animation controls at the bottom of the window to bring up the next keyframe to continue this pattern in frames 65, 85, 105, 125, 145, 165, 185, and 205.

As you can see in Figure 8.3, the Biped swaggers when he walks but appears to be a little stiff. We can change that by adjusting his spine to compensate for the swagger.

1. Using the **Key Mode**, go to each keyframe and rotate the spine forward around the Z-axis approximately 8 degrees.

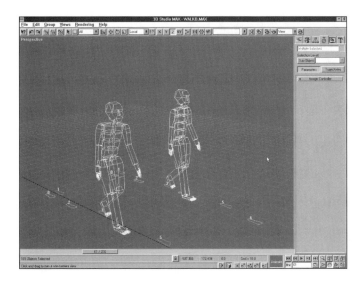

Figure 8.3

The Biped on the left has more of a swagger but is still a little stiff.

TIP *You can only select one arm or leg at a time to link the object. However, after you've linked one, you may choose another to link as well. So if you have a Biped doing chin lifts, for instance, you can attach both hands to the bar.*

2. Alternately select the Biped's fore-arms and bend them in the Z-axis to give them more back-and-forth movement as the Biped walks. Remember, as the right arm swings to the front, the opposite foot is forward and visa versa.

3. Load Tut 8_1a.MAX and check your animation with this one.

Attaching an Object to Your Biped

Objects in MAX can be linked. The problem is that you can't unlink an object during an animation sequence. With Character Studio, you can link and un-link an object during an animation allowing you to throw a ball or carry a sword. However, you need to follow a specific order of steps to make your attempt successful. This procedure isn't easy, and it's not explained clearly in the program's documentation. So go through it a couple of times and make sure you have the steps in the right order for the best results. The tutorial following this one will take you through a more complicated animation.

1. Load Tut8_1b.MAX. A basic Biped appears with a horizontal bar in his right hand, as seen in Figure 8.4. A running motion has already been applied to the Biped.

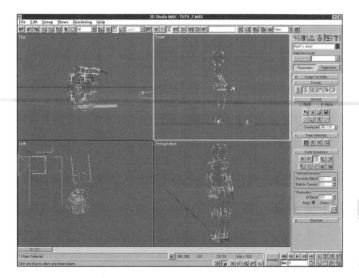

Figure 8.4

The Biped is holding the tube.

2. Play the animation. You can see that the Biped runs off without the tube. In order for the Biped to carry the tube, it also has to have its own animation applied.

3. Go to frame 0 and select the right lower arm (Bip01Arm2).

4. Click on **Select Object Space Object** (the arrow under the **Object** button) in the Kinematics section of the Track Operations rollout in the Motion panel. See Figure 8.5.

5. Click on the tube. It will not turn white; however, the name will appear in the Name Selection box in the Kinematics section.

You will note that the hand is already in position for you. If it wasn't, however,

you could adjust the hand position at this point.

6. Click on the **Right Arm Anchor** to activate it.

Note: If you want the hand to change positions during an animation, for instance, when sliding along a handrail, you should leave the anchor off.

7. Select **Object** in the Kinematics section to select the Object space coordinates, and move the IK Blend spinner to 1.0.

8. Click on the **Set Key** button. Now the tube is linked to the hand with a MAX-type IK link. Select the tube and move it around to see that the

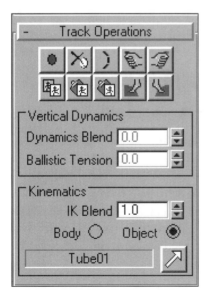

Figure 8.5

*The **Select Object Space Object** is shown in the Kinematics section of the Track Operations rollout.*

hand is attached and follows the tube's movement. Now click on the hand and move it around. It doesn't stay attached to the tube as it moves.

9. Run the animation. The Biped runs off without the tube. However, because the hand is still trying to hold the tube, as the Biped runs, the arm is pulled in a backward position toward the tube.

Animating the Tube

In order for the Biped to carry the tube, the tube must be animated using standard keyframe animation.

1. Go to frame 0, and click on the **Animate** button.
2. Maximize the Front viewport and select the tube.
3. Go to frame 22, and move the tube up and slightly forward in ZX with World coordinates.
4. Go to frame 31, the mid-air point in the running movement, and move the tube up and forward until the hand is just in front of the Biped's waist.
5. Go to frame 39, the next frame where a foot is flat on the ground, and move the tube forward so that it's even with the waist.
6. Continue to go through the animation and move the tube at every frame where a foot is flat on the ground or is at the highest mid-air point between footsteps until you get to frame 177. Remember to move the right arm forward when the right leg is back and vice versa.

7. At frame 177, move the tube to the ground and play the animation.

The Biped runs while holding the tube and drops it just before the jump. The hand is still not looking right, however, and still pulls toward the tube.

1. Go to frame 0 and select the right lower arm.
2. Go to frame 24, select Object, and set IK Blend to 1.0. Then click on the **Set Key** button.
3. Click on Next Key to go to the next keyframe, select Object, set IK Blend to 1.0, and then click on the **Set Key** button.
4. Repeat Step 3 until you get to frame 176. This is the first frame where the hand no longer is in contact with the tube.
5. At frame 176, select Object but this time set IK Blend to 0.0, as shown in Figure 8.6.
6. Click on the **Anchor Right Arm** button and play the animation.

Using Free Form Motion

Free form editing is used for any motion, such as flying or diving, that needs to be free of vertical dynamics or gravity. However, free form editing can only be accomplished in between footsteps. Therefore, at least two footsteps are needed: one to start the animation and one to end it.

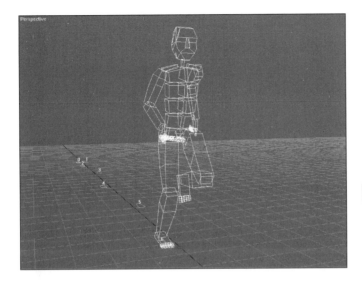

Figure 8.6

The Biped is running with the tube in his hand.

Assigning a Free Form Area

Before you can make your Biped fly, jump, or dive without vertical dynamics, you have to assign a place in the animation where the vertical dynamics can be turned off. This tutorial will show you how to set up a series of frames in an animation to be used as a free form area. After you are able to do this, you can animate your Biped with standard keyframe animation to make it do whatever you wish.

1. In the Front viewport, create a basic Biped.
2. Go to the Motion panel. Click on **Footstep Track** in the Track Selection rollout. Choose **Jump**, and click on **Create Multiple Footsteps**.
3. In the Create Multiple Footsteps dialog box, set the number of footsteps to 4, as shown in Figure 8.7.
4. Go to Track view by pressing F4. Select Objects\ Bip01 Footsteps. The blue and green blocks, which indi-

IK BLEND

The IK Blend allows you to change the motion parameters from forward kinematics to inverse kinematics or a blend of the two. When IK Blend is set at 0.0, the arm or leg track selected will have a free swing-type or sweeping movement that is controlled from the joints at the set keys. If the IK Blend is set at 1.0, the arm or leg track selected will follow a more planned spline path that the hand or foot is leading, like throwing a baseball or hitting a punching bag.

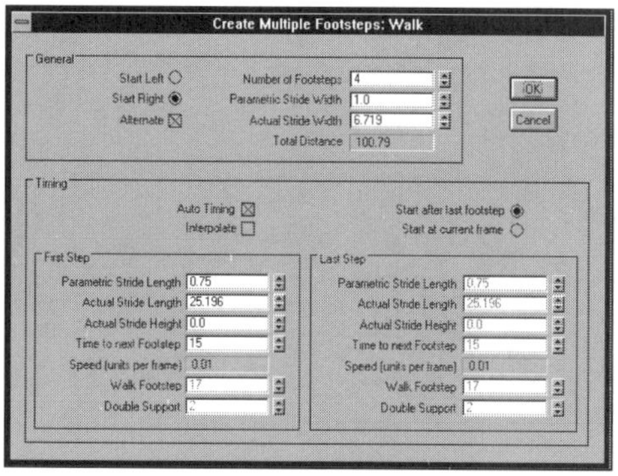

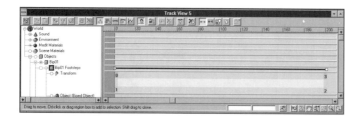

Figure 8.7

The Create Multiple Footsteps dialog box.

cate the placement and duration of the footsteps, appear. See Figure 8.8.

5. Place the cursor over the right end of the black slider in the **Footsteps Track**, and drag it to 200.

6. Put the cursor over footstep box 2, and double-click on the left side of the footstep box. Doing this will show you that the footstep can be stretched to the left while the right side stays in place. Drag the footstep to the left to approximately 198. Do the same with the footstep box 3.

7. Scroll back in the **Footstep Track** to footstep box 0 and 1. Double-click the left side of the box, and drag the left side of the box back to approximately 2. Do the same for footstep box 1.

Now you have several frames in between footsteps to create a free form sequence.

8. Right-click on the **Footstep Track**; the Bip01 Footstep Track dialog box appears, as shown in Figure 8.9. Select Edit Free Form (no physics). Close the dialog box.

A hollow yellow box appears in the **Footstep Tracks** between the footsteps. This shows the area where free form is possible.

9. To activate the free form area, click on the yellow box. It will turn solid to indicate that it is active, as shown in Figure 8.10.

10. Click on **Create Keys** for Inactive Footsteps. The footsteps are now active. Click on the **Footstep Tracks** button to deactivate it.

11. Click on the **Save File** icon in the General rollout, and save the free form steps as an .stp file so you can apply the free form steps over any Biped.

Figure 8.8

The Track view shows the footstep placement.

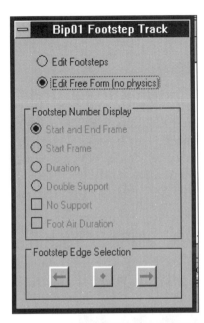

Figure 8.9

The Footstep Track dialog box.

Figure 8.10

The solid box in the middle of the Footstep track is the Free Form Edit area.

Note: To make your Biped move without vertical restraints, you can use keyframe animation using the Animate Key.

Dribbling a Ball

Learning how to animate the dribbling of a basketball will give you some basic in-

formation about linking and unlinking an object during animation.

Creating the Biped with a Basketball

The first thing we need to do is create a basic biped to dribble the ball.

It is important to note that if you had a series of footsteps, there would be small yellow boxes between each set of footsteps. You have to have a jump or a spread in the footsteps to allow enough frames to finish whatever movement you require without the vertical dynamics being in place.

Animation keys cannot be set without footsteps, or with footsteps that are not activated.

1. Create a basic biped in the Front viewport with a height of 70 units at 0,100,0.
2. Go to the Motion panel and click on **Footstep Track** button in the Track Selection rollout.
3. Select **Jump** and click on the **Create Multiple Footsteps** in the Footstep Creation rollout. The Create Multiple Footstep dialog box appears.
4. Set the number of footsteps to 2, and click on OK.
5. Press Shift + \ to bring up the alternate viewport layout, or press F4 for Track view.
6. Click on Object/Bip01 Footsteps. Scroll down to see the blue and green blocks representing the two footsteps.
7. Drag the black slider in the footsteps track over to 100. Double-click on each footstep until a small arrow appears, and stretch it from frame 1 to frame 100. Close Track View.
8. Click on **Create Keys for Inactive Footsteps** in the Footstep Creation rollout.

The footsteps are now active and the Biped will stand in one place throughout the animation.

Creating the Basketball

Now that we have our basketball player, he really needs something to play with.

1. Go to the Create panel and in the Standard Primitives rollout. Click on Sphere.
2. Go to the Left viewport and create a sphere at coordinates 0,70,40, with a radius of 5 units and 16 segments.

Now there is a ball in the scene with the Biped. Click on the **Play Animation** button. The Biped and the ball are motionless. See Figure 8.11.

Animating the Ball

Because you will be animating the ball using regular keyframing techniques, the **Animate** button will be active.

1. Click on the **Animate** button to select it. Move the ball up 50 degrees in the Z-axis.
2. Go to frame 16 and move the ball to -50 degrees in the Z-axis.
3. Go to frame 36 and move the ball 50 degrees in Z-axis.
4. Go to frame 40 and, leaving the ball in position, set another key.
5. Go to frame 56 and move the ball back down -50 degrees.
6. Go to frame 76 and move the ball up 50 degrees.
7. Go to frame 80 and, leaving ball in position, and then click on the **Set Key** button.
8. Go to frame 94 and move ball -50 degrees.

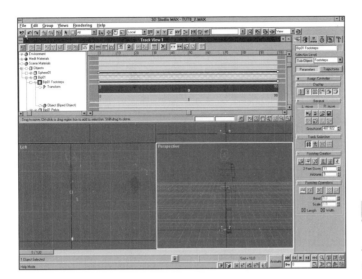

Figure 8.11

Player with the basket-ball in the scene.

9. Click on the **Animate** button again to deselect it. Play the animation.

Now when you play the animation, the bouncing basketball stays in mid-air slightly before it returns to the floor.

10. Load Tut8_2.MAXto check your animation.

IK Linking the Biped

Linking the Biped to an object with IK can be tricky. You should do the steps in the following order for best results.

1. Select the Biped's right arm. Go to the Kinematics section of the Track Operations rollout and click on the **Select Object Space Object** (the arrow directly under **Object**).

2. Click on the ball. It will not turn white; however, sphere01 will appear in the Name selection box.

3. Click on the **Animate** button. Now rotate the arm in the Z-axis so that the hand rests on the top of the ball.

4. Page down to select each set of finger links, and rotate them to match the curve of the ball.

5. Create two footsteps and stretch them over the length of the animation in the Track view. Click on **Create Keys for Inactive Footsteps** to activate them, as shown in Figure 8.12.

6. In the Track operations rollout, select **Anchor Right Arm**.

7. Select **Object** (also referred to as **Object Space Object**) in the Kinematics section of the Track Operations rollout. By doing this, you are telling the program that the Biped hand is linked to the object's space, not the body's center of mass.

8. Set IK Blend to 1.0.

9. Click on the **Set Key** button.

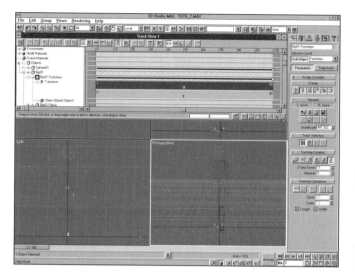

Figure 8.12

The footsteps in the Track view have been stretched over the entire animation.

Note: IK Blend allows you to change from forward kinematics at setting 0.0, which is used in animations where the motion is starting in the joints and shown in wide, sweeping arcs. This is useful if the figure is walking and swinging its arms. A setting of 1.0 will give the motion inverse kinematics. This is especially useful if the figure's arms are moving along a predetermined path, say, in a punching motion or when throwing a ball. If the setting is somewhere between 0.0 and 1.0, IK Blend will blend the two together.

10. Go to the first frame where the hand is no longer in contact with the ball. Click on **Object** and set IK Blend to 0.0. Then click on the **Set Key** button.

11. Go to next frame where the hand has contact with the ball again. Click on **Object** and set IK Blend to 1.0. Then click on the **Set Key** button. Continue this pattern throughout the animation.

12. Click on **Right Arm Anchor** to deselect it.

13. Click on the **Animate** button. The Biped bounces the ball rather stiffly up and down as it stands in one spot.

14. Load Tut8_2a.MAX to check your animation.

Now, let's get a little action into this dribble. Complete the next tutorial to have your basketball star run and move more realistically as he bounces the ball.

If you select the Object Space with an IK Blend of 1.0, the Biped and the object are linked just as though you were using standard MAX linking tools. If you set IK Blend to 0.0, the link is disconnected. When you give these two commands on two separate keys, the program will blend the information from the two keys to make the transition from linked to unlinked smooth.

TIP You must select the Object Space keys both before and after you have selected Object. These keys are called an Object Space Interval. If any of the keys are set to Body space, the program assumes that all should be reverted back to the default Body space.

Basketball Dribbler on the Run

The first thing that we need to do is animate the basketball player.

1. In the Perspective viewport, create a basic Biped at 0,100,0 with a height of 70 units.
2. Go to the Motion panel and click on the **Footstep Track** in the Track Selection rollout. Select **Running**, and click on the **Create Multiple Footsteps** button. The Create Multiple Footsteps dialog box will appear.
3. Set the Number of Footsteps spinner to 12, leaving everything else at the default setting. Click on OK.

4. Click on **Create Keys** for Inactive Footsteps.

You now have a Biped with 161 frames of running motion. Click on Play Animation and watch the Biped run. This running movement might be OK for timid little ladies, but let's give your basketball star a forward bend as it runs to make it more realistic.

5. Maximize the Left viewport and click on **Footstep Track** to deselect it.
6. Click on **Figure Mode** and **Bend Links Mode** in the Tracks Operations rollout.
7. Select any of the Biped Spine objects and rotate it about the Z-axis 25 degrees. Note that the head stays in an upright position. See Figure 8.13.

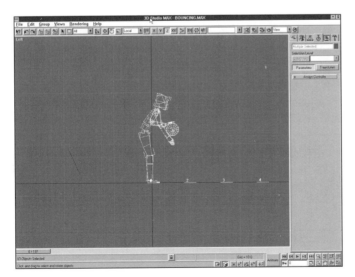

Figure 8.13

The basketball player is bent over but the head stays in an upright position.

8. Click on the **Figure Mode** to deselect it. Then click on the **Bend Links
Mode**. Play the animation.

The figure now runs in a funny, hunched-
over position. Let's give him something
to do.

Link and Create
the Basketball

Now we'll create the basketball and link it
to the Biped's hand.

1. In the Left viewport, create a sphere
at coordinates 0,70,40 with a radius
of 5 units and 16 segments.
2. Click on the Select and Move transform, and move the sphere in the
X-axis to -8.5.
3. Go to the Motion panel and select
the Biped's lower right arm (the
Biped's right side is shown in green).
4. Select the **Select Object Space Object** (the arrow directly beneath

Object) in the Kinematics section of
the Track Operations rollout.
5. Click on the sphere. It will not turn
white; however, the name Sphere01
will appear in the Name Selection
box.

*Note: If you want to change the sphere's name,
go to the Modify panel, select the sphere and
click in the Name Selection Box at the top of
the Command panel where it currently says
Sphere01. Type in "Basketball". The name
will be updated in the Kinematics Name
Selection box as well.*

6. Go to the Front viewport and move
the Basketball in the X-axis 9 units
to place it outside the Biped's right
foot, as shown in Figure 8.14.
7. Select the Biped's right hand.
Using Select and Move with ZX
constraints, set the Reference Coor-
dinate System to World, and move
the hand up to the top of the
basketball.

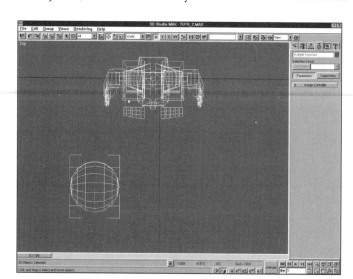

Figure 8.14

*The ball is placed
outside the players
right foot.*

Character Animation with 3D Studio MAX

8. Rotate the hand about the X-axis to approximately 90 degrees to lay it palm-down on the basketball.

9. In the Left viewport, rotate the hand about the YZ-axis to lay the fingers onto the ball surface, as shown in Figure 8.15.

10. Click on the **Anchor Right Arm** in the Track Operations rollout.

11. Click on Object in the Kinematics section of the Track Operations rollout and set the IK Blend spinner to 1.0.

12. Click on the **Set Key** button.

Now the Biped IK is linked to the basketball. Run the animation again. The Biped runs while trying to keep attached to the ball. However, the basketball still must be animated with regular keyframe animation to keep up with the Biped's movements.

Animate the Ball

Now we'll animate the ball so it can keep up with the player.

1. Open the Track view.

2. Click on the Transform under Sphere01, and open Object|Bip01 Footsteps. Scroll down until the blue and green footstep boxes are visible in the **Footstep Tracks**.

3. Click on the **Animate** button.

4. In the Left viewport, select the basketball and go to frame 18.

5. Right-click over the Select and Move tool. The Move Transform Type-In dialog box appears, as shown in Figure 8.16. Enter Y-44 and Z-5 in the Absolute: World fields. Close the dialog box.

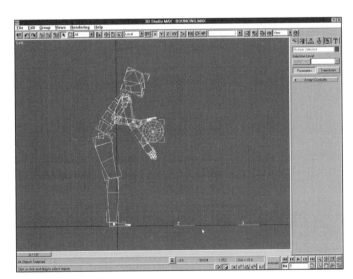

Figure 8.15

The hand is placed on the basketball.

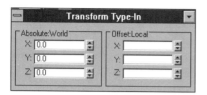

Figure 8.16

The Move Transform Type-In dialog box.

6. Go to frame 36, and using the Select and Move tool, move the basketball up in front of the Biped to approximately Y-16 and Z-35. Now scratch the time slider back and forth to see how the basketball moves. Notice that the bounce is still not realistic.

7. Go to frame 0. The basketball should still be selected.

8. Go to the Key Info (basic) rollout in the Motion panel so you can adjust the tangents of the motion curve. See Figure 8.17. We want the basketball to accelerate as it drops to the ground. Go to the drop-down window in the Out tangent box and choose the fifth selection down.

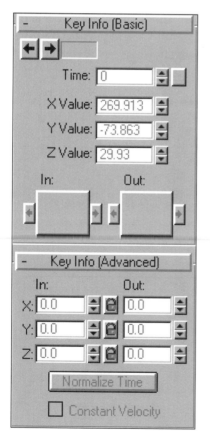

Figure 8.17

The Key Info (basic) rollout.

9. Go to frame 18. When the ball bounces, we want it to bounce sharply and come up sharply. So this time, go to the In tangent box and choose the fourth selection down. Now click on the right-pointing arrow on the right side of the In tangent. Doing this will transfer the same selection to the Out tangent.

10. Go to frame 36. At the top of the bouncing basketball's arc, we want to slow the ball down a little, so in the In tangent, choose the fifth selection down and transfer it to the Out tangent as well.

Scratch the time slider again and see how much better the ball bounce looks.

Clones-R-Us

The ball's position keys can be cloned in the Track View to produce a series of bounces rather than animating them one at a time. In the following steps we'll clone the down position of the bouncing ball to each corresponding frame.

1. In the Track view, go to Objects/Ball and select the key at frame 18 in the Ball Position track. It will turn white to signify it is selected.

2. Hold the Shift key down, drag the selected key to frame 51 to clone it, then release the mouse button. In the same manner, hold the Shift key

down again, drag the key to frame 81, and release the mouse button. Continue to clone the key at frames 111 and 141.

This completes all of the down positions. Now we have to do the same for all of the up positions.

3. Go to frame 36 and select the ball position key there. Hold down the Shift key and drag the key to frame 66 to clone it. Release the mouse button. Repeat this step and clone the key to frames 96, 126, and 156.

Look at the animation again. The ball is now bouncing in place without the Biped.

Moving the Ball with the Biped

In order to move the ball so it keeps up with your basketball star, we must move the ball in the Y-axis every time the ball touches the ground plane. Remember that the **Animate** button must be on for all of these steps.

1. Go to frame 51, and using the Select and Move tool, move the ball in the Y-axis -56 units. Then click on the **Set Key** button.

2. Go to frame 81. Move the ball along the Y-axis to -112 units. Then click on the **Set Key** button.

3. Go to frame 111 and move the ball along the Y-axis to -170 units. Then click on the **Set Key** button.

4. Go to frame 141 and move the ball along the Y-axis to -221 units. Then click on the **Set Key** button.

The ball is now bouncing along, but it's returning to the original top position at every bounce. That's not realistic, of course, but when we adjust the top position of each bounce, it'll be fine.

5. Go to frame 66, which is the second bounce up. Move the ball along the Y-axis -56 units. Then click on the **Set Key** button.

6. Go to frame 96, which is the third bounce up. Move the ball along the Y-axis -115 units. Then click on the **Set Key** button.

7. Go to frame 126, or the fourth bounce up. Move the ball along the Y-axis -166 units. Then click on the **Set Key** button.

8. Go to frame 156, the fifth bounce up. Move the ball along the Y-axis -220 units. Then click on the **Set Key** button.

9. Scratch the animation. The ball should now be bouncing quite nicely along the track next to the Biped.

Now we have the ball moving nicely, but you'll notice that the hand motion needs a little adjustment to follow through on the action.

Adjusting the Hand Follow-Through

In this section we are animating the right hand to follow the motion of the ball and complete the action after the ball has left the hand. The first step is to go to each frame that has the Biped hand attached to the ball and set IK Blend and Object Space.

1. Click on the **Animate** button to deselect it. Then swap the viewport layout by pressing Shift + \.

2. Maximize the Left viewport.

3. Go to frame 10, and select **Object** and an IK Blend of 1.0 in the Kinematics section of the Track Operations rollout. Then click on the **Set Key** button.

4. Go to frame 36, and select **Object** and an IK Blend of 1.0. Then click on the **Set Key** button.

5. At frame 66, select **Object** and an IK Blend of 1.0. Then click on the **Set Key** button.

6. At frame 96, select **Object** and an IK Blend of 1.0. Then click on the **Set Key** button.

7. At frame 126, select **Object** and an IK Blend of 1.0. Then click on the **Set Key** button.

8. At frame 156, select **Object** and an IK Blend of 1.0. Then click on the **Set Key** button.

All these frames are the center frames where the hand is on the ball. They are now set to act like a regular MAX IK link between the ball and the Biped hand.

IK Keys Chart

Frame	IK Blend	Coordinate System
0	1.0	Object
11	1.0	Object
18	0.0	Object
31	1.0	Object
36	1.0	Object
42	1.0	Object
51	0.0	Object
62	1.0	Object
66	1.0	Object
72	1.0	Object
81	0.0	Object
93	1.0	Object
96	1.0	Object
102	1.0	Object
111	0.0	Object
122	1.0	Object
126	1.0	Object
132	1.0	Object
141	0.0	Object
151	1.0	Object
156	1.0	Object
161	1.0	Object

The IK Keys Chart shows frames that have keys set to **Object Space** with an IK Blend of 1.0, or all the keyframes where the hand has contact with the ball, and all the keyframes that are still in **Object Space** but have an IK Blend set to 0.0, showing that the hand no longer is in contact with the ball and therefore no longer is linked to it.

Now we will adjust the hand and arm as the ball leaves the hand and the arm continues its follow-through action.

1. Go to frame 18 and select **Object** and an IK Blend of 0.0. Then click on the **Set Key** button.
2. elect the right lower arm and rotates it about the Z-axis approximately 50 degrees. Page down to select the hand and rotate it down in the Z-axis slightly until you have the end position you desire for the follow-through motion. Then click on the **Set Key** button. See Figure 8.18.

Scratch the time slider to see the motion. Looks a little funny, doesn't it? The arm is moving in a haphazard motion because the Anchor Right Arm is still active. Turn the anchor off and watch the animation again.

We have one good bounce with correct arm movement. You can either repeat these steps at every bounce of the ball (sounds pretty time-consuming to me), or you can just copy and paste to each keyframe. The following steps will show you how:

1. Select Bip01R Arm.
2. Right-click over the selected part and choose Select Children from the dialog box. Now the entire arm is selected.
3. Click on **Copy Posture** button in the Track Operations rollout.
4. Go to frame 51. Click on **Paste Posture** in the Track Operations rollout. Then click on the **Set Key** button.

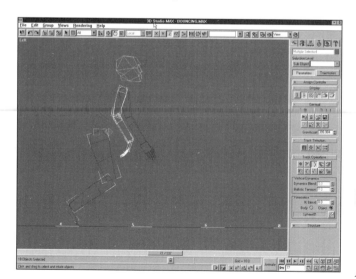

Figure 8.18

The hand is adjusted to the follow-through position.

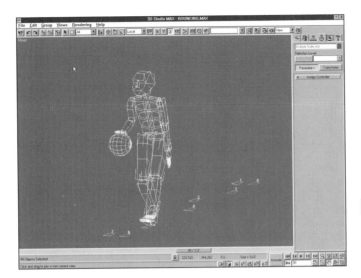

Figure 8.19

The left arm is dangling without motion.

5. Go to frame 81 and click on **Paste Posture**. Then click on the **Set Key** button.
6. At frame 111 click on **Paste Posture**. Then click on the **Set Key** button.
7. At frame 141 click on **Paste Posture**. Then click on the **Set Key** button.

Now we have a downward follow-through hand motion.

1. Go to frame 15. Select the Biped's right hand and rotate it down in the Z-axis slightly as the hand starts to come off the ball (10 degrees or so). Set to Object Space with an IK Blend of 0.0. Then click on the **Set Key** button. Now we will copy the posture to the other keyframes (six frames before the ball touches the ground).
2. Select the Biped's right arm and the children. Then click on **Copy Posture**.

3. Go to frame 46 and click on **Paste Posture**. Then click on the **Set Key** button.
4. Go to frame 78 and click on **Paste Posture**. Then click on the **Set Key** button.
5. Go to frame 107 and click on **Paste Posture**. Then click on the **Set Key** button.
6. Go to frame 138 and click on **Paste Posture**. Then click on the **Set Key** button.

Play the animation. The movement of the right arm and ball is good, but the left arm is dangling lifeless to the Biped's side, as shown in Figure 8.19. We want the arm to be bent at the elbow as it runs with the movement coming from the shoulder. If there is a lot of movement coming from the elbow, it starts to look loose and sloppy. Remember, if the left leg is back, the left arm is forward, and vice versa. As you go through these keyframes and adjust the arm position, watch where the leg is and adjust accordingly.

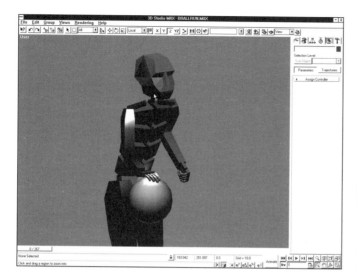

Figure 8.20

The arm and wrist are in position for copying and pasting.

1. Go to frame 0. Select the Biped's left lower arm (it's shown in blue). Rotate the arm up in the Z-axis to -55 degrees.

2. Go to frame 10, select the left upper arm, and rotate it about the Z-axis approximately 20 degrees to bring it back slightly. Page down to select the lower arm, and bend it slightly in the Z-axis to keep it bent.

3. Page down until the first row of finger links are selected and rotate them about the Z-axis to curve them inward. Now page down to the next set of finger links and rotate them to curve inward. Finally, press Page Down to select the last set of finger links and rotate them around the Z-axis as well to form a fist. The thumb sticks out because it sits on a different plane on the hand than the fingers.

4. Select the first thumb link and rotate it about the Y-axis to bring the thumb into the fist. Then click on

the **Set Key** button. See Figure 8.20.

5. Select the Bip01L Arm and select its children.

6. Click on **Copy Posture**.

7. Go to frame 29 and click on **Paste Posture**. Then click on the **Set Key** button.

8. Go to frame 48 and click on **Paste Posture**. Then click on the **Set Key** button.

9. At frame 68, click on **Paste Posture**. Then click on the **Set Key** button.

10. At frame 89, click on **Paste Posture**. Then click on the **Set Key** button.

11. At frame 107, click on **Paste Posture**. Then click on the **Set Key** button.

Now we have the backward movement of the free arm as the Biped runs. To get the forward movement follow the following steps.

1. Go to frame 19. The left arm is at its most forward position. Click on **Copy Posture**.

2. At frame 39, click on **Paste Posture**. Then click on the **Set Key** button.
3. At frame 59, click on **Paste Posture**. Then click on the **Set Key** button.
4. At frame 79, click on **Paste Posture**. Then click on the **Set Key** button.
5. At frame 99, click on **Paste Posture**. Then click on the **Set Key** button.

Play the animation. You'll notice that the runner looks much more lifelike.

Here is another trick you might keep in mind when you are working with Biped. If you want to animate two objects together, separate them and then animate them individually. To do this:

1. Create a "Master" dummy object.
2. Link the object to the master dummy.
3. Link the Biped center of mass to the master dummy.

4. When every thing is animated together, animate the dummy.
5. When the Biped and object need to separate, stop animating the dummy and animate them individually.
6. If they need to come together again, stop animating separately and start animating the dummy again.

Next Chapter...

In the next chapter we will look at Character Studio's Physique plug-in. With Physique we can attach any mesh to our Biped. This allows us to apply any motion file to our meshes and see a troll do the boogie or watch powerlines walk drunkenly down the street.

Chapter 9

Adjusting the mesh to fit the Biped for realistic movement

Attaching the Physique modifier so your mesh and skeleton will move together smoothly

Preventing mesh spikes and deformations

Assigning and reassigning vertices

Physique

In this chapter we will use the Physique modifier to attach more complicated meshes. We used a very simple version of this in the first Quick Start Tutorial. Now, we will adjust and attach a physique to a more complicated mesh.

Loading the Mesh

We will be attaching a Biped to the Olaf the Troll mesh you received with Character Studio. The Troll is a good example of a mesh that is not a typical human form, so adjusting the Biped is a little more complicated.

1. Load Tut9_1.MAX. The Troll mesh comes up on the screen in the standard reference pose: with the arms in a straight-out position. See Figure 9.1.
2. Maximize the Front viewport and select the mesh.
3. Type in "Mesh All" in the Named Selection Set in the toolbar. Press Enter.
4. Go to the Freeze by Selection rollout in the Display panel, and click on the **Freeze Selected** button. This will freeze the mesh and allow you to adjust the Biped over it without selecting the mesh by mistake.
5. Go to the Create panel, click on the **Systems** button, and choose Biped. The button turns green indicating it is active. The Body Parameters rollout appears.
6. Drag the cursor from the bottom of the Troll's feet to the top of its head to create a Biped figure. A default Biped appears over the mesh.

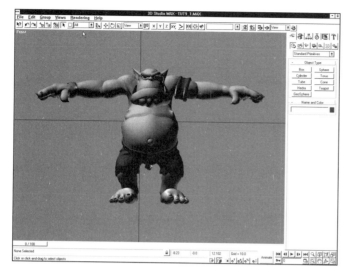

Figure 9.1

The Troll in a reference pose.

7. In the Body Parameter rollout, change the Fingers and Toes spinners to 4 and add a three-linked tail. The Biped will make these changes instantly. See Figure 9.2.

Adjusting the Biped

You have now created a basic Biped over the Troll mesh. Before you can attach the Biped to the mesh, you must adjust it to fit properly. This is a very important part of making your mesh move accurately when Physique is applied. If the Biped is not adjusted correctly, your mesh might spike and deform as the Biped moves.

Adjust the Torso

The basic Biped does not fit the mesh at this point. Because one adjustment affects another and so on, when adjusting the Biped you need in a specific order. You need to adjust the pelvis first since it is the parent object of the Biped (except for the center of mass), and it will not move separately from the rest of the Biped.

Note: *To ensure proper assignment of vertices in the body, always align the Biped to the center of the mesh. Don't try and fit it so the spine runs along the back of the body.*

When you are aligning a Biped with a mesh, it's always good to have your mesh in a standard reference pose. This brings the arms away from the body, ensuring the vertices will be linked to the right area of the body when Physique is applied.

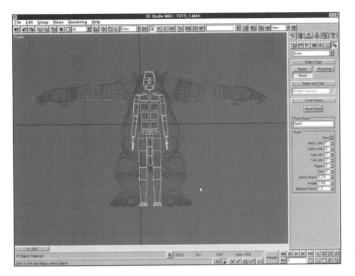

Figure 9.2

The default Biped with four fingers and toes and a three-linked tail.

1. While still in the Front viewport, go to the Motion panel and click on the **Figure Mode** button. The button turns yellow indicating it is active.

2. Click on the **Center of Mass** button and move the entire Biped down in the Z-axis until the pelvis is centered in the pelvis area of the mesh.

3. Select the pelvis and non-uniform scale it in the Z-axis approximately 333 percent, or until the legs are moved far enough apart to be in position over the mesh legs. Scale the pelvis up in the X-axis 200 percent so the pelvis has some height as well.

4. If the Center of Mass object is not in the lowest point of the pelvis, click on the **Center of Mass** button. Click on the **Rubber-Band** button in the General rollout and move the Center of Mass object down to the lowest point in the Troll's pelvis area. This will pull down the Troll's center of gravity and give him the appearance of having more weight.

5. Click on the **Rubber-Band** button to deselect it.

Adjust the Biped Legs

The default Biped has human proportions. In order to get the arms and legs to move naturally for the Troll's body shape, the arms and legs must be adjusted to fit the Troll's body.

1. Select Bip03 R leg. Click on the **Symmetrical Tracks** in the Tracks selection rollout. Now both the right and left legs are selected.

2. Using Non-uniform scale in the X-axis, shorten the thighs to the knee joint on the mesh. The thighs can also be enlarged to match the mesh in the Z -axis approximately 200 percent and the Y-axis approximately 200 percent.

3. Rotate the thighs outward to 25 degrees around the X-axis to match the mesh.

Always check your mesh from the side when adjusting for length. Make sure the upper leg comes down just to the knee joint so the leg will bend at the correct place.

4. Press Page Down to select both lower legs, and non-uniform scale them in the X-axis until they are at the ankle joints.

5. Using non-uniform scale, enlarge the lower legs in the Z-axis to 200 percent and in the Y-axis to 200 percent to match the mesh legs.

Adjust the Biped Arms

Now that the legs are adjusted, we'll adjust the Biped arms to match the mesh.

1. Select the Bip01 R arm1 and click on the **Symmetrical Tracks**. Rotate the arms in the Y-axis until they are even with the mesh arms.

2. Press Page Down to symmetrically select Bip01 R and L Arms. The clavicle objects are selected. Non-uniform scale them in the X-axis 170 percent to bring them out to match the shoulder width. If the shoulders and arms do not line up with the mesh, the clavicles can be rotated around the Y-axis to angle them up and align them properly.

3. Press Page Down, select Bip01-Arms1, and non-uniform scale them in the X-axis to match the mesh elbow. Scale them in the Y- and Z-axes to approximately 200 percent.

4. Press Page Down to select the Bip01 Arm2. Scale them in the X-axis to align with the wrists, then scale them

in the Y- and Z-axes to 200 percent to resize to match the mesh.

Note: Don't forget to use your spacebar to lock your selections. It makes it easier to adjust without selecting another part accidentally.

Adjust Body Posture

Every mesh is different in body posture. The Biped has to be adjusted to correspond to the bend and stance of each figure so as the mesh moves, the stance and posture remains true to the character.

1. Maximize the Left viewport. The Biped does not line up with the body mesh, as shown in Figure 9.3.

2. Select the Bip01 Spine object, and rotate it around the Z-axis to about 30 degrees.

3. Select Spine 1 and rotate it around the Z-axis to -40 degrees.

4. Select Spine 2 and rotate it to -20.

5. Select Spine 3 and rotate it to 15.

6. Select Spine 4 and rotate it to 15.

This should align the spine curve with the mesh back. Now we will adjust the legs.

1. Select the upper legs. Rotate them around the Z-axis approximately 15 degrees to match the angle of the upper leg mesh.

2. Click on the **Rubber-Band** button to select it. Select the lower legs and

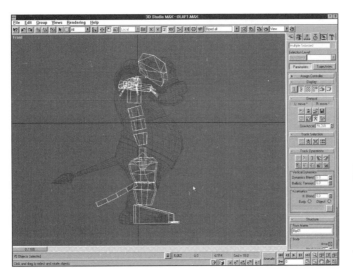

Figure 9.3

The body is not aligned to the mesh until the posture and stance can be adjusted.

rotate them back to -30 degrees to match the angle of the lower leg.

3. Page down to select the feet. Non-uniform scale the feet 200 percent in the Y-axis, 300 percent in the Z-axis and 400 percent in the X-axis. We will adjust the feet more accurately later, but this gives us a better view of how the feet and legs go together. At this point you can go back

and fine-tune the length of the legs to make sure they don't overlap the joints. See Figure 9.4.

Adjust the Head and Neck

The Troll is difficult because it has a hunch-back and the face does not have human proportions. The jaw is very large and the forehead, eyes, nose, and ears are in the top

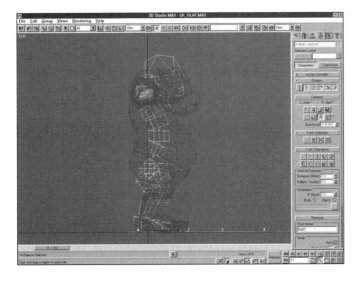

Figure 9.4

The Troll's legs and spine adjusted from the side.

one-third of its face. However, it is still possible to adjust the Biped to work with figures that are not human proportions.

1. Select the biped head. Non-uniform scale the head in the XY-axis to 170 percent and in the Z-axis to 235 percent. This gives you a Biped head roughly the same size as the Mesh.
2. Go to the Body Parameters in the Structure rollout. Raise the neck spinner to 4. The added links will not only make the neck longer, but will give the neck more flexibility.
3. Select Bip01Neck. Non-uniform scale in the X-axis to 167 percent, and rotate in the Z-axis to -25 degrees.
4. Select Bip01Neck1 and scale it 190 percent in the X-axis. Rotate it 15 degrees in the Z-axis.
5. Select Bip01Neck2 and scale it 196 percent in the X-axis. Rotate it 65 degrees in the Z-axis.
6. Select Bip01Neck3 and scale it 350 percent in the X-axis. Rotate it 25 degrees in the Z-axis.

This will give the neck a bent appearance but will bring the head out and down to match the mesh. With the biped head sticking out of the mesh, it appears that the mesh is wearing a football helmet, as shown in Figure 9.5.

Adjust the Hands and Feet

This is the most difficult part of aligning the Biped to the mesh. Because the Phy-

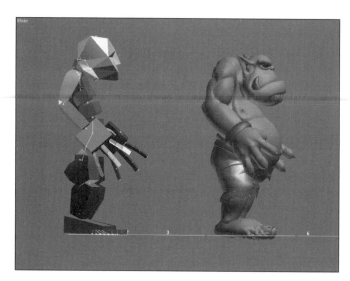

Figure 9.5

The biped neck has been aligned with the mesh.

The Biped fingers and toes can be moved around the hands or feet using the Move transform. This can be done by selecting the first finger joint closest to the palm and then moving it to the desired position. The entire finger will move. You cannot move the finger by selecting the second or third link.

sique modifier links the mesh to the Biped by assigning cylinders of vertices to the nearest Biped link, miscalculations can occur easily if the Biped isn't adjusted correctly inside the mesh.

Adjust the Hands

Adjusting the hands is one of the more time consuming jobs when adjusting a biped to a mesh. The more accurate you are in this section, the less time-consuming it will be later to reassign your vertices.

1. Maximize the Top viewport.
2. Select both Bip01 hands. Non-uniform scale them in both the X-axis (approximately 240 percent) and Z-axis (approximately 450 percent) to fit the mesh palm. Make sure that the palm does not go over the joint line where the fingers attach to the hand. As you can see, the fingers are not in the same position on the palm as the mesh.
3. Press Page Down. All the first finger links are selected.
4. Non-uniform scale in the X-axis until the joints are even with the first finger joints.
5. Press Page Down to select the next set of links, and scale them to line up with the second finger joint.
6. Press Page Down to select the last finger links, and scale them so they are longer than the actual mesh fin-

gers. That is, the Biped fingers will actually come through the ends of the mesh fingers. Remember: If the Biped does not come all the way through the mesh, the vertices will not be attached properly.

7. After you have scaled all the fingers, you can select them individually and move or rotate them to align along the midline of each corresponding mesh finger. See Figure 9.6.

*Note: If the hands are not in identical positions, the hands and fingers will have to be adjusted separately. However, if just one hand is adjusted, and the other hand is in a similar position, the adjusted hand can be copied by selecting the part you want copied, clicking on the **Copy Posture** button in the Tracks rollout, and then clicking on the **Copy Opposite** button.*

8. Now, look at those thumbs! I'm sure you have already noticed that the thumbs are not only coming out of the side of the palm, they angle downwards. Simply move the Biped thumb with the Move transform in the XY-axis to the location of the hand from which the thumb protrudes. Then rotate in the Biped thumb in the Z-axis until it's lined up with the mesh. Don't forget that the last thumb link has to be longer than the mesh thumb.

Figure 9.6

The fingers can be moved around the palm to align with the mesh hand.

Now that the hands are adjusted, we need to adjust the feet.

Adjust the Feet

Adjusting the feet is similar to adjusting the hands.

1. Go to the Top viewport. Using Arc Rotate, rotate the body so you have a clear view of the top of the feet. Now using Region Zoom, drag a box around the feet area.
2. Select both feet. In the X-axis, rotate outward until the feet line up with the mesh.

You might find one foot lines up and the other isn't quite right. Using the Move transform in the XY-axis, you can fine-tune the position of each foot individually.

3. Press Page Down to symmetrically select all the first toe links. Using non-uniform scale, adjust the length of the link to the first toe joint.
4. Press Page Down and scale the next set of toe links to the next joint. Remember not to scale the link past the joint or the mesh toes will not bend properly.
5. Press Page Down and scale the last set of toe links so they are slightly longer than the mesh toes and protrude out the end of the mesh.
6. Using the Move transform in the XY-axis, align each toe with the center

 Just as with the fingers, the toes aren't automatically lined up in the right position. We can move them around the foot just as the fingers were. Make sure the Biped foot is wide enough to cover the whole mesh foot, especially if the mesh foot has a wide, spread-toe arrangement.

With the Attach to Node button active, the cursor changes between the international symbol for No (a circle with a diagonal line running through it) and a stick figure. Only when the cursor is a stick figure will Physique attach to the Biped.

of the corresponding mesh toe. Remember, you can only move the whole toe by selecting and moving the first toe link.

Now that the body is adjusted to fit the mesh as shown in Figure 9.7, we can attach them with Physique.

If your Biped foot does not appear to fit inside the mesh, you can adjust it by using the Ankle Attach spinner in the Body Parameters to slide the foot to the back or front.

Attaching Physique

Now that you've adjusted the Biped to your mesh, you can attach the Physique

modifier so your mesh will move smoothly with the Biped skeleton.

1. Maximize the Front viewport.
2. Go to the Display panel and click on Unfreeze All in the Freeze by Selection rollout.
3. Go to the Modify panel and select the mesh.
4. Click on More in the Modifiers rollout. A dialog box will appear with several new modifiers listed. See Figure 9.8.
5. Click on Physique and answer OK. The Physique and the Physique Level of Detail rollouts appear. Physique is now listed in the Modifier stack.
6. Using Region Zoom, drag a box around the pelvis.

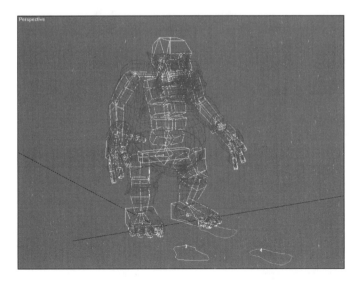

Figure 9.7

The Biped adjusted to the mesh.

Figure 9.8

The More Modifier dialog box.

7. Click on the **Attach to Node** button in the Physique rollout. The button turns green to signify it is active.

8. Place the cursor over the pelvis. The orange line of the Biped pelvis will be visible through the mesh. Move the cursor around the line of the Biped pelvis and click on it when the stick figure appears. After a few moments an orange line appears following the line of the Biped skeleton and passing through the mesh objects.

Note: If you apply Physique to the Biped and you get extraneous lines or multiple Physique bodies, you can try a couple of things before you throw up your hands in despair. First, delete the Physique modifier from the modifier stack and apply Physique again; sometimes it will attach correctly the second time. If that doesn't work, your skin might have too many mesh objects. The program can't handle too many and in fact does best with a single mesh. To remedy this you can boolean them together to form one mesh and then try Physique again, or you can replace the Biped geometry with the mesh objects by linking them with the MAX linking tool.

Physique is now applied to your Biped and mesh. You can see in Figure 9.9 that the Physique appears inside the body as links and nodes, or lines and crosses. The links or lines are what Physique uses to assign the vertices in the mesh. The nodes act like flexible joints. The vertices are assigned to the closest link in cylindrical groups. If the mesh is more complicated, sometimes the vertices get assigned to the wrong link and spiking and deformation of the mesh skin appears when you apply a motion file to it. I've even had my 3D person's hair slide right off its head as it walked. Therefore, even though you have very carefully adjusted the Biped to the mesh and applied Physique, sometimes the mesh will still need some manual adjustment so the mesh will move smoothly.

Who Needs Stinking Adjustment?

To check to see if your mesh needs some adjustment, let's apply a motion file to it and see how it moves.

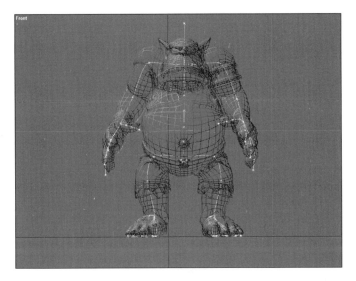

Figure 9.9

The Physique modifier is applied to the mesh.

1. Go to the Motion panel and click on the **Figure Mode** to deselect it.
2. Load 3DSMax/Tut/basic.bip. The Biped and mesh will disappear. Click on Extents All for the mesh to appear in the viewport at the starting position of the animation.
3. Play the animation and watch the Biped and mesh move. It will probably be easier to detect stray vertices if you change the viewport to Smooth + Highlight. If the mesh moves with no stray vertices apparent, you are ready to play with your figure because once the Physique is applied correctly to the mesh, you can use any .bip or .stp file with it.

Adjusting Stray Vertices

Okay, so your mesh spiked in fifteen different directions and you're about to commit hara-kiri. Don't worry, a little vertex adjustment ought to do take care of the problem. Let's round up those stray doggies and assign them to the right links.

Finding the Strays

Before you can reassign those vertices, you have to find which ones are assigned incorrectly.

1. Make sure to click on the **Figure Mode** to deselect it.
2. Maximize the Front viewport. Select the mesh and go to the Modify panel.

You should see the white mesh with the yellow links and nodes running through it.

3. Click on Sub-Object in the selection level. It turns yellow to signify it's active. Select Vertex in the drop-down window. The Physique Selection Status and Physique Vertex Assignment rollouts appear. See Figure 9.10.
4. Make sure all colors—red, green, and blue—are selected in the Vertex Type box in the Vertex Assignment rollout.

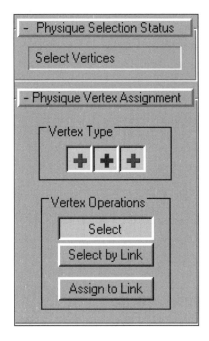

Figure 9.10

The Physique Selection Status and Physique Vertex Assignment rollouts.

5. Click on the **Select by Link** button in the Physique Vertex Assignment rollout. Now you can click on any of the yellow links in the mesh body, and the vertices already attached to that link will appear in the color they are assigned. This will give you an idea of how the vertices were assigned to the links by the Physique modifier.

Reassigning Vertices

If you find that the vertices were assigned to the wrong links, have no fear, you can reassign them to the proper link.

1. Click on Select in the Vertex Operations section of the Physique Vertex Assignment rollout. Leave the three colors active and hold down Alt while using the Fence Select tool to select the upper arm including the shoulder to the elbow. When you release, those vertices selected disappear and remain attached to their original link.

2. Using Fence Select, select the torso from under the arms to the navel. The vertices you selected will turn red, as shown in Figure 9.11.

3. Click on Assign to Link in the Vertex Operations section of the Physique Vertex Assignment rollout, and select the red vertex button. Notice that when you have the **Assign to Link** button active, only one color can be selected.

4. Click on the mid-torso link. The vertices selected will turn red and blue. The blue vertices are unable to be assigned to that link. They can, however, be assigned to the links adjacent to that one.

5. Click on Select again and this time click on the **Blue Vertex** button. Select an area that shows blue vertices. Only the blue vertices will be selected. Red vertices in the selected area will not be selected.

6. Click on Assign to Link and click on the **Red Vertex** button. Now click on the next link to see if the blue vertices will assign to that link. If they do, they will turn red. Continue

WHAT'S IN A COLOR?

The three color buttons in the Physique Vertex Assignment rollout identify different attributes that can be assigned vertices.

- *Red is for deformable vertices, or any vertices that will display movement, such as torso, legs, arms and, so forth. Most of the mesh vertices will probably be red.*

- *Green is for immovable vertices or vertices that won't be displaying much movement such as the head. Making vertices green also helps when you want deformation limited.*

- *Blue is the color the Physique modifier gives a vertex when it can't decide which color it should be. The vertices will turn blue if you want to manually reassign it to a link the Physique modifier doesn't want to link it to. Never leave vertices blue. Always reassign them either red or green.*

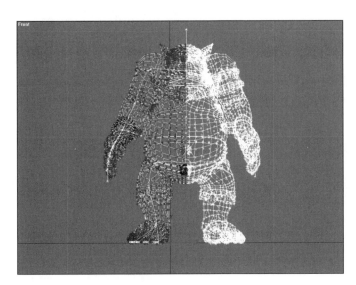

Figure 9.11

All vertices are originally assigned to red by Physique. Before any reassignment has taken place, any area selected will show selected vertices as red.

these steps until all the blue vertices have been assigned.

You'll notice that since the Troll's jaw hangs down over the torso, it is included in the group of vertices that are assigned to the torso link. We must go in and select only the head and jaw to reassign it.

1. Go to the Left viewport.
2. Click on Select. With the red vertex selected, Fence Select the head and jaw vertices from the side being careful not to include any shoulder or back vertices.
3. Click on the **Assign to Link** button and activate the **Green Vertex** button.
4. Click on the head link to reassign the vertices as green or non-deformable.

The areas that always seem to need a little help are under the arms, where vertex assignment gets a little tight if the arms aren't straight out. Fingers and toes tend to have

stray spikes, especially if the Biped doesn't go all the way through the mesh, and anything sticking up from the head like ears and horns. The head, face, and immovable items such as bracelets, glasses, and such need to be reassigned as green vertices.

Note: Sometimes even after the vertices have all been reassigned, the mesh still doesn't look quite right. This happens sometimes if a mesh doesn't have enough faces to stretch evenly and smoothly. You might be able to overcome this by tessellating the mesh in the areas needing more faces.

When applying a motion file to a Physique mesh, there is no collision detection to prevent body parts from going through other body parts as the figure moves. This means that a motion file originally created with a thin mesh or simply a Biped skeleton will not allow room for large-bodied or differently proportioned meshes, such as the Troll. When these motion files are used adjustments have to be made.

COLLISION DETECTION AND YOU

Collision Detection in Character Studio is limited to the footstep. The program defines the ground plane and adjusts to make sure the foot always stays on the ground level, whether that's an uneven terrain or a flat surface. Of course, this feature can be overcome to allow airborne flight.

If you get all the vertices assigned on your mesh and you still have one or two stray spikes, don't despair, just bring the mesh into the Modify panel (Figure Mode button off) in a position that shows the offending spike. You can select it individually and assign it to the proper link. If it will not reassign to the right link and continues to deform incorrectly, assign it to the correct link as a green vertex.

Next Chapter...

In the next chapter we will be doing some cartoon and exaggeration animations. You can get your figures to sneak and strut or make those muscles bulge like Popeye's.

Chapter **10**

Adjusting movement for cartooning

Exaggerating the body

Making cartoon features

Using linked controllers for facial expression

Exaggeration and Cartoon Movement

If you've ever watched a Disney cartoon one frame at a time, you know that animators sometimes "cheat" a bit to get the effect they want. The first one I can remember watching was *Roger Rabbit*. I was dying to see how they put the animated Roger in the film so seamlessly with the human actors. I was amazed to discover that some frames had only portions of Roger, not even a whole rabbit! They made special effects in some frames by using only an outline of Roger and white blobs. In some frames, there was no Roger at all, just background. As the scene played, all this deception was invisible to the human eye because, at 20 to 30 frames per second, your eyes see only the illusion of action, not every movement frame by frame.

This "cheating" is easy in 2D cel animation because every picture is hand-drawn and the animator is in complete control. When animating in 3D though, things are a little different. You have an entire 3D object to manipulate in every frame of the animation and still get those same effects that are taken for granted by the general animation viewer. So, even though some aspects of 3D animation might be more convenient than 2D animation, (like only building a character model once) you also lose the ability to have total control over the cartoon effect shots just by drawing them. This is one reason why animators are still using 2D cel animation with 3D modeling. Pixar's *Toy Story* was the first to use 100 percent 3D modeling, but you sure didn't see much in the way of Looney Tune imagery.

In this chapter we'll make our 3D models look more cartoonish and move in a more cartoonlike manner.

Exaggeration in Movement

Exaggeration is the key word in cartooning. Everything from movement to body styles is exaggerated. First let's look at the sneak example of exaggerated movement.

We described the differences between the slow and fast sneak in Chapter 5. Now let's see how to make your Biped move in a slow sneak.

The Sneak Biped— First Steps

All Bipeds are created equal—it's what happens afterwards that makes them unique. In this case, we're going to make some unusual adjustments in the automatically created footsteps to start building our slow sneak.

1. In the Front viewport, create a Biped that is 70 units in height.
2. Go to the Motion panel, and with the Left viewport maximized, click on the **Footstep Track** button.

3. Choose the **Walk** button and click on **Create Multiple Footsteps**.
4. In the Create Multiple Footsteps dialog box, set the number of footsteps to 7. Then click on Auto Timing to deselect it, and click on Start Right.
5. Adjust Walk Footstep to 30 and Double Support to 5. This adjustment will give us a slower stride with a longer overlap.
6. Click on OK.

You'll notice on the Create Multiple Footsteps rollout, Total Distance shows the total number of units covered by the selected Biped in this set of footsteps.

Total Distance is determined by the number of footsteps, the stride length, and whether you have Interpolate activated. If Interpolate is on, you can adjust the start and end speed, making your Biped speed up or slow down over the duration of the animation.

7. Click on the **Create Keys for Inactive Footsteps** button. The footsteps are activated.
8. Go to the Time Configuration dialog box and turn off Real Time Playback.

Now we will bend the spine so that the Biped moves in a sneak-type motion.

As you change the number of frames per footstep in the Walk Footstep field, you'll automatically set the speed of each step in units per frame. The higher the Walk Footstep value, the lower will be the speed in units per frame.

1. Turn off the **Footstep Track** button.
2. Select the **Biped Center of Mass** button.
3. Click on the Select and Move transform in the Z-axis.
4. Right-click over the Move transform in the toolbar; the Transform Type-In dialog box appears. See Figure 10.1.
5. Set the Z-axis to 30 units in the Absolute: World. Press Enter.

Now the Biped's center of gravity is lower, and it is bending its knees slightly, as seen in Figure 10.2. This will give the Biped a more hunched appearance as it sneaks along. Note, however, that the hunched motion is only on the first frame. To make the Biped hunched over the entire animation we need to go to the Track view.

6. Press F4 to bring up the Track view. Click on the **Filters** button and choose Animated Tracks in the Show Only section. See Figure 10.3.
7. Open Objects/Bip01 Transform Vertical.
8. Select all keys except the first in the Transform Vertical track. The selected keys turn white.

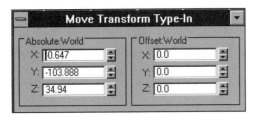

Figure 10.1

The Transform Type-In dialog box.

Figure 10.2

The Biped appears to be hunched when the Center of Mass object is moved down in the Z-axis.

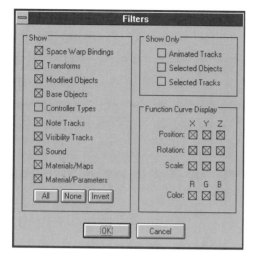

Figure 10.3

Filters dialog box.

9. Right-click over any track except Footsteps; the Change Multiple Keys dialog box appears. See Figure 10.4.

10. Click on Apply Increment. The last change made to the Biped will be applied over all selected keys.

Now let's rotate the spine.

Bending the Spine

Now, we will bend the spine so that the Biped moves in a sneak-type motion.

1. While still in the Left viewport, select Bip01 Spine, and click on the **Bend Links Mode** button. As you look at the General rollout, you'll see

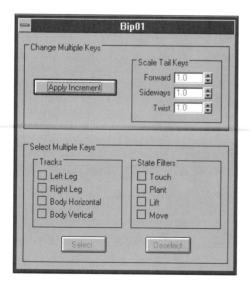

Figure 10.4

The Change Multiple Keys dialog box allows you to change a transform over an entire animation.

Change Increment applies to Move and Rotate only. It will not work with Scale.

two windows that say L Touch and R Touch (Figure 10.5). These windows tell you what position the right and left feet are in at any point in the animation.

Note: The Biped's leg motion is separated into four categories: touch, plant, lift, and move. The two windows in the General rollout tell you what phase the leg is in at that particular frame in the animation.

Touch: *This is shown when the foot first comes in contact with the ground and corresponds with the first frame of a footstep in the Track view.*

Plant: *This is shown after a foot is on the ground, but before it lifts off again. It is always in between the start and end frames of a footstep in the Track view.*

Lift: *This is shown at the frame when the foot first lifts off the ground. It always corresponds to the end frame of each footstep in the Track view.*

Move: *This is shown during the interval when the foot is moving in air and not being*

supported at any point. It is also always in between steps in the Track view.

With a sneak, we want to bend the spine backward just as both feet are coming together under the Biped to give it support, and then bend the spine forward at the halfway point as the foot is moving to the next footstep.

2. Turn on Angle Snap.
3. Go to frame 63. Since the Biped stands in place for a few frames, this is the first frame where the two legs are coming together.
4. Rotate in the Z-axis to -20 degrees. Click on the **Set Key** button.
5. Select all the Spine objects and click on the **Copy Posture** button.
6. Go to frame 88 and click on the **Paste Posture** button. Then click on the **Set Key** button.
7. At frame 112, click on **Paste Posture** button. Then click on the **Set Key** button.
8. At frame 138, click on **Paste Posture** button. Then click on the **Set Key** button.

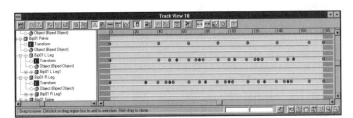

Figure 10.5

The Leg Position windows in the General rollout.

9. At frame 168, click on **Paste Posture** button. Then click on the **Set Key** button.

Now that all the backward spine movement has been applied (Figure 10.6), let's give the Biped some forward motion.

1. Go to frame 51.
2. Select Bip01 Spine and rotate it 50 degrees in the Z-axis. Then click on **Set Key** button.
3. Select all the Spine objects and click on the **Copy Posture** button.
4. Go to frame 76 and click on the **Paste Posture** button. Then click on **Set Key** button.
5. At frame 101, click on the **Paste Posture** button. Then click on the **Set Key** button.
6. At frame 126, click on the **Paste Posture** button. Then click on the **Set Key** button.
7. At frame 151, click on the **Paste Posture** button. Then click on the **Set Key** button.

Now the Biped has a forward and backward movement as it walks. (See Figure 10.7) But it still needs some swagger-type motion to really give it a more natural-looking spine movement.

Spine Swagger

Now that the spine bends forward and backward in an appropriately sneaky fashion, we're going to add a bit of shoulder twist to make it still sneakier. (It also makes the body movement more natural.)

1. With all the Spine objects still selected, go to frame 50.
2. Rotate the spine 10 degrees in the X-axis. Then click on the **Set Key** button.
3. Click on the **Copy Posture** button.
4. Go to frame 100 and click on the **Paste Posture** button. Then click on the **Set Key** button.
5. At frame 150, click on the **Paste Posture** button. Then click on the **Set Key** button.

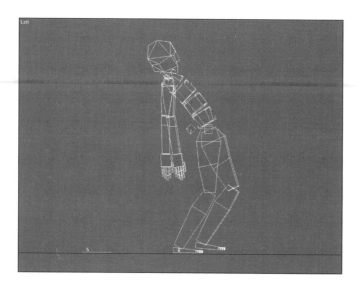

Figure 10.6

The Biped with backward spinal bend.

Character Animation with 3D Studio MAX

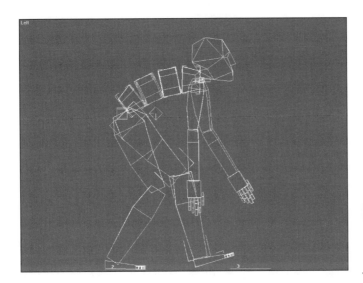

Figure 10.7

The Biped with a forward spinal bend.

Now to complete the swagger motion, we need to rotate the spine in the other direction.

1. Go to frame 75.
2. Rotate the spine -10 degrees in the X-axis. Then click on the **Set Key** button.
3. Click on the **Copy Posture** button.
4. Go to frame 125 and click on the **Paste Posture** button. Then click on the **Set Key** button.

Scratch the time slider back and forth to view the animation. You'll notice that the spine has pretty good movement, but the arms need a little more action.

Forward Arm Swing

The sneak uses a very exaggerated arm swing, one that no one would use under normal conditions. But that's part of what makes the cartoon-y sneak so fun. First, we'll set the forward arm swing of the right arm.

1. Go to frame 75, select the Bip01 R Arm1, and rotate it in the Z-axis -65 degrees.
2. Press Page Down to select the lower arm; rotate it in the Z-axis -25 degrees.
3. Press Page Down to select the hand, and rotate it about the X-axis -90 degrees. Then click on the **Set Key** button.
4. Press Page Up twice to reselect Bip01 R Arm1. Right-click over the selected part and choose Select Children.
5. Click on the **Copy Posture** button.
6. Go to frame 125 and click on the **Paste Posture** button. Then click on the **Set Key** button.

Now we'll set the forward arm swing for the left arm.

1. Go to frame 50. Select Bip01 L Arm 1.
2. Click on **Paste Posture Opposite** button. Then click on the **Set Key** button.

3. Go to frame 100 and click on **Paste Posture Opposite** button. Then click on the **Set Key** button.

4. At frame 150, click on **Paste Posture Opposite** button. Then click on the **Set Key** button.

Now we have the forward arm swing on both the right and left arms. See Figure 10.8. We'll do the backward swing now.

Arm Backswing

The forward sneak is pretty nice now; it's starting to look like a classic cartoon movement. But the back swing still needs work—it's just not exaggerated enough. We'll start with the left arm.

1. Go to frame 75 and select Bip01 L Arm1.
2. Rotate it 50 degrees in the Z-axis.
3. Press Page Down to select lower arm. Rotate it -15 degrees in the Z-axis.
4. Click on the **Set Key** button.
5. Select Bip01 L Arm1 and choose Select Children.
6. Click on the **Copy Posture** button.
7. Go to frame 125 and click on the **Paste Posture** button. Then click on the **Set Key** button.

Now for the right arm.

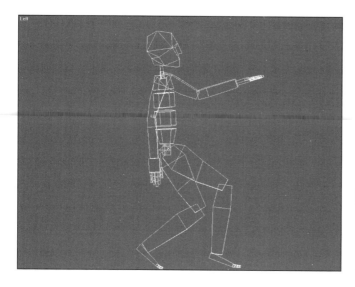

Figure 10.8

The forward arm motion has been applied.

1. Go to frame 50 and select Bip01 R Arm1.
2. Click on the **Paste Posture Opposite** and the **Set Key** button.
3. Go to frame 100 and click on **Paste Posture Opposite** button. Then click on the **Set Key** button.
4. At frame 150, click on **Paste Posture Opposite** button. Then click on the **Set Key** button.

Watch the animation (Figure 10.9). You'll notice that the upper body movement is good, but your sneak really needs some leg movement.

Exaggerating Leg Motions

In a cartoon sneak, the leg motions are also exaggerated—high lift and dainty touch-downs. We can add these features by careful keyframing.

1. Click on Angle Snap to de-select it.
2. In the Track view, select all the key dots except the last two in both Leg Transform tracks. The selected keys turn white, as shown in Figure 10.10.
3. Press Delete. Now only the red dots remain in the leg tracks.

Play the animation. Now the Biped comes down hard on its heels when it walks because we deleted all its interpolated keys. Not very sneaky.

4. Go to frame 50. You'll see that this is the first frame where a foot (this one happens to be the right foot)

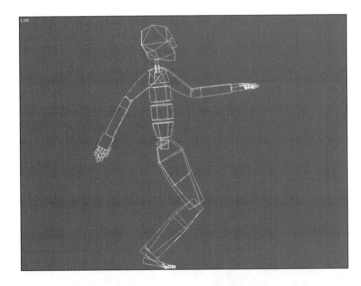

Figure 10.9

The forward and backward arm movement has been applied to both arms.

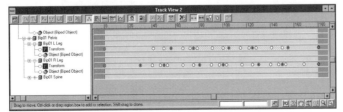

Figure 10.10

The Leg Transform tracks show selected keys.

comes down to touch the ground. See Figure 10.11.

5. Select the right foot and rotate it 120 degrees in the Z-axis.

6. Press Page Down to select the first toe links. Rotate the toes -35 degrees in the Z-axis.

7. Press Page Up to reselect the foot, and with the Move Transform selected, move the foot down in the Z-axis until the toes rest on the ground plane.

8. Click on the **Set Key** button.

9. Page Up to R Leg and select the children. Click on the **Copy Posture** button.

10. Go to frame 100. Click on the **Paste Posture** button and the **Set Key** button.

11. At frame 150, click on the **Paste Posture** and the **Set Key** button.

Copying Motion from Leg to Leg

Biped lets you work on one side of the body, get it right, and then copy that perfected motion to the other side. We'll use this wonderful feature to copy the right leg positions to the left leg at the right frames so that the left leg will mirror the right leg.

1. Go to frame 75 and select the left leg. Click on the **Paste Posture Opposite** and the **Set Key** button.

2. Go to frame 125. Click on the **Paste Posture Opposite** and the **Set Key** button.

3. At frame 175, click on **Paste Posture Opposite** and the **Set Key** button.

Scratch the time slider to view the animation. The leg movement is better, but we still need the Biped's foot to bend as it accepts more body weight.

Refining the Leg Movement

In order to make the foot bend more realistically, we need to work on specific key frames right around where the feet touch down. We'll start by refining the movement of the right leg.

1. Press F4 to look at the leg tracks in the Track view. In the Right Leg track

Figure 10.11

The first frame where the right foot comes down and touches the ground plane.

you'll notice a red key dot at frame 50. This is the frame where the Biped first touches its foot to the ground. We want to place a key just before and just after the red key to tell the Biped where to place its foot as it puts all of its weight on it.

2. Select Right Foot and go to frame 63 (thirteen frames past 50 and where we have determined that all the Biped's body weight would now be resting on the foot).

3. Rotate the foot about the Z-axis to -60 until the toes touch the ground plane. Then click on the **Set Key** button.

4. Press Page Up to select Bip01 R Leg. Then select its children.

5. Click on the **Copy Posture** button.

6. Go to frame 113. Click on the **Paste Posture** button, and the **Set Key** button.

7. Go to frame 163. Click on the **Paste Posture** and the **Set Key** button.

Now let's paste to the left leg.

1. Select L Leg.

2. Go to frame 88 (thirteen frames past where the foot was first touching, as above). Click on the **Paste Posture Opposite** and the **Set Key** button.

3. Go to frame 138. Click on the **Paste Posture Opposite** and the **Set Key** button.

Scratch the time slider and watch the animation. We have a pretty good position on the ground, but since we deleted our

interpolating keys, we have no keys set defining where the legs go while they're in the air in between steps.

1. Go to frame 40 and select R Leg.

2. Rotate the leg up 25 degrees in the Z-axis and the **Set Key** button.

Now scratch the time slider back and forth and see what a difference one key makes. We need a second key because the leg still drags below ground level, but we have a nice sneaky motion.

1. Go to frame 33 (three from liftoff).

2. Select R Foot, and using the Move transform, move the foot up about 2 units. Then click on **Set Key** button.

3. Go to frame 40. Select R Leg and select children.

4. Click on the **Copy Posture** button.

5. Go to frame 90 and click on the **Paste Posture** button. Then click on the **Set Key** button.

6. At frame 140, click on **Paste Posture** button, and click on **Set Key** button.

To adjust the left foot in the same way:

1. Go to frame 65 and select L Leg. Click on **Paste Posture Opposite** and **Set Key** button.

2. At frame 115, click on **Paste Posture Opposite** and **Set Key** button.

Now let's go back and adjust the right leg.

Full Step versus Half-Step Adjustments

Scratch the time slider and check the animation. Notice that this last move should have worked, but it didn't. This is because we started from a two-foot support step. The parameters are different in a full step and what's essentially a half step. But never fear, we can fix this too.

1. Go to frame 33 and select R foot.
2. Using the Move transform, move the R Foot up 3 units in the Z-axis. Then click on the **Set Key** button.

Now if you scratch the time slider, you'll see the foot is up at frame 83 but still drops down before it reaches the footstep.

1. Go to frame 87.
2. Move the R Foot up 3 units in the Z-axis. Then click on **Set Key** button.
3. Go to frame 90 and move the R Foot up 3 units in the Z-axis. Then click on the **Set Key** button. Because of the difference between the first step and the rest of the animation, the key we copied from frame 40 to frame 90 didn't raise the foot as far. Now that the foot has been raised at key 90, try deleting the key at 87. When you watch the animation, you'll notice that the Biped now makes a deliberate, quiet step.

Now, let's finish up the leg motion.

1. Go to ten frames before the right leg touches the ground plane, which is frame 90. Click on **Copy Posture** button.
2. Go to frame 140 and click on **Paste Posture**. Then click on the **Set Key** button.
3. At frame 83, click on **Copy Posture** button.
4. At frame 133, click on **Paste Posture** and **Set Key** button.

The left leg can be adjusted the same way.

1. Go to ten frames before left leg touches down, or frame 65.
2. Select L Leg and click on the **Paste Posture Opposite** button. Then click on the **Set Key** button.
3. Go to frame 115. Click on **Paste Posture Opposite** and **Set Key** button.

Watch the animation. You'll note that the left leg is still dragging a bit after takeoff.

TIP *You can only set a key between footsteps, so if you want to adjust the position of a foot or leg following the last footstep, the program will not accept a key. You must make your animation longer by appending footsteps and then rendering the frames you wish to complete the action.*

If you attempt to region-select a link, the Cross Section Editor will close. To select a link and still keep the Cross Section Editor window open, click on the Pin Stack button next to the Modifier Stack rollout in the Modify panel. This keeps all Physique controls open while you make a selection.

1. Go to frame 83 (three after liftoff) and select R Leg and its children.
2. Click on the **Copy Posture** button.
3. Go to frame 59 and select L Leg. Click on **Paste Posture Opposite**. Then click on the **Set Key** button.
4. At frame 108, click on **Paste Posture Opposite** and the **Set Key** button.
5. At frame 158, click on **Paste Posture Opposite** and the **Set Key** button.

To compare your final animation, load Tut 10_1 and view the Sneak.

Now you see the basic problems you run into doing cartoon movement with a 3D model. It's doable, but it takes a little work to get the model to do what you want. There are no easy answers.

Body Exaggeration

In the previous tutorial we exaggerated body motion. But that's not the only way to get a cartoon effect. In this tutorial we will exaggerate the body by using the Cross Section Editor.

1. Load Tut 10_2. The baby appears on your screen.
2. Go to the Modify panel and select the mesh skin. The mesh turns white, and the orange Physique links appear.
3. In the Physique rollout, click on the **Cross Section Editor** button. The

Cross Section Editor window appears. See Figure 10.12.

The Cross Section Editor actually allows you to reshape and adjust the skin on your Biped. We want to create an exaggerated bulge in the baby's right upper arm that resembles a Popeye-type muscle.

1. In the Bulge Angle drop-down field at the right of the Cross Section Editor, you'll see Biped link names followed by a bulge number. By default, each link has one bulge angle. To activate the link you want to adjust, in this case Bip01 R Arm1, click on the **Previous Link** button on the toolbar until Bip01 R Arm1Bulge 0 appears in the Bulge Angle drop-down field.
2. In the Front viewport, the Bip01 R Arm1 link has colored lines around it. These represent the same link profile as in the Cross Section Editor.
3. The Cross Section view shows four black control points around the red band. Click on the bottom control point in the 6 o'clock position. It will turn white.
4. Now click on the **Select and Scale Control Points** button in the toolbar.
5. Drag the selected control point down to the outer circle. A bulge appears in the Biped right upper arm. You might notice in the Cross Section view that a green line has appeared.

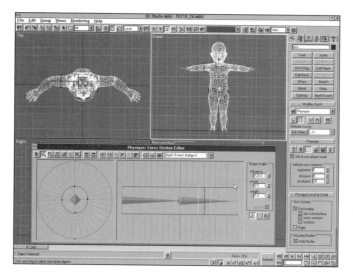

Figure 10.12

The Cross Section Editor window.

This is the angle of the actual mesh skin. See Figure 10.13.

Cartoon Bulges

Now we want to limit the area of the upper arm that will bulge to make it a little more cartoon-like.

1. Load Tut 10_2a.MAX.
2. Select the mesh and click on the **Cross Section Editor** button in the Physique rollout under the Modify panel.
3. Select the Bip01 R Arm1 link.
4. In the Link view on the right side of the Cross Section Editor window,

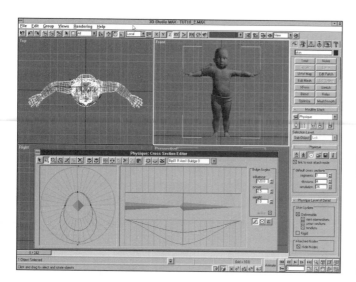

Figure 10.13

The bulge shows on the baby's right upper arm. The Cross Section view also shows the deformation of the bulge angle.

The single red wire band encircling the arm is the default cross-section. This is the point on the arm where the bulge will occur. On the left side of the Cross Section Editor, the section view shows the same red band. In the profile view, the red control spline shows the side view of the bulge. The green circles at the ends of the arm link in the front viewport show the two ends of the link that's shown in the Profile View. The green deformation spline also appears along the length of the link to show the actual mesh skin when it differs from the red control spline. The yellow half-outline has no effect on the deformity of the mesh; it simply tells you the current profile view orientation. You can change the orientation by dragging the yellow profile bar around in the Cross Section View window. The green deformation spline also rotates so that you can see the current deformation at all points around the mesh.

you'll see two links: the link selected (Bip01 R Arm1) on the right in the arrow formation and the parent on the left.

5. Click on the **CS Slice** button in the toolbar. The cursor changes into a small oval with two black lines coming from the top and bottom.

6. Click on the center of the right link at the fifth gray grid line. A new cross section is added to the link.

Now we want to add new cross sections on either side of the new one we just added.

7. Click to the left of the new link two gray grid lines toward the center. A second new cross section is added.

8. Click to the right of the center cross section two gray grid lines over and add a third new cross section, as shown in Figure 10.14.

9. Click on the middle new cross section. It will turn red to show it is selected.

10. Select the bottom control point in the Cross Section view.

11. Select the **Select and Scale Control Points** button in the toolbar, and

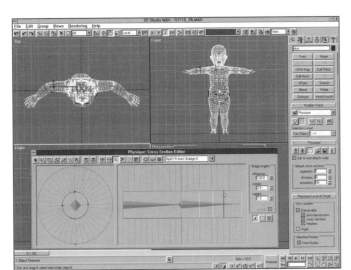

Figure 10.14

The three new cross sections appear in the Links view of the Cross Section Editor window.

RADIAL SCALE PARAMETERS USEFUL IN CARTOONING

There are other functions in Physique that affect the size and shape of the mesh skin. Radial Scale parameters expand or contract the skin by scaling the radial distance perpendicular to the link. In other words, they will scale the cylindrical body of skin vertices around the link in or out to make the radius of the selected part larger or smaller (Figure 10.15). Some parameters, like Stretch and Breathe, can be used only with a non-biped skeleton because the stretching and scaling of biped links can't be animated. However, you might be interested in the following radial scale parameters:

Link Scale: This parameter scales the radius of the entire link independent of any cross section alterations. The settings range from 0 to 10, with 1.0 as the default. Changing this setting can give your mesh a variety of appearances instantly, from really buff to emaciated.

CS Amplitude: Unlike Link Scale, CS Amplitude has no effect unless the part has cross sections. The CS Amplitude exaggerates the cross section effect. So if you have a bulging muscle, you can make it bulge more by adjusting this parameter. At a setting of 0.0 it has no effect.

Bias: This lets you shift the effect of the radial scaling. At the default setting of 0.5, the scaling is equal between the selected link and its child. You can shift from all the effect being towards the selected link at a setting of 0.0, or all the effect towards the child with a setting of 1.0.

drag the selected control point down to the outer circle.

The bulge is now limited to between cross sections. As a result, it appears to be a point. However, the bulge can be adjusted.

1. Click on the **Cross Section** button below the Bulge Angle parameters. The Cross Section parameters appear.

2. Change the segment number to 8 and the divisions to 12. The arm now has eight cross sections and the Cross Section view now has twelve control points.

One of the remarkable features of the Physique Cross Section Editor is the control you have over the bulging shape.

Character Animation with 3D Studio MAX

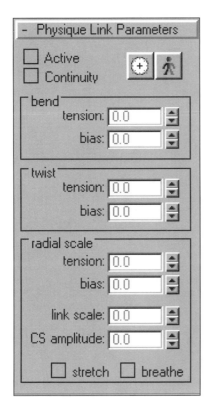

Figure 10.15

The Radial Scale parameters in the Physique Link Parameters rollout.

3. Click on the **Draw Control Points** button in the toolbar. With this tool activated, you can either draw a cross section shape in the Cross Section view or draw the side view of muscle shape in the Profile view. The shape changes with the cursor as it moves. In the Cross Section view, control points are added as you draw. Try drawing different shapes and watch how the arm muscle changes.

Refining the Bulges

Now let's make some adjustments with the Radial Scale parameters.

1. Make a muscle bulge on the baby's right upper arm.
2. Go to Link Scale spinner in the Physique Link Parameters rollout.
3. Drag the spinner up to a setting of 1.7. The baby's upper arm swells and looks more muscular. See Figures 10.16a and b.

The more cross section segments you apply to your link, the more control you have over the shape.

4. Drag the spinner down to 0.66 and see the upper arm start to thin out. See Figures 10.16a and b. The further down you set the spinner, the thinner the upper arm will become. Try it with different body links.

5. Go back to the baby's upper arm and make sure you have additional cross sections on the link. CS Amplitude has no effect if there are no cross sections.

6. Go to the CS Amplitude spinner in the Physique Link Parameters rollout.

7. Drag the spinner up and note how the bulge gets higher as the area on either side of the bulge gets thinner. When the spinner is dragged back to 0.0, it has no effect.

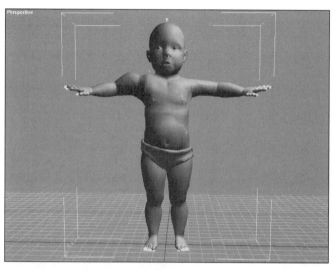

a.

Figure 10.16

In Figure a., the Link Scale spinner is set at 1.7, causing the baby's arm to be much more muscular-looking. In Figure b., with the spinner adjusted to 0.66, the baby's arm looks very thin.

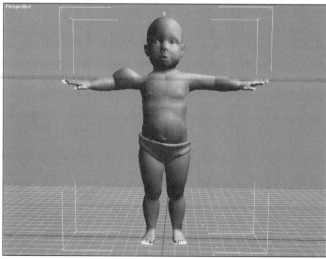

b.

Character Animation with 3D Studio MAX

Animating Muscle Bulges

Now let's set new bulge angles and animate them.

1. Reload Tut10_2.MAX.
2. Go to the Display Panel and click on Unhide All in the Hide by Selection rollout. The Biped skeleton can now be seen.
3. Go to the Motion Panel. Select Bip01and click on the **Footstep Track** button.
4. Create two walking footsteps and stretch them in the Track view over 240 frames.
5. Click on the **Create Keys for Inactive Footsteps** button.

We now have a Biped with footsteps that will allow it to stand in place. Now let's animate an arm bulge.

1. Go to the Modify panel and select the mesh skin.
2. Turn on the **Animate** button and go to frame 120.
3. Select Bip01R Arm1 and rotate it around the Z-axis to -65.
4. Press Page Down and select the lower arm. Rotate it around the Z-axis to -85.
5. Press Page Up and reselect the upper arm. Rotate it in the Y-axis 90 degrees.

6. Click on the **Cross Section Editor** button in the Physique rollout and select Bip R Arm1 in the Bulge Angle drop-down window.
7. Click on the **Insert Bulge Angle** button in the CS toolbar. The name in the Bulge Angle drop-down window changes from Bip01R Arm 1Bulge0 to Bip01 R Arm 1 Bulge1.

We now have a new bulge angle set with the arm flexed up. But as you can see, there is no change in the actual arm bulge itself.

1. Click on the cross section at the right of the links in the Profile view. It turns red to show it is selected.
2. Click on the **Cross Section** button at the bottom of the dialog box at the right of the Profile View window. The Cross Section dialog appears.
3. Change the Segments spinner to 4. There are now four cross sections in the Bip01 R Arm1 link.
4. Select the middle cross section and click on **Select and Scale Control Points** button.
5. Go to the Cross Section view and select the control point at 6 o'clock.
6. Drag the control point down to the outer circle. The baby now has a bulgy muscle.

For a mesh with Physique applied, you can't set keys without footsteps—even if you are only animating the mesh's arm and bulge angles

7. Play the animation. The baby's arm moves up, and a bulgy muscle appears and then disappears as the arm moves down.

8. To check your animation, load Tut 10_2b.

Cartoon Faces

The Cross Section Editor can be used for more than just limbs. In this section, we'll use it to make cartoon changes to the troll's head.

1. Load Tut 10_3.MAX. The troll appears with footsteps already applied.

2. Go to the Modify panel and click on the **Cross Section Editor** button in the Physique rollout.

3. Select Bip 01 Head Bulge 0.

4. Select the right link in the Profile view and add ten cross sections.

5. Select different cross sections and scale them with the **Select and Scale Control Points** or the **Draw Control Points** buttons. Have some fun with the character—for instance, by making his lips smaller and his forehead larger.

6. If you want to adjust a part of the troll's face that isn't controlled by the existing cross sections, add more in the area you need with the **Insert CS Slice** button on the CS toolbar.

Now let's try using the standard MAX tools to make cartoon eyes.

Stretch

The basic MAX transformations can also produce pretty authentic-looking cartoon characters when applied judiciously. You may even have produced cartoon-like characters using them when you didn't intend to do so! We're going to do it on purpose here.

1. Load Tut 10_4 .MAX. A cartoon dog head appears.

2. Select both eyeballs. The eyeballs turn white to indicate that they are selected.

3. Go to the Modify panel. Click on Edit Mesh and drag a selection box around the eyeballs again. This time, the eyeballs turn red, indicating the mesh can now be edited.

4. Select Stretch in the Modifier rollout. The Stretch parameters appear in the Parameters rollout. See Figure 10.17.

5. Click on the Z-axis in the Stretch Axis parameter. Run the Stretch spinner up and down to see the results. Now try it in Y- and X-axes. The eyes stretch in different directions.

6. This time, set the Stretch Axis to Z and set Stretch to 2.0. The eyes elongate but are much too thin.

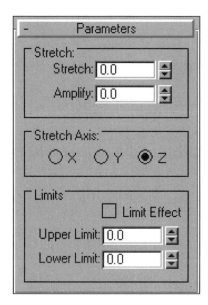

Figure 10.17

The stretch parameters appear in the Parameters rollout.

7. Set Amplify to -25. This brings the width back out on your eyes. Try the other axes using Stretch and Amplify. See Figure 10.18.

Taper

Taper can produce exaggerated features quickly—and you can vary its effects along several axes to see which one works best for you in a particular situation.

1. Reload Tut 10_4. MAX and select both eyeballs.
2. Select Edit Mesh in the Modify panel and reselect the eyeballs.
3. Click on Taper in the Modify rollout. The Taper parameters appear in the Parameter rollout. See Figure 10.19.
4. Raise the Taper spinner up to 1.0. Leave everything else at default levels. The eyes curve up. See Figure 10.20.

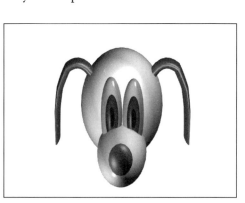

Figure 10.18

An example of the Stretch Modifier on the eyeballs.

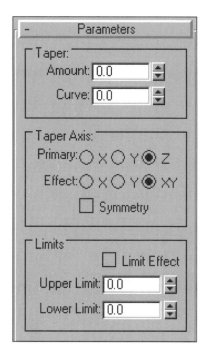

Figure 10.19

The Taper parameters appear in the Parameters rollout.

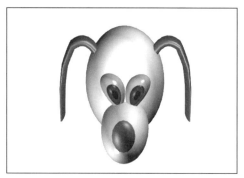

Figure 10.20

The eyeball curve up with the Taper Modifier applied.

5. Now raise the Curve value to 1.0. The eye tapers outward at the top of the eyeball only. Move the Curve spinner up and down and check the Left viewport to see the effect.

Now let's make some other adjustments and see what type of effect we can get.

1. Return the settings to 0.0.
2. Go to Y Primary Axis and leave Effect in the XZ-axis. Raise the Taper spinner to 2.0. The cartoon eyes grow in a cone shape toward the middle plane, so the pupils are now to the inside edge of the eye. See Figure 10.21.

Character Animation with 3D Studio MAX

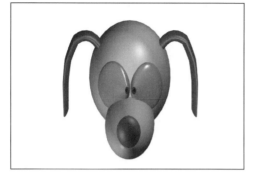

Figure 10.21

The eyes grow in a cone shape toward the middle plane.

3. Click on the Symmetry box to activate it. The eyes now have pupils looking straight ahead.

Now you have some idea how you can adjust your cartoon figures using a few of the MAX modifiers. Play with the others and see what effects you can come up with.

Facial Expression with Controllers

In this section we will learn how to adjust facial expression with controllers by using 3D Studio MAX's standard tools. This is very useful for cartooning as well as for achieving natural facial adjustments.

1. Load Tut10_5.MAX. A female face mesh appears. See Figure 10.22.
2. Go to the Create panel, click on Standard Primitives, and select Box in the Object Type rollout.
3. In the Front viewport, create a vertical rectangular box to the right of the mesh face with a length of 4.0, a width of 0.3, and a height of 0.2.
4. Go to the Modify panel and select the face mesh.

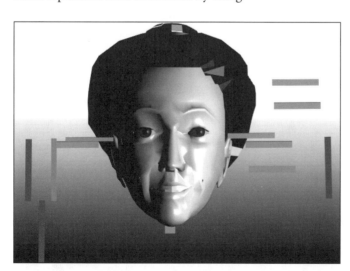

Figure 10.22

Facial vertices can be moved with controllers.

5.   Select Edit Mesh in the Modifiers rollout. Notice Sub-Object is on in the Selection Level of the Modifier Stack, and Vertex is chosen. You'll see that eight vertices have been selected for you on each side of the face. These are the vertices we will use to raise the cheeks. If they had not been selected, you could select the area of the face you want to animate by pressing the Ctrl key while clicking on the individual vertices.

6.   Select More in the Modifier rollout and click on Link X-Form. Click on OK.

7.   Click on the **Pick Object** button in the Parameters rollout. The cursor will turn into a cross. Select the box. The box now controls the vertices we chose.

8.   Go to the Front viewport. Using the Select and Move transform, move the vertices up in the Y-axis .27 degrees. The cheeks move up.

Using the muscle maps in Chapter 5, you can link controllers to the entire face to make it move just as you want. To play with a face with controllers already added, load Tut10_5a.MAX.

Next Chapter...

In the next chapter we explore Bones Pro by Digimation, another plug-in program for 3D Studio MAX. With Bones Pro we can animate four-legged creatures as well.

Chapter 11

Using Bones Pro MAX

In the previous chapters, we have been working with bipedal characters, those with two-legged motion. But what if you want to animate a four-legged mesh? For this, you can use Bones Pro MAX from Digimation. Bones Pro MAX makes the simple animation of a multiped surprisingly fast and easy. You will find a limited version of Bones Pro MAX on the CD-ROM, courtesy of Digimation.

Bones Pro MAX

Bones Pro MAX is a Space Warp plug-in for 3D Studio MAX. It has features similar to Character Studio in that it uses an IK-linked skeletal system to deform a solid mesh. However, unlike Biped, the Bones Pro MAX skeleton is not automatically created inside the Bones Pro MAX program. Instead, a basic skeleton is created using Bones, the demonstration IK plug-in that comes with 3D Studio MAX. After you assemble a skeleton with Bones, the Skeleton portion of the Bones Pro MAX package replaces them with a box skeleton that you can manipulate within the Bones Pro MAX program.

Bones Pro MAX is relatively easy to use and can be used in other types of meshes that don't require the motion and gravity dynamics of a bipedal figure. You can also fine-tune your meshes in the Influence Editor and adjust the influence each bone has on the mesh vertices attached to it. In addition, the Bones Pro MAX package includes a Blend modifier to help make booleaned meshes appear smoother. It's great for fixing those little glitches that always seem to happen when you join two meshes.

Snapshot Plus is another part of the Bones Pro MAX package that adds to your 3D Studio MAX arsenal. With it, you can create copies of mesh objects that have been deformed using the Bones Pro MAX skeleton system *or any other space warp.*

Finally, you can use Bones Pro MAX in conjunction with Character Studio to create complex bipedal models with secondary skeleton-controlled motion, thus giving you the best of both programs.

In this chapter, we'll begin with the system requirements for Bones Pro MAX. We'll also learn the basic controls in Bones Pro MAX, and how to use the Skeleton, Blend, and Snapshot Plus functions.

System Requirements

System requirements for using Bones Pro MAX are similar to those of Kinetix Character Studio; see Chapter 6 for Character Studio system requirements. Like 3D Studio MAX, Bones Pro MAX needs a minimum of 32 MB RAM to run.

Digimation, however, recommends 64 MB RAM, and I can only say that you probably shouldn't even think of doing production work in MAX with less than 128 MB.

Authorizing Bones Pro MAX

The first time you use Bones Pro MAX, you will need to obtain an authorization code from Digimation to run the program.

Note: You don't need an authorization code to run the special version of Bones Pro MAX that's on the CD-ROM that came with this book. These instructions apply to the commercial version only.

1. After you've finished installing Bones Pro MAX from the CD-ROM, click on the Space Warps icon in the Create panel.
2. The Bones Pro MAX Command rollout appears.
3. Click on the **Authorize** button. It will display a system code.
4. Contact Digimation at the number in your software package. You will need your package serial number and the system code to get your authorization code from Digimation.

Keep a copy of your authorization code in case it is accidentally erased. The same authorization code can be used again on your system to reauthorize Bones Pro MAX. It's keyed to the hardware lock, so you can only use the authorization code on a single workstation.

Character Animation with 3D Studio MAX

Before doing anything with Bones Pro MAX—or Character Studio for that matter—examine the mesh you intend to animate and tessellate any areas that look like they have too few faces to animate smoothly. Then, collapse the Modifier Stack to reduce animation overhead.

A Bone Pro MAX Quick Start

In this tutorial we will be learning the basics of Bones Pro MAX and how it creates smooth, believable movement by deforming a solid mesh. We'll use a cow as a model—not unlike the flying cow created by ILM for *Twister*. We won't be flying her in this lesson, but this tutorial should get you off the ground with Bones Pro MAX.

Load Tut 11_1.MAX. A cow mesh appears on your screen as shown in Figure 11.1. Note that the cow's hide is unevenly tessellated. I added additional faces in those areas I knew were going to be animated in order to ensure smooth movement. The areas I wanted animation-ready included the four haunches and legs, the neck, and the tail.

Bones Pro MAX works most easily with one-piece meshes. With multiple meshes, a number of special considerations can arise that complicate matters. (I'll cover how to create and bind these in Chapter 12.) Our cow—dear old Bessie—is made up of several meshes. The main mesh is named hide, and there are separate meshes named horns, face, udder, tail, hoof rr, hoof rf, hoof lr, and hoof lf. Before we can move the cow intact, we'll need to attach all of these objects to the main mesh.

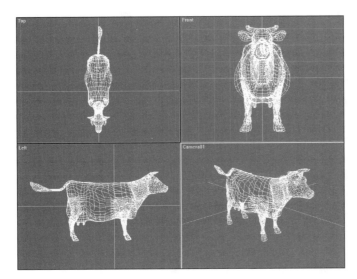

Figure 11.1

Our cow. May she stay away from twisters.

If you attach objects to one another, make sure that you have already applied the right materials to them before attaching. If not, you have to go through extra work creating Multi/Sub-Object materials to assign materials by faces. The Tut11_1.MAX file has a typical Multi/Sub-Object material in slot #2 that includes all of the materials needed for Bessie.

If you haven't worked with Multi/Sub-Object materials, start now. They're a great way to combine a number of materials in a single tree for application to different parts of a mesh.

1. Select hide and then go to the Modify panel.
2. Click on the **Sub-Object** button in the Modifier Stack rollout to deselect it. The Edit Object rollout appears.
3. Click on the **Attach** button and use the Select by Name tool to bring up the Pick Object dialog box, then select Face and click on the **Pick** button. The Face object, consisting of the eyes, nostrils, and mouth, is now attached to the body mesh. If you look in the Select by Name dialog box, you'll note that face is gone from the list.
4. With the body still selected, repeat the Attach operation with the horns.

The horns are now attached to the body mesh as well.

5. Now attach the udder, tail, hoof rr, hoof rf, hoof lr, and hoof lf to the hide mesh.

Binding Bessie to Her Skeleton

I've already included a full set of bones for you in this version of the cow, but they were hidden for the first part of the Quick Start. We'll need to unhide them now. In the Display panel, open the Hide by Selection rollout and click on Unhide All to display our skeleton. The skeleton is now visible, as shown in Figure 11.2.

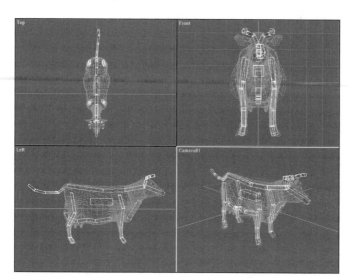

Figure 11.2

Our cow mesh with her Bones Pro MAX skeleton.

TIP *There's another, faster way to attach more than one object to a mesh. Just under the Attach button in the Edit Object rollout is the Attach Multiple button. Click on this button and the Attach Multiple dialog box appears. Select the objects you want to attach and click on Attach. Note that even hidden objects are listed in the Attach Multiple dialog box, so be careful!*

If you have worked through the Digimation tutorials, these bones might look a little odd to you. In order to create smooth animation of all of the subsidiary parts—and keep them positioned properly throughout the animation—I had to create a complex of bones to do the job. Trust me, they're all there for a reason, and I'll explain the details in the next chapter.

The next step is to attach the mesh to the Bones Pro MAX skeleton, much the same way Physique is applied to attach a mesh to a Biped skeleton. Bones Pro MAX works differently than Biped and Physique, however. Physique is a modifier that was applied in the Modify panel to each mesh we wanted to be controlled by Biped. Bones Pro MAX uses the MAX Space Warp system to bind each mesh to a Space Warp controller.

1. In the Create panel, click on the Space Warps icon to reveal the Object Type rollout.
2. Select Bones Pro from the Object Type rollout. The Bones Pro Space Warp rollout appears, as shown in Figure 11.3.

3. Click anywhere on the Front viewport. The Bones Pro MAX icon appears as three crossed bones, as shown in Figure 11.4. It's selected when created.
4. Click on the **Bind to Space Warp** button in the MAX toolbar. It turns green to show that it is active.
5. Drag the Bind to Space Warp cursor to the cow and release the button. The cow mesh turns white. Now it's selected and the Bones Pro MAX Space Warp is deselected.
6. Reselect the Bones Pro MAX icon and open the Modify panel. The Bones Pro Space Warp rollout appears.
7. In the Bones section of the rollout, click on Assign. The Add/Remove Bones for Bones Pro dialog box appears. See Figure 11.5.
8. In the Add/Remove Bones for Bones Pro dialog box, select all the skeleton parts—that is, those with "bone" in their names—and click on Select. (The only objects that appear in the dialog box that you shouldn't select are Camera01.target and Hide.)

TIP *If you are using the commercial version of Bones Pro MAX, you must authorize it by contacting Digimation (if you haven't already) or you will not be allowed to proceed to the next step. However, if you are using the special version of Bones Pro MAX that is included on your CD-ROM, you don't need to authorize it.*

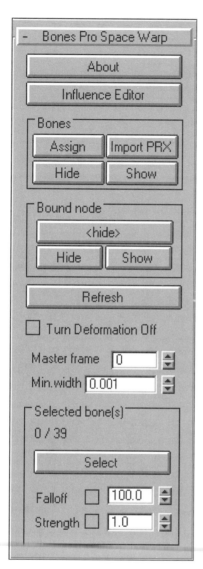

Figure 11.3

The Bones Pro Space Warp rollout.

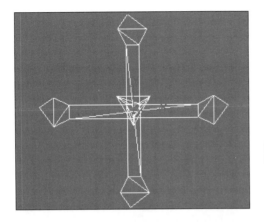

Figure 11.4

The Bones Pro MAX icon is three crossed bones. No skull, though.

Figure 11.5

The Add/Remove Bones for Bones Pro dialog box.

Note: When you create bones using the MAX Bones system, each bone created is given a default name that includes the word "bone." When you use the Skeleton portion of Bones Pro MAX to convert MAX bones to Skeleton parts, the bones are renamed by default to include the word "Skeleton." The bones in this file were named in this manner to be clear for your use.

9. Click on the button labeled **<None>** in the Bound Node section of the rollout. The Select Bound Node dialog box appears. See Figure 11.6

10. Select Hide in the Select bound node dialog box and click on the **Select** button. This attaches the cow's body to the skeleton. The button in the Bound Node section of the Bones Pro Space Warp rollout now reads **<Hide>**. The **Bound Node** button doesn't actually bind the node to the Bones Pro MAX space warp; it simply enables the Influence Editor to display the mesh for vertex level control.

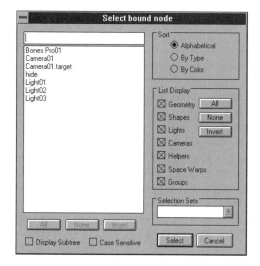

Figure 11.6

The Select bound node dialog box.

Animating Bessie

With Bones Pro MAX, you can animate a skeleton either before or after binding the mesh to the space warp. Whichever method you choose, however, you still must manually keyframe the skeleton to animate the mesh. Bones Pro MAX, however, handles all mesh deformations for you when you animate the skeleton—no more morphs, bends, or skews.

If you save an animated Bones Pro skeleton by itself, you can then merge it into a scene with another similar mesh. Then, you can use the pre-existing motion to animate the new mesh. Bones Pro MAX has nothing like Biped's .bip files, how-

ever; all animation is strictly manual keyframing.

To save just the skeleton, select the bones you want to save, then select Save Selected from the File menu.

I've predefined a few movements so that you can see how Bones Pro MAX works. Bessie's head, tail, and her right foreleg all move over the thirty frames of the animation.

1. Click on the **Time Configuration** button to bring up the Time Configuration dialog box, as shown in Figure 11.7. Turn off Real Time in the Playback section of the dialog

The Bound Node and Bones sections of the Bones Pro dialog box each has Hide and Show buttons that make it easy to control what's displayed. You can hide all of the skeleton in one shot by clicking on the Hide button in the Bones section, or you can hide the mesh by clicking on the Hide button in the Bound Node section. This saves having to select them first and then going to the Display panel to hide or unhide them. It's a nice touch.

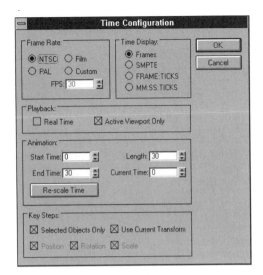

Figure 11.7

The Time Configuration dialog box.

box so that you can see how the mesh deforms at each frame as you play the animation.

2. Click on the **Play Animation** button and watch the cow move. There's a lot of computation going on in order to deform everything during playback, so the displayed movement will probably be quite slow.

Note that Bones Pro MAX is not "gravity-aware." It doesn't try to rebalance Bessie when we lift her leg. That's the price you pay for a more versatile animation system.

Now let's add a few more movements to the old girl.

1. Turn on the **Animate** button.

2. Click on the **Time Configuration** button again, and in the Time Configuration dialog box, change Length in the Animation section to 60 frames. Click on OK. There are now sixty frames in the animation, but the animation that's already on the cow ends at frame 30.

3. Go to frame 35. Select the Skeleton box in the cow's face (Backbone04).

4. Using the Select and Rotate transform in the toolbar, rotate the skeletal link in the Left viewport 30 degrees around the Z-axis. The cow's head tilts upward, as shown in Figure 11.8.

The Animate button must be on for the mesh to move along with the bone when you reposition part of the skeleton and for you to click on the Set Key button, of course.

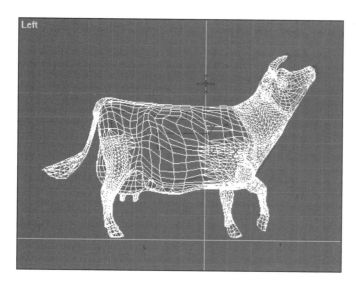

Figure 11.8

The cow's head tilts upward 30 degrees.

5. In the Top viewport, select the Tail-bone03 object and rotate it around the Z-axis -25 degrees.

Remember that you can move up and down a hierarchy by using the Page Down and Page Up keys. Watch the name field as you move through the hierarchy, and you won't have to worry about which bone is which—just page to the right one!

6. Go to frame 50. Select FL legbone02. Rotate it around the Z-axis upward 30 degrees. Press Page Down, select the lower leg (FL legbone03), and rotate it -40 degrees around the Z-axis to bend her leg at the knee. If it looks like it would be painful, you've probably gone the wrong direction!

7. Select the neck link (Backbone03) and rotate the neck -30 in the Z-axis.

If you find yourself waiting for the system to catch up to you as you adjust the bone's position interactively, here's a solution. Use the Rotate Transform Type-In dialog box and enter new values directly in the Off-set fields. Then you only have to wait once.

8. Select the Bones Pro MAX space warp and go to the Modify panel. Click on the **Hide** button in the Bones section to quickly hide the skeleton. Then with the Camera viewport active, press the W key to enlarge it.

TIP
To smooth out an existing animation, increase the length and then use Re-Scale Time. Don't try this with Biped, however; you can seriously confuse it.

Never change the position of your mesh or its bones at frame 0. MAX uses the frame 0 position as a reference position, and Bones Pro MAX does so as well.

311

Chapter 11: Using Bones Pro MAX

9. Play the animation. Notice that the mesh bends smoothly as the bones move.

You can go back anywhere in the animation and change or refine the movements to create the ones you want. As with all MAX keyframe animation, you must have the **Animate** button on and you can't make changes at frame 0.

Using the Influence Editor

The Influence Editor lets you select and assign vertices to bones and then adjust how much influence the bone has over the vertices assigned to it.

The Influence Editor can only be viewed after the skeleton has been assigned to the Bones Pro MAX space warp. However, although the Bounding Node need not be assigned before you use the Influence Editor, you won't accomplish much because there will be no vertices to adjust.

1. Load Tut 11_1a. The complete cow and Bones Pro Skeleton appear.
2. Select the Bones Pro MAX icon and go to the Modify panel.
3. Click on the **Influence Editor** button. The Influence Editor dialog box appears; the cow skeleton should be visible in the edit window, as shown in Figure 11.9. If it's not, click on the **Draw Bones On/Off** button in the Influence Editor (IE) toolbar.

THE BEST MESH TYPES FOR BONES PRO MAX

Bones Pro MAX works best with single, unjointed meshes. However, it will work with objects composed of multiple meshes, as we saw in the Quick Start tutorial. Although you could simply bind all of the other meshes to the same Bones Pro MAX space warp, Digimation discourages this. If you try this, the additional meshes will not appear in the Influence Editor, and therefore, the Influence Editor can have no control over them.

Complex meshes with larger mesh parts can be booleaned together and then blended using Digimation's Blend modifier to create a mesh without noticeable seams. However, you must be certain that the parts to be booleaned overlap with a sufficient number of intersecting faces. If not, you might be quite surprised at the result.

Figure 11.9

The Influence Editor dialog box.

4. If the cow mesh is not visible in the edit window, click on the **Draw Mesh On/Off** button in the IE toolbar. The cow mesh appears on the screen over the skeleton. Enlarge it in the IE edit window, if necessary, by clicking on the **Zoom Extents** button in the IE toolbar. See Figure 11.10.

5. From the IE Views menu, select Left. The cow is now shown from the left side.

6. Scratch the MAX time slider and notice that as the cow moves in the viewports, its position also changes in the IE edit window.

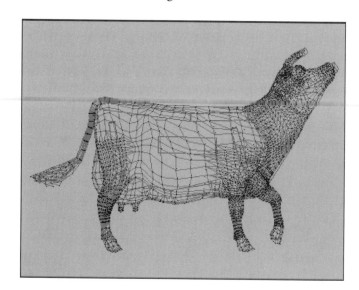

Figure 11.10

The mesh now appears over the skeleton in the edit window.

Being able to see the mesh animate in the Influence Editor can be quite useful if you need to have a part in a particular position to see the vertices you need to adjust. For example, you might need to adjust an arm. If it's away from the body in one part of the animation, that might make adjustment easier.

7. Go to frame 8 and click on the **Visualize Bones Influence** button in the IE toolbar.

8. Click on the neck link of the skeleton (Backbone03) in the IE edit window. The cow changes to a bright blue, and the neck portion of the mesh is green with a small, light-blue fringe area. See Figure 11.11. Refer to the color section of this book to see this in color.

These colors indicate the influence the bone has over the vertices in the bound node (the mesh), as shown in Table 11.1. A red area indicates the portion of the mesh that is *totally controlled* by the bone. Green areas show *overlapping* vertex control between the bone and the next one

linked to it, while bright blue areas indicate *no* vertex control at all.

With the default settings for Falloff and Strength of 100 and 1, respectively, applied to all bones in the skeleton, no one bone has exclusive control over any vertices in the mesh. This results in smooth but somewhat sloppy movement. If we localize the control a bit, we can adjust each bone to produce the result we want.

9. Scroll the Bones Pro Space Warp rollout up until the Selected Bone(s) section of the rollout is visible. See Figure 11.12.

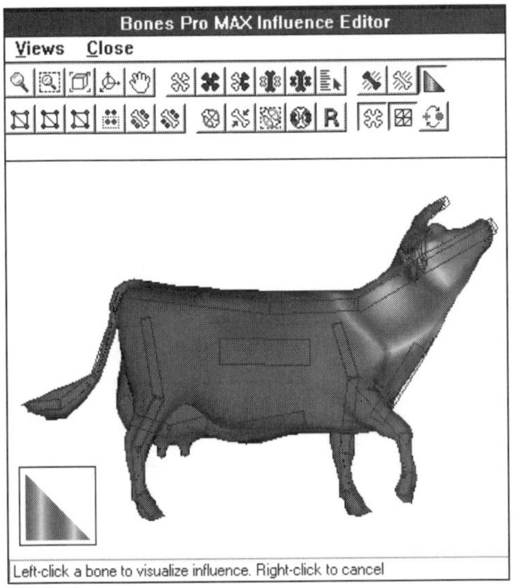

Figure 11.11

The bone's influence over the mesh is shown in the edit window by shades of red, green, yellow, and blue. In this case, the default settings produce a primarily blue and green display. See color section.

Table 11.1

The Influence Editor uses these colors to display how each bone controls the adjacent vertices in the mesh.

Displayed Color	Influence Over Vertices
Red	Total control
Bright Blue	No control
Green	Some or shared control
Light Blue	Transition color
Yellow	Transition color

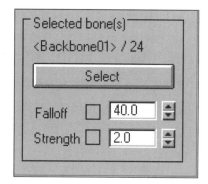

Figure 11.12

The Selected bone(s) section of the Bones Pro Space Warp rollout.

The Selected bone(s) section of the rollout lets you assign specific Falloff and Strength values to bones that are linked to the selected space warp. The fraction at the top of the section shows how many bones are in the skeleton and how many are selected. In our case, there are thirty-nine bones and none (0) are selected. We'll now change the values for all the bones.

10. Click on the **Select** button in the Selected bone(s) section. The Select bones for group operations dialog box appears. Click on the **All** button to the far left, then the **Select** button. The fraction changes to 39/39,

indicating that we have all of the bones selected.

Note: Selecting bones in the Select bones for group operations dialog box does not select them for other MAX operations. It does, however, select them for IE operations.

11. Change the Falloff spinner to 40 and the Strength to 2.0, then check the boxes next to the Falloff and Strength spinners.

12. Open the Influence Editor again, click on the **Visualize Bones Influence** button, and click on the neck link again. Notice how the color dis-

> *The checkboxes next to the Falloff and Strength spinners must be checked in order to make the changes effective. In this way, you can change one spinner value for the selected bones without interfering with the other.*

tribution has changed with the new settings. See Figure 11.13 and the Influence Editor color images in the color section of this book.

By selecting one or more bones in the Select Bone(s) section of the rollout, you can set their influence without calling the Influence Editor. This sounds like a pretty convenient arrangement—and it is—until you get bit the first time!

Editing Strength and Falloff in the IE

If you are in the Influence Editor, you can click on either of two buttons to adjust the strength or falloff. One, the **Edit**

Bones' Influence Interactively button, lets you edit one bone at a time. The other, **Edit Influence of Selected Bones** button, lets you edit multiple bones.

1. Click on the neck bone, or Backbone03, in the IE. It turns green to show that it is not selected. Notice that the fraction in the Selected bone(s) section of the rollout still reads 39/39.

2. Now click on the **Invert Bones' Selection** button in the IE toolbar. All of the previously selected bones are now deselected and only the neck bone is selected. The fraction in the Selected bone(s) section of the rollout still reads 39/39, however.

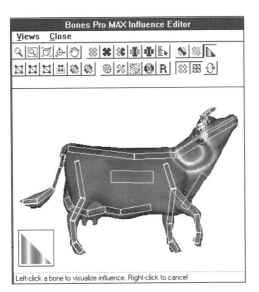

Figure 11.13

Notice how the influence of the neck bone has changed with Strength increased and Falloff decreased. See color section.

3. Click on the **Edit Influence of Selected Bones** button in the IE toolbar. The Bones' Influence dialog box again appears. Note that the Strength and Falloff values show those we set in the rollout.

4. Change the values in the Strength and Falloff fields to 25 and 1, respectively, and uncheck the two boxes if they are checked. Click on OK, then examine the Strength and Falloff values for the neck bone by moving the cursor over the bone in the IE edit window. Notice that they are still 40 and 2, respectively. Why? Think it over while you read the next tip.

Quiz answer: The Strength and Falloff values did not change for the neck bone because the checkboxes were unchecked when we closed the Bones' influence dialog box.

5. Click on the **Edit Bones' Influence Interactively** button in the IE toolbar and then on the Backbone03 bone. The Bones' influence dialog box appears with the name of the bone, Backbone03, at the top, indicating that this is the bone we are editing.

6. Change the values in the Strength and Falloff fields to 25 and 1, respectively, and check the two boxes if they are not checked. Click on OK.

7. Now examine the Strength and Falloff values of the neck bone. They should now be updated to 25 and 1.

8. Look at the influence color distribution of the neck bone with these values. It mostly shows the result of reducing the strength from 40 to 25; the red area is much smaller, as shown in Figure 11.14.

INFLUENCE EDITOR KEYBOARD SHORTCUTS

Here's a list of handy Influence Editor keyboard shortcuts:

- *Click on a bone to toggle its selection on and off.*
- *Press Ctrl + Click to add a bone to the current selection.*
- *Press Ctrl + Shift + Click to select a bone while deselecting all the others.*
- *Press Alt + Click to deselect a bone from the current selection.*
- *Press Alt + Shift + Click to deselect a bone while selecting all the others.*

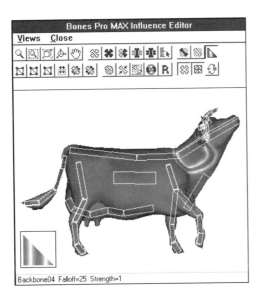

Figure 11.14

Falloff is set to 25 and Strength to 1. The area of influence is much smaller.

9. Close the IE by clicking on the Close menu item. The fraction in the Selected bone(s) section of the rollout now reads <Backbone03>/39. It updates only when you close the IE.

10. Notice that the Strength and Falloff values in the Selected bone(s) section of the rollout now match the values we assigned in the IE. Change them in the rollout to 50 and 6, and click on both checkboxes.

11. Reopen the IE and examine the Strength and Falloff values for the neck bone. They are now 50 and 6, just as you set them in the rollout.

You can set a bone's influence in three ways: in the Selected Bone(s) section of the rollout, by clicking either the Edit bones' influence interactively, or the **Edit Influence of Selected Bones** button in the IE toolbar. The two **IE** buttons both bring up the Bones' influence dialog box, but the Edit Bones' Influence Interactively lets you edit one bone at a time by first clicking on the bone you want to edit. With the **Edit Influence of Selected Bones** button, you can edit more than one bone at a time; however, you must first select them either in the IE or by using the **Select** button in the Selected bone(s) section of the rollout.

This all might seem confusing at first, but just keep an eye on the fractions, the checkboxes, and which bones are selected, and you'll be able to keep it straight.

To check the Strength and Falloff values of a bone, move the cursor over it in the Influence Editor edit window. The status line at the bottom of the edit window shows the current values of the bone under the cursor.

ABOUT FALLOFF AND STRENGTH

The Falloff value represents how far a bone's influence over the mesh can extend, expressed as a percentage of the overall length of the bone. It might help to think of it as the size of a magnetic field that surrounds the bone. The larger the value, the larger the potential field and the larger the area that's not bright blue.

In order to provide a smooth movement transition from one bone to the next, the bones must share control over the mesh's vertices at their adjacent ends. The Falloff value determines the extent of vertex control overlap between two linked bones based on the two bones' sizes. In our second cow example, there was a large red area where the vertices were totally controlled by the neck bone. The green areas showing overlapping vertex control between that bone and the ones linked to it were moderate in size. But remember when we first looked at the cow with Falloff of 100 and Strength of 1. The green shared control areas were large, and no red areas, indicating exclusive control, were present.

The Strength value represents the strength of a bone's influence over the attached vertices. The lower the Strength value, the easier it is for the bone to give up its influence over the attached vertices. If you go back to the cow and set the neck bone's Strength to 5, you'll see in the IE that the red area covers all of the neck and part of the head, while the green areas have diminished proportionately. The higher the Strength value, the less vertex control the bone will give up to the neighboring bone.

Assigning Vertices

No matter how careful you are in setting up your bones and adjusting them within the mesh, sometimes the vertices just don't attach to the right bone. Bones Pro MAX is pretty good about assigning them, but not perfect. Just like Physique, we sometimes have to reassign them manually.

Bones Pro MAX has a slightly different method of assigning vertices than Physique. Where Physique has a three-color system for assigning vertices as deformable vertices, rigid, or root node, Bones Pro MAX has only one type: deformable. The Physique system is more flexible, but the Bones Pro MAX system works fine, once you understand it. (See Chapter 9 for more detailed information on Physique.)

When you bind a node to a Bones Pro MAX skeleton, it assigns each vertex to a bone, depending on whether the vertex is in the bone's zone of influence. Once assigned, that bone controls the vertex deformation, unless you either reassign it to another bone or exclude it from the bone's influence. Sometimes, vertices in Bones Pro MAX are stubborn and won't accept reassignment to another bone, as we'll see in a minute. The only alternative then is to exclude the stubborn vertices from the bone's influence so that the bone's movement doesn't deform the mesh incorrectly.

Fixing Those Problem Cow-Butt Vertices

In this tutorial, we'll look again at Bessie, but this time from a new angle. Bessie has several vertices in her butt region that fall within the zone of influence of one of the tailbones. To avoid a painful case of butt distortion when she swishes her tail, we're going to exclude these misguided vertices from the tailbone. First, to speed up redraw time while we work in the Bones Pro MAX Influence Editor, first hide the skeleton and the mesh in the MAX viewports.

1. In both the Bones and Bound Node sections of the Bones Pro Space Warp rollout, click on the **Hide** buttons. The skeleton and mesh both disappear from the viewports.
2. Click on the **Influence Editor** button to bring up the IE. Whichever view was last active should still be displayed; the User view in the edit window is the default.
3. From the IE Views menu, select Left. The green skeleton should now appear in the Edit window in left view; although depending upon how you last left the IE, you could have the skeleton and mesh, just the mesh, or just the skeleton.
4. If the mesh and skeleton are not visible in the Edit window, click on the **Draw Mesh On/Off** button and the

TIP *By default, when you first enter the Influence Editor, all the bones are green, indicating that they are not selected. When a bone is selected, it turns white, just as in MAX.*

Draw Bones On/Off button until both mesh and skeleton are visible.

5. Click on the **Select All Bones** button in the IE toolbar. All the bones turn white to indicate they are selected. See Figure 11.15.

6. Click on the Exclude Unlinked from **Selected Bones** button. This examines all of the linked bones in the skeleton and determines which are not linked directly to one another; it then disconnects any interaction of the bones or the vertices of adjacent parts.

7. Use the **Region Zoom** button in the IE toolbar to zoom in on the area at the base of Bessie's tail, as shown in Figure 11.16.

8. Click on the **Deselect All Bones** button in the IE toolbar. All bones turn green to indicate they are deselected.

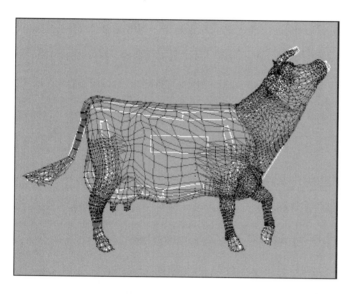

Figure 11.15

All bones are white to indicate they are selected.

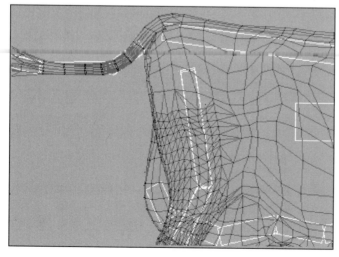

Figure 11.16

This is the region where we need to operate.

If you have trouble seeing the red vertices, click on the Toggle vertex Display Mode button to increase the size of the vertices. The dot display can sometimes be too large in close quarters, however.

9. In the IE edit window, click on the tailbone closest to the body, Tailbone03, to select it.

10. Now, click on the Select vertices in the zone(s) of **Selected Bone(s)** button. The vertices in Tailbone03's zone of influence turn red, as shown in Figure 11.17.

11. Click on the **Select Vertices by Region** button and deselect just the

vertices in the tail. Following standard MAX selection procedure, you may hold down the Ctrl key to add more vertices to the current selection, or the Alt key to deselect them. When you've finished, only the few vertices on the body should still be red, as shown in Figure 11.18.

12. Click on **Exclude Selected Vertices from Selected Bones** button.

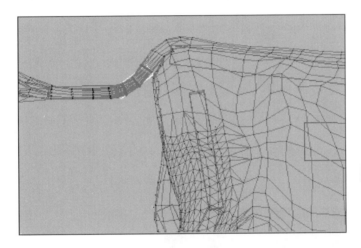

Figure 11.17

These vertices should be selected.

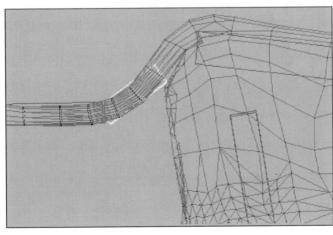

Figure 11.18

Only these vertices should still be selected before moving on.

This excludes the vertices on Bessie's butt from being influenced by the tailbone.

You can try reassigning these vertices to other bones, but they resisted my attempts to do so. In other situations with vertices closer to other bones or higher Strength values for other bones, you can usually reassign them. If the vertices are outside any other bone's zone of influence, you won't be able to reassign them, only exclude them.

If you are setting Influences on complex meshes and find a bone that just doesn't behave right, first do a major exclusion, as in Steps 5 and 6, above. Then, adjust the Strength spinner for the troublesome bone. If that doesn't solve the problem, exclude the vertices from the bones using **Exclude Selected Vertices from Selected Bones** button in the IE toolbar.

We'll do more interesting things with Bessie in Chapter 12, like breathing and walking. For now, let's look at how some of the other parts of the Bones Pro MAX package can help you.

Blending Meshes

It's always frustrating to see the results you get with a jointed model. Even though a model might move well, those joints are almost always tough to hide (unless you're animating a robot with visible mechanical joints, of course). You can combine the parts with booleans, but often the joints still show. The Bones Pro MAX Blend modifier smoothes joints that have been booleaned into a smooth mesh. Blend can also use be used more generally, however, to smooth out rough spots. Note that Blend does this by moving an object's vertices; none are deleted and no new ones are added.

1. Load Tut11_2.MAX. A dinosaur mesh appears on your screen, as shown in Figure 11.19. Note that

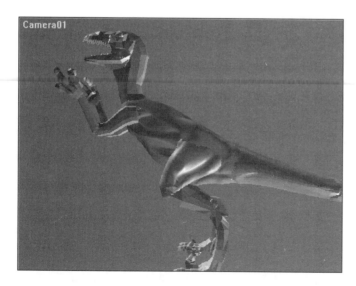

Figure 11.19

The dinosaur mesh before booleaning and blending.

Character Animation with 3D Studio MAX

there are a variety of different tessellation levels so that you can experiment with booleans and Blend. The body and upper left leg were tessellated to create enough faces to provide a smooth surface, and I applied an Edit Mesh modifier with Auto Smooth on. Finally, I collapsed the Modifier Stack to reduce overhead. In Version 1.1 of 3D Studio MAX, this produces an *editable mesh.*

2. In the Create panel, choose Compound Shapes in the Object Category drop-down list.

3. Select the dinosaur's body, named appropriately, Body.

4. Click on the **Boolean** button in the Object Type rollout. The Pick Boolean and Parameters rollouts appear. See Figure 11.20.

5. Click on the **Pick Operand B** button in the Pick Boolean rollout, then select Union in the Operation section of the Parameters rollout.

6. Click on the dinosaur's left upper leg to create a single object from the two meshes.

Now render the Camera view. Even though the two boolean components had been smoothed and joined, a definite joint line still appears where the two come together, as shown in Figure 11.21. With Bones Pro MAX's Blend modifier, we can smooth this joint.

1. In the Modifier panel, select Blend in the Modifiers rollout. If it doesn't appear in the button panel, click on the **More** button and select it from

the Modifiers dialog box. The Blend Modifier rollout appears. See Figure 11.22.

2. Make sure Concave zones only is selected.

3. Raise the Tension spinner to approximately 11.0. The leg smooths out along the top joint edge.

4. Click on the **Quick Render** button and notice the difference in the dinosaur leg, as shown in Figure 11.23.

Blend Vs. MeshSmooth

MAX Version 1.1 includes a modifier named MeshSmooth. MeshSmooth does some of the same things that Blend does (and actually can do a bit more), but at a cost. See Figure 11.24. MeshSmooth is not only much more demanding in terms of time and processor resources, it also produces many more faces in the final mesh and requires resmoothing. Blend is quick, easy, and predictable.

Now let's smooth the joints of the tail.

1. Select the body and boolean the first tail section to it.

2. Go to the Modify panel and select Edit Mesh in the Modify rollout.

3. In the Top viewport, use a Fence Selection Region and Window Selection to select the vertices around the first tail joint, as shown in Figure 11.25.

4. Click on the **Blend Modifier** button, and this time, choose Selected Ver-

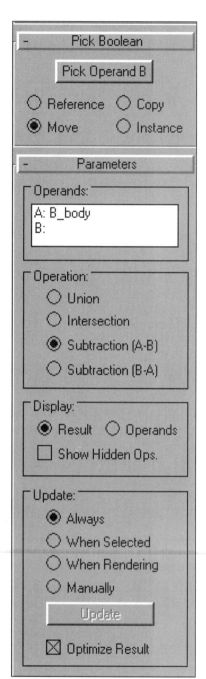

Figure 11.20

The Pick Boolean and Parameters rollouts.

Character Animation with 3D Studio MAX

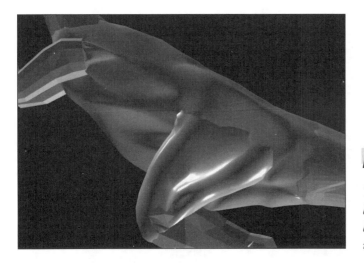

Figure 11.21

The dinosaur leg has been booleaned together, but the seam is still visible.

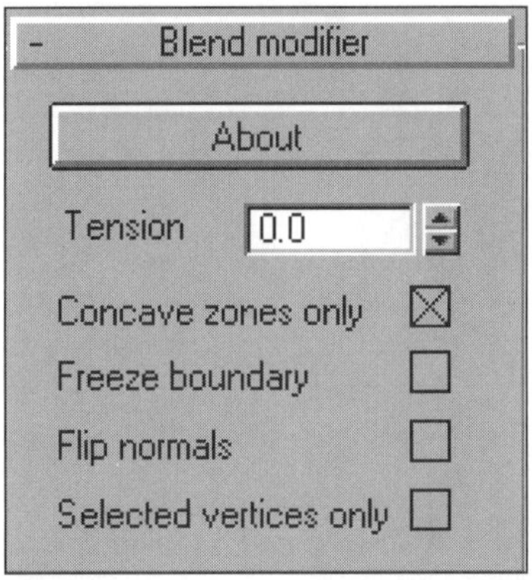

Figure 11.22

The Blend Modifier rollout.

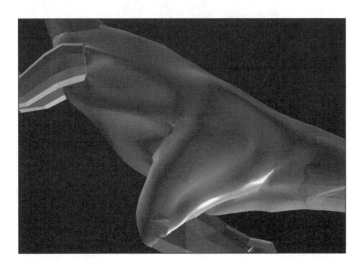

Figure 11.23

The dinosaur leg has been blended.

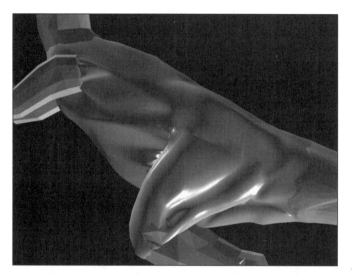

Figure 11.24

Here is the result of using MeshSmooth at its default settings, followed by an Edit Mesh modifier with AutoSmooth on, and the Modifier stack collapsed. It looks good, but has almost 42,000 faces versus just over 7,000 for the Blended mesh.

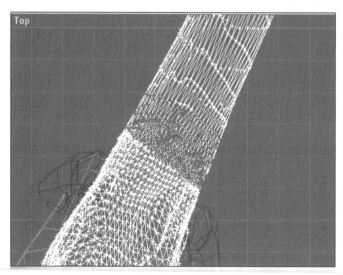

Figure 11.25

Select these vertices (more or less).

TIP

It's usually better to adjust the Blend tension slowly and check the mesh to see when the blending is at the best point. If you raise the Blend spinner too high, the mesh can distort.

tices Only. Now adjust the Tension spinner until the tail joint is smooth, approximately 20.

At this point, you can apply an Edit Mesh modifier and use the Auto Smooth function, or you can blend all the joints you need and then smooth them all at once.

5.   Render the scene again. The dinosaur is looking much better. See Figure 11.26.

Use Snapshot Plus for Quick Modeling

Another part of Bones Pro MAX, Snapshot Plus, is a valuable tool for making copies of mesh objects that are bound to space warps. For example, you can use it with a Bomb space warp to create a treeful of leaves, as Digimation suggests. You can also use it with Bones Pro MAX itself.

Snapshot Plus cures a deficiency in the MAX Snapshot function. Snapshot Plus can create snapshot meshes during the deformation of the object by a space warp. 3D Studio MAX Snapshot will only create copies of the original object before space warping occurs.

Note: Snapshot copies generated by Snapshot Plus are no longer bound to the space warp that generated them. This means that other Space Warp tools such as Bomb, Wave, Wind, and of course, Bones Pro MAX can then be applied to them.

You might be asking yourself, "I'm a character animator—what good is Snapshot Plus to me?" It's actually a fast and easy way to create a forest full of trees with leaves or a herd of animals all in different positions. You can even use Snapshot Plus to create bulging, cartoon-y eyeballs.

Creating a Herd o' Cows

First let's multiply Bessie into a herd.

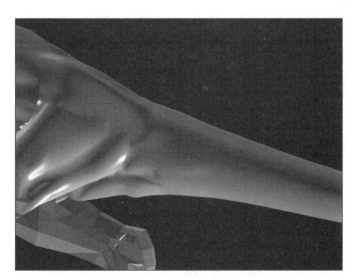

Figure 11.26

The dinosaur after the Blend modifier has been applied to the tail/body joint and the mesh smoothed.

1. Reload Tut 11_1a. Ol' Bessie's back.
2. Select the Bones Pro MAX space warp, go to the Modify panel, and click on Hide in the Bones section of the Bones Pro MAX Space Warp rollout. The skeleton is hidden.
3. Select the cow mesh and go to the Utility panel.
4. In the Utilities category drop-down list, select Snapshot Plus. The Snapshot Plus rollout appears, as shown in Figure 11.27.
5. Click on the **Snapshot** button. The Snapshot Plus dialog box appears, as shown in Figure 11.28. The mesh name Hide appears in the Node name field.
6. Click on Range to create a herd of cows, rather than a single copy.
7. From and To are set at 0 and 30, respectively. These values define the range of frames over which the snapshot meshes will be created.
8. Set Step to 3 and Copies to 1 to create one copy every three frames, or ten copies.
9. Click on OK. Snapshot Plus generates ten new cows in different poses that you can arrange to produce the look of a herd.

Figure 11.27

The Snapshot Plus rollout.

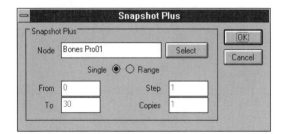

Figure 11.28

The Snapshot Plus dialog box.

Next Chapter...

In our last chapter, we'll go deeper into Bones Pro MAX and show you how to make your characters breathe and walk. We'll take Bessie apart bone-by-bone (sob!) so that you'll understand why the skeleton is as it is. Finally, we'll see how to combine Bones Pro MAX and Biped.

Chapter **12**

Creating a Bones Pro MAX skeleton

Creating secondary motion with Bones Pro MAX

Adding lifelike touches

Using Bones Pro MAX with Biped

Advanced Bones Pro MAX

In the last chapter, we explored the basic features of Bones Pro MAX. Now we'll get into the "bones" of the program and see how it really works.

Them Bones

In Chapter 11, I provided a pre-made skeleton for you to use with Bessie the cow. Now you will learn the ins and outs of creating your own Bones Pro MAX skeleton from the ground up. How you create a Bones Pro MAX skeleton is very important to the final outcome of your animation.

The easiest and quickest way to create a skeleton for Bones Pro MAX is to use the 3D Studio MAX Bones utility to create a linked skeleton inside the mesh body. You can then convert the linked skeleton to a boxed skeletal system by using the Bones Pro MAX Skeleton utility. Skeleton maintains the hierarchy and pivot points of the original Bones and lets you adjust the width of the skeletal links. This gives you more control over the mesh vertices surrounding each link.

The boxed skeleton has several advantages over the Biped skeleton or even Bones. The boxed skeleton links are easy to see and can be twisted, resized, and scaled to perform otherwise difficult animations such as breathing. (You'll do this later in this chapter.)

If you're going to use Skeleton, don't waste time setting up the joints in the IK panel. Although Skeleton maintains the hierarchical tree and pivot points from Bones, it doesn't pass on IK constraints or joint limits.

Bones Pro MAX doesn't require that the skeleton be linked together. In fact, in some instances, like the breathing technique shown later in this chapter, you can get better results sometimes by not linking them and then animating the bones independently of each other. However, in most cases having a linked skeleton makes animation keyframing much easier.

A good rule of thumb is that the simpler the skeleton, the easier it will be to use. Usually one bone per section is enough, unless your mesh will require more detailed manipulation. The beauty of Bones Pro MAX is that it lets you add bones to an existing skeleton; you can start with a few key bones, and then add to it after you've decided where the control is needed. It makes building the skeleton much easier. All you need to do is create the new bones, and then simply assign them to the existing skeleton.

The bone size determines how well Bones Pro MAX assigns vertices to them. That's one of the reasons that Skeleton lets you change the size of bones. As with Biped, the bones should be similar in size to the part it controls and be centered in its mesh. The closer in size the bone is to the part, the less likely the part's vertices are to be assigned incorrectly and pulled away by an adjacent bone when the part is moved.

Creating Mootilda's Skeleton

Mootilda is Bessie's faux Holstein cousin. We'll create her skeleton using MAX Bones first. Let's start on her spine, head, and tail.

1. Load Tut 12_1.MAX. Mootilda appears with no skeleton. See Figure 12.1.
2. Select Mootilda's unified mesh, then go to the Display panel.
3. Click on Freeze All in the Freeze by Selection rollout. The cow mesh turns gray, indicating it is frozen. Anytime you are creating or manipulating a skeleton inside a mesh, it's always better to freeze the mesh so you don't move the mesh accidentally.

Even though you don't have to link Bones Pro MAX skeletons, unlinked skeletons work best when the skeletal links are close together or even overlapping.

Figure 12.1

*Mootilda in all
her glory.*

4. Select the **Systems** button in the Create panel, then select Bones in the Object Type rollout. The button turns green, indicating it is active.

5. In the Left viewport, click on Moo's body at the center of the back. Drag the first bone to the base of the neck, and click. Next, click and drag the next bone up, and click at the top of the neck. Now click and drag a bone to the nose. Right-click to end the bone link. Figure 12.2 shows all of the bones, including these. Refer to this illustration while creating all of the bones.

6. Go back to the first link. Click on the start of the first link (Bone01) and drag the new link down to the

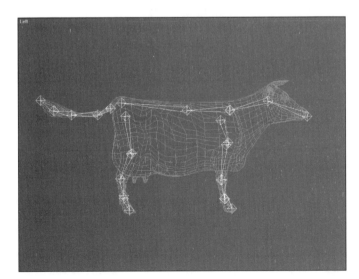

Figure 12.2

*Mootilda with the
spine, head, tail, and leg
bones created.*

base of the tail. Right-click to end the bone link. This is Mootilda's lower back link. Now we need to link her tail.

7. Click on the highest point of the tail, then drag and click down the length of the tail to make three tailbones. Make sure to position the intersection between the last two tailbones where the tail plume attaches to the tail body. Right-click to end the bone link. Now that the tail is linked together, the legs are next.

Creating the Leg Bones

Now let's make bones for Mootilda's legs. In this critter, you'll notice that the leg bones aren't attached to the rest of the skeleton. Only the jointed parent and children links for each leg have to be linked together. Doing it this way eliminates undesirable interaction between the leg bones and body bones for vertex control of the body mesh.

For a mesh that will be animated without locomotion, this type of skeleton is fine. For figures that will be walking, running, and so on, a completely linked skeleton is easier to manipulate.

1. Start at the top of Mootilda's right front shoulder. Click and drag a bone to the elbow, click and drag one to the wrist, and click and drag a final bone for the hoof. Right-click to end the link.

2. Starting at the right rear hip, click and drag a bone down to the knee, click and drag one to the ankle, and click and drag a bone to the hoof. Right-click to end the link.

In the front viewport, you'll notice that the leg bones looked great from the side but are positioned in the center of the body. We'll have to position them so they are centered in the leg.

3. Select the first bone in the front leg we created at the shoulder. Right-click over the bone and choose Select Children. All the front leg bones are selected.

4. Lock your selection and make sure the **IK** button is off.

5. In the Front viewport, use the Select and Move transform and move the leg in the XY-axis until it matches the position of the anatomy of the right leg. It's best to do this adjustment while checking both Front and Left viewports.

6. Repeat Steps 1 through 5 for the left leg.

7. Repeat this procedure for the rear legs. Now Mootilda's back, head, tail, and leg bones are created.

In Chapter 11, Bessie's cow mesh had a line of linked bones running parallel to her

Because of a bug in the 3D Studio MAX versions 1.0 and 1.1, mirroring a hierarchical tree may cause unpredictable results. Thus, each leg must be built separately.

337

lower body profile. Because the cow body is so large and the shape of the lower profile is complicated, we gave it a line of linked bones to make it easier for the program to assign vertices correctly and to give us more control.

Mootilda—What a Profile!

In this section let's give Mootilda a linked skeleton along her lower profile to ensure proper vertex assignment and keep her shape.

1. In the Left viewport, start behind the front legs and create five bones running along the bottom profile of the cow's belly and curving up around the bottom curves of the udder.
2. Right-click to end the bone links.

These bones need not be linked to any other part of the skeleton. They won't be used to animate the cow, just to help keep control of Mootilda's girlish figure.

Now that we have added a line of linked bones to the lower body profile, we will add bones to Mootilda's horns so the horn vertices will assign correctly as well.

Note: Anytime a mesh has parts standing away from the body, like Bessie's horns, add bones to make it easier for Bones Pro MAX to assign vertices correctly.

Adding Those Horn Bones

Let's add some bones for the horns.

1. In the Left viewport, starting at the intersection of the neck and head bones, click and drag a bone straight up to the top of Mootilda's head.
2. Following the curve of the horns, create three bone links in the right horn. Right-click to end the bone link.
3. Repeat Step 2 for the left horn.

Mootilda now has a complete skeleton, as shown in Figure 12.3.

But wait—parts of Mootilda's skeleton still need to be linked together.

Linking Mootilda

Before we can animate the Bones Pro MAX skeleton, we need to know that the areas we will be animating are linked together. To check the bones currently linked, we'll go to the first bone we created on Mootilda's back.

Click on bone01 and right-click, then select its children. The first three bone links turn white, indicating they are selected. The rest remain unselected, telling us that only the first three links are in this hierarchical tree. For Mootilda, we want the entire back, tail, and horns to be linked together so that we can move them using IK.

Figure 12.3

Mootilda with a complete bones skeleton.

1. Select the first tail link.
2. Click on the Select and Link tool in the MAX toolbar. It turns green to indicate it is selected.
3. Click on the **Select by Name** button in the MAX toolbar. The Select Parent dialog box appears.
4. Select bone04 and click on the **Link** button. The tail is now connected to the lower backbone. However, the lower backbone is still not connected to the upper half of the backbone.
5. Click anywhere in the viewport away from Mootilda to deselect all objects, then select bone04.
6. Link bone04 to bone01. Bone01 is the parent.

Now all the spine and the tail are linked. All that's left are the horns.

Click on the main horn bone, the one you created from the intersection of the neck and head bone to the top of the cow's head.

Right-click over the bone and select its children. All the horn bones should be selected. If they aren't, link the first bone of each horn to the main horn bone attaching the horns to the head. Now link the main horn bone to bone01.

Now when you go back to bone01 and select its children, the spine, tail, and horns should all be selected.

Note: After linking parts of a skeleton together that were created independently, be sure to check that the pivot points are located correctly to allow bending at the mesh joints.

Now that we have the Bones, let's turn them into a Skeleton.

Turning Bones into a Skeleton

MAX bones can be used to do simple animations, but can't be scaled and twisted like Skeleton bones. This is one of the real pluses of Bones Pro MAX. Thus, before we can use Moo's Bones, we must first convert them to Skeleton boxes using Skeleton.

Skeleton "boxes" should be generated close to the size of the part animated to keep vertices from being pulled away to an adjacent box. The boxes can be generated individually or in groups to make different-sized boxes in the same skeleton. Simply select the bones you want sized the same, and click the **Generate Boxes** button. Change the box width to the desired size, and click on OK. Only those boxes selected will have boxes generated around them. Do the same for the rest of the skeleton.

If you want your individual bones to be individually named or as a group, as in backbone, leg bone, and so on, it's easier

to name them when they are created than to go back later and rename them. Instead of selecting all the bones, select a named group like Front left leg bones, and generate boxes as above. Continue on to select each group of bones you want named and sized and repeat. Above all, plan first!

1. If all the Bones aren't selected, do so now.
2. In the Utility panel, select Skeleton in the Utilities drop-down.
3. Click on Generate Boxes. The Generate Boxes dialog box appears.
4. In the Box Width field, change the number to 2.0, and click on OK. Boxes appear around the selected bones, as shown in Figure 12.4; the Bones are still selected.
5. Press the Delete key to delete the original Bones. Only the boxed skeleton remains. Notice that unless you have renamed your bones as in the tip above, the name *Bones* have been

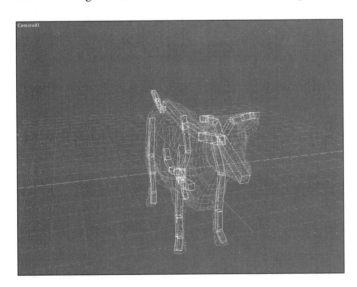

Figure 12.4

The Bones have been converted to skeleton boxes.

replaced by *Skeleton* in the Select by Name dialog box. The skeleton is now a series of linked boxes, as shown in Figure 12.5.

6. Save your file as Cowlink.MAX.

Mootilda's Body-Lift

The skeleton is now ready to take control of Mootilda's body. Bones Pro MAX, like Physique, assigns vertices to a bone in cylindrical groups. This makes it important to have your mesh in a position that is easy for the program to assign vertices correctly. You'll notice that in Chapter 11, we edited the cow mesh so the tail stood out away from the body. When the skeleton was attached to the mesh, the tail vertices don't overlap and accidentally become assigned to the wrong bone. This is very helpful in eliminating the need to reassign vertices later.

It is also important to know your mesh.

Finding, in the middle of an animation, that the mesh is incomplete, or missing faces because parts have been created attached to each other, makes it difficult to save hours of work.

Trial and Error... Lots of Error

Even with all the careful planning, sometimes a mesh just doesn't cooperate and needs additional modification before it can be attached to the skeleton. The cow we animated in Chapter 11 needed little adjustment because it was animated standing in place. If you tried to move its rear haunches much, you would have noticed that the udder moves with the legs, causing an unnatural stretch of the udder vertices, as shown in Figure 12.6. The first logical step to fix this would be to reassign the udder vertices to another bone and deselect them from the leg bones to which they are currently attached.

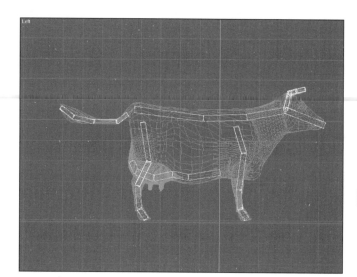

Figure 12.5

The skeleton is now comprised of linked boxes.

Figure 12.6

The udder stretches in an unnatural way when the vertices are attached incorrectly.

Ahh, but wait, if you try to reassign these vertices, you'll see they won't reassign. There's no bone close enough to be in control. If you try to simply deselect them, it makes no noticeable difference; the udder still deforms and stretches as the legs move. In this case, we can't reassign vertices because, as we discovered, the udder mesh is actually attached to the back legs.

Our first step to correct this was to go back and reattach the cow body, minus the udder, to the Bones Pro MAX space warp. After we did so, we found that the udder mesh itself was incomplete, as shown in Figure 12.7. The legs are now free to move away from the udder, but a large gap appears where the udder has been left unfinished.

The Modify panel was the next stop. We couldn't leave the cow with a painful and ugly gap in her udder, so we selected the udder and built faces on either side to close

the gap. Since the udder was an Editable Mesh, we could go to the sub-object level and use Build Face in the Miscellaneous section of the Edit Face rollout. (Remember to build faces in a counterclockwise direction.) If the udder hadn't been an editable mesh, we could have applied an Edit Mesh modifier, and then proceeded.

Now the udder was complete, but no longer a part of the cow mesh. Since this little part moves little itself, we linked it directly to the Bellybone04.

1. In the Left viewport, select the udder.
2. Using the Select and Link tool in the MAX toolbar, link the udder to the next-to-last bone.
3. Save the file as Newmoo.MAX.

Now when you move the cow, the udder will be attached to the rest of the cow mesh.

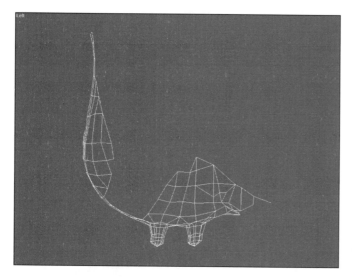

Figure 12.7

The udder on poor Mootilda was painfully incomplete.

There's Life in the Old Cow Yet

Bones Pro MAX lets you scale or otherwise transform boxed skeleton links over time. Scaling them carefully lets you create a nice breathing effect. In the following tutorial, we will give our cow mesh a breath of fresh air.

Breathing Life into Mootilda

The first breathing technique creates that subtle motion of breathing at rest. Or if you want to make her breathe a little harder, you can also use it to create a pant. This tutorial limits Mootilda to the more subtle breathing pattern.

1. If you don't already have the cow mesh on screen, reload Newmoo.MAX.

2. Select the cow mesh and freeze it.
3. In the Left viewport, click and drag a bone along the midsection of the cow's body in the rib area where you want breathing to occur. Click to set the bone, and right-click to end the link.
4. Click and drag another bone along the front chest from just under the neck to where the chest starts to protrude. Click to set the bone, and right-click to end the link. See Figure 12.8.
5. Save the file as Newmoo1.MAX.

These bones needn't be linked to any other cow bones because they don't affect any other body movement. However, they must be sized properly so that they can affect a large area of the mesh, and they must be assigned in Bones Pro MAX to control the mesh.

Figure 12.8

The two links in the cow's chest and body will control its breathing.

Converting Lung Bones into Lung Boxes

Now that we have the "lung bones" placed in Mootilda's body, select them and create custom-sized skeleton boxes. Using Skeleton, generate boxes with a width of 6.0. This larger size lets us control a larger number of vertices in the mesh. Delete the lung bones.

Animating the Breathing

Now we'll pump some air into Mootilda's lungs.

1. Select the skeleton link at the center of Mootilda's body, and turn on the **Animate** button.
2. Move to frame 3, and using the Select and Non-uniform Scale tool in the toolbar, scale it up 3 percent along the Z-axis.
3. Go to frame 6 and scale the bone down 3 percent along the Z-axis.

4. Repeat at frames 12 and 15.
5. Save file as Cowbrth1.MAX.

The cow's body now moves in and out as the cow breathes. You can load Tut12_2.MAX to check your animation.

A Little Sniff or Two

To get a different type of breathing motion, more like sniffing, use the same breathing technique using the chest bone.

1. Reload Newmoo1.MAX.
2. Select the chest link and turn on the **Animate** button.
3. Go to frame 2. Using the Select and Non-uniform Scale tool, scale the chest up 3 percent along the X-axis.
4. Go to frame 4, and scale the chest down 3 percent along the X-axis.
5. Repeat at frames 6, 8, and 12.

When you use this technique, be careful that you don't scale the bone too much. It can look unbelievable if there is too much movement—unless, of course, that's the look you're going for.

6. Click on the **Play Animation** button and watch the movement of the cow's head as it breathes. Load Tut12_3.MAX to check your animation.

These breathing animations can be used together or separately, depending on what else your cow is doing.

Breathing is a *secondary movement*. Secondary movements add those little touches that make an animation lifelike. Observe a cow standing in a pasture and watch for the small, subtle movements: a tail swish, skin twitch, or maybe an ear flick. These movements let you know that there is life there. We'll give Mootilda a little ear flick for an additional touch.

A Flick of the Ear

Sometimes a girl's gotta do what a girl's gotta do...in this case, flick her ears.

1. Load Newmoo1.MAX. Mootilda is back.
2. Select the Bones Pro MAX icon, and in the Modify panel, click on the **Influence Editor** button in the Bones Pro Space Warp rollout. The Influence Editor dialog box appears.
3. Click on the **Draw Bones On/Off and Draw Mesh On/Off** buttons. The cow bones and mesh appear in the edit window.

4. Click on the Front view in the IE Views menu. The cow is now facing you.
5. Click on the **Visualize Bones' Influence** button in the IE toolbar and select the face bone. The Influence colors appear.

As you can see, the ears are green; no specific bone has total control over their vertices.

Attaching New Bones for Flicking

In order to have control over Mootilda's ears, we must place bones inside them.

1. Merge Earbones.MAX into the scene. A pre-made set of skeleton boxes appear. If you haven't moved Mootilda around at frame 0, they should be positioned correctly. See Figure 12.9.
2. Select EarboneinnerR and EarboneinnerL, and link them to Skeleton03.

The ear bones are now all attached to the Bones Pro MAX skeleton.

3. Click on the **Influence Editor** button, and click again on the **Draw Mesh On/Off** button to hide the mesh. The skeleton is displayed in the edit window, but the ear bones

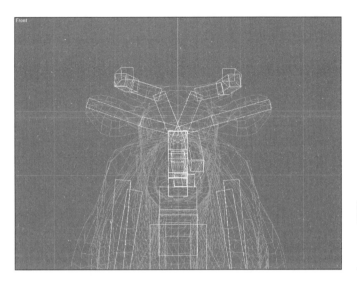

Figure 12.9

The ear bones are shown in position.

are not visible, even though we linked them to the skeleton. Why not? We never assigned them to the space warp.

4. Click on the **Assign** button in the Bones section of the Bones Pro Space Warp rollout. Click on All, and then on the **Select** button. All the bones in the cow are now assigned. Since

hide is already shown as the Bound Node, you do not need to reassign it.

5. Click on the **Influence Editor** button again. This time the ear bones appear in the edit window, as shown in Figure 12.10.

6. Scroll down in the Bones Pro Space Warp rollout until you come to the Selected Bones section. Click on the

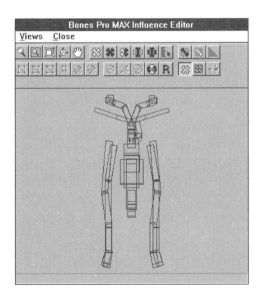

Figure 12.10

The ear bones appear in the Influence Editor.

If you want to animate a figure moving along a path with Bones Pro MAX, you must attach a dummy object to the Bones Pro Skeleton and animate the dummy object, just like we did with the basketball in Chapter 8.

Select button. The Select bones for group operations dialog box appears.

7. Select the four ear bones, and click on Select. The fraction above the **Select** button in the rollout now reads 4/46.

8. In the Falloff spinner, change the value to 40. In the Strength spinner, change the value to 4. Check both checkboxes next to Falloff and Strength.

Now check the cow's ears in the Influence Editor. You'll see that the ear bones have total control over the ear meshes. See Figure 12.11.

Animating a Flick

Now that the added ear bones are in sole control of the ears, we can add a little flick.

1. Click on the **Animate** button and move to frame 10.

2. Select the EarBoneOuterR and rotate it about the X-axis to -20 degrees.

3. Go to frame 15 and rotate the EarboneOuterR about the X-axis 30 degrees.

Now scratch the time slider and watch the ear flick.

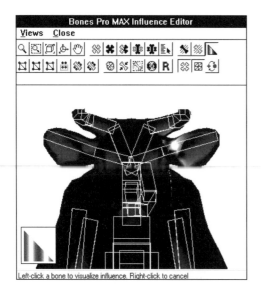

Figure 12.11

The Influence Editor shows the total control of the ear bones over the ear mesh. See color section.

Using Bones Pro MAX with Character Studio

One of the things that makes Bones Pro MAX special is that you can use it *with* Character Studio to add secondary movement to your Biped. We saw in the tutorial above how you can use Bones Pro MAX to make a cow breathe. In this tutorial, we'll see how to animate those added parts that Biped just doesn't cover, like wings, a headful of Medusa snakes, or that nagging second head. With Bones Pro MAX, not only can you link more bones to the Biped skeleton, you can deform the extra mesh parts as well.

Keeping a Griffon from Molting

In this section, we'll attach a Bones Pro MAX space warp to wings, while the main body is controlled by a Biped. This gives you the best of both worlds: the ease of Biped's footstep animation with secondary control using Bones Pro MAX.

This technique is a little tricky because the Bones Pro MAX space warp uses frame 0 as a starting point. *The mesh controlled by Bones Pro MAX cannot be modified in this frame without being distorted.* But often a .bip file moves the Biped to a different starting position, which can be a headache if not handled precisely right.

Linking the Wings to the Biped

First, we'll attach preexisting bones to the Biped. We've done the grunt work for you in this tutorial, creating and positioning MAX Bones, converting them to skeleton parts, creating a Biped, and adjusting the Biped to fit the griffon character's odd proportions.

1. Load Tut12_5.MAX. A griffon with wings appears, as in Figure 12.12.

Figure 12.12

The griffon with wings and all.

This griffon—George—is not a single mesh like Bessie, but a series of separate meshes that are simply linked to the Biped skeleton, rather than attached with Physique.

Note: For more information on this technique, see Tutorial 5 in the Character Studio User's Guide and Tutorials.

2. Link LeftWing01 and RightWing01 to Bip01Spine2, the closest Biped "bone."

In this tutorial, we'll create footsteps from the Biped's position in place. If we were loading a .bip file that relocates the Biped from its current frame 0 position, we'd first want to *temporarily* link the wings to the griffon torso, so that when the torso moves to its starting position, the wings follow. We'd then unlink the wings from the torso and bind them to a Bones Pro space warp.

3. Select the Bip01Pelvis.
4. In the Motion panel, click on the **Footstep Track** button.
5. Click on the **Run** button in the Footstep Creation rollout.
6. Click on Create Multiple Footstep and create fifteen footsteps.
7. Click on the **Create Keys for Inactive Footsteps** button in the Footstep Creation rollout.

The griffon now stands in position at frame 0 for its run. See Figure 12.13.

Attaching Bones Pro MAX to the Wings

Now we'll attach the Bones Pro MAX space warp to the wings.

1. Create a Bones Pro MAX space warp, as shown in Figure 12.14. Name it R Wing Controller.

Figure 12.13

The griffon in starting position at frame 0 with wings temporarily linked to its torso.

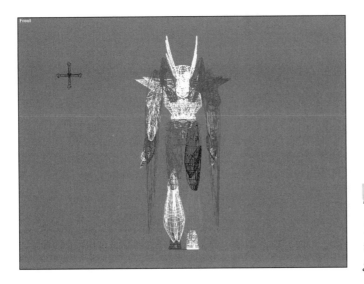

Figure 12.14

The Bones Pro space warp controller to the griffon's right.

Although we created it in the Front viewport, a Bones Pro MAX space warp can be located anywhere in the MAX world and still control the mesh. It's handy to have it near the mesh it controls, however. It's easier to remember which is which that way.

2. Bind the R Wing Controller space warp to the right wing.

3. Click on the **Select** button and select the R Wing Controller.

4. In the Modify panel, assign the bones named RightWing01 through RightWing07 to the Bones Pro space warp. (If you've forgotten how to do this, use the **Assign** button in the Bones section of the Bones Pro space warp rollout.)

5. Click on the button in the Bound Node section of the Bones Pro space warp rollout that now reads <**None**>. The Select Bound Node dialog box appears.

6. Select the object named right wing and click on Select. The right wing can now be controlled using the Bones Pro Space warp. To have control over the left wing, create a separate controller for it. If the wings were a single mesh, only one controller would be necessary; however, in this case, since you can only bind a *single* object to a space warp and have control over it in the IE, we will use two for our two wings.

7. Repeat Steps 2 through 6 for the left wing. First, create the space warp to the left of the griffon and name it L Wing Controller. Bind it to the left wing mesh, then link it to bones LeftWing01 through LeftWing07, and assign the left wing object as the bound node. This makes it easier to tell at a glance which controller controls which wing. See Figure 12.15.

Now both wings are controlled by the Bones Pro MAX space warp.

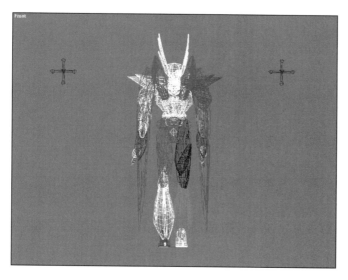

Figure 12.15

The griffon with both controllers in place.

Animating the Wings

With the space warps controlling the wings, we now can move them and deform the mesh to give it a more interesting, lifelike appearance.

1. Turn on the **Animate** button and move to frame 16.
2. Select Skeleton01 and rotate it in the Z-axis -20 degrees.
3. Press Page Down and rotate the next wing link in the Z-axis -10 degrees.
4. Select Skeleton04 and rotate in the Z-axis 30 degrees.
5. Repeat Steps 2 through 4 for the skeleton links in the right wing.

Scratch the time slider to see the effect. The wings come up as the griffon runs.

See Figure 12.16. If you want the griffon to flap his wings as he runs, go to frame 32 and rotate the wings down in the Z axis using the same techniques you used in Steps 2-4 to bring them up. Repeat the up and down movements at appropriate frames through the rest of the animation.

Notice that you can also use the scale technique to make the griffon's wings seem to fill with air as it runs. Just use Nonuniform Scale to scale the links in the mid-wing area along the XY axes. See Figure 12.17.

Now that you have some idea about how to use Bones Pro MAX with Biped, here's a few do's and don'ts (see sidebar). Read them carefully.

Figure 12.16

The wings come up as the griffon runs.

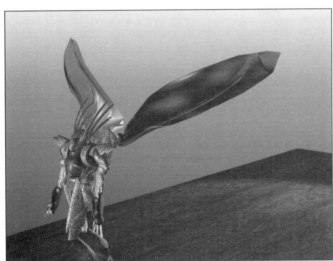

Figure 12.17

The griffon's wings are scaled to illustrate them filling with air as it runs.

In Conclusion

That's it, there is no more. If you've made it this far, you now know much more about anatomy, motion, cartoon movement, Bones Pro MAX, and Character Studio than you probably ever thought there was to know. I hope you enjoyed the trip.

DO'S AND DON'TS FOR USING BONES PRO MAX WITH BIPED

Bones Pro MAX and Biped are a powerful combination, but they are also tricky to use just right. Here is a baker's dozen rules that you should read and reread before using both together.

1. **Don't** *link the mesh controlled by Bones Pro MAX to the Biped-controlled mesh. The Bones Pro MAX mesh must be free of any attachments to the Biped.*
2. **Do** *link the Bones Pro MAX-controlled mesh to the Biped-controlled mesh temporarily while moving the Biped to its starting position at frame 0.*
3. **Don't** *forget to unlink the Bones Pro MAX-controlled mesh from the Biped-controlled mesh before animating it with Bones Pro MAX.*
4. **Don't** *bind the Bone Pro MAX space warp to the mesh it will control until after the biped motion has been placed on the figure and it is in place at frame 0.*
5. **Do** *create separate controllers for each mesh to be controlled by Bones Pro MAX.*
6. **Don't** *bind more than one mesh to a Bones Pro MAX controller. However, you can have as many controllers as you have meshes to control.*
7. **Don't** *use Bones Pro MAX on meshes that are controlled with Biped.*
8. **Don't** *use the Mirror Selected Objects tool in the MAX toolbar to mirror MAX Bones hierarchies.*
9. **Do** *use keyframe techniques to animate with Bones Pro MAX.*
10. **Don't** *attempt to change the Bones Pro MAX controlled mesh at frame 0.*
11. **Do** *check the Influence Editor in Bones Pro MAX to ensure that the Bones Pro MAX skeleton has complete control over its surrounding mesh.*
12. **Do** *link the Bones Pro MAX bones to the Biped skeleton to ensure that the new bones—and the mesh they control—move along with the Biped.*
13. *When animating Bones Pro MAX meshes, always move from frame 0 and turn on the* **Animate** *button.*

Appendix A

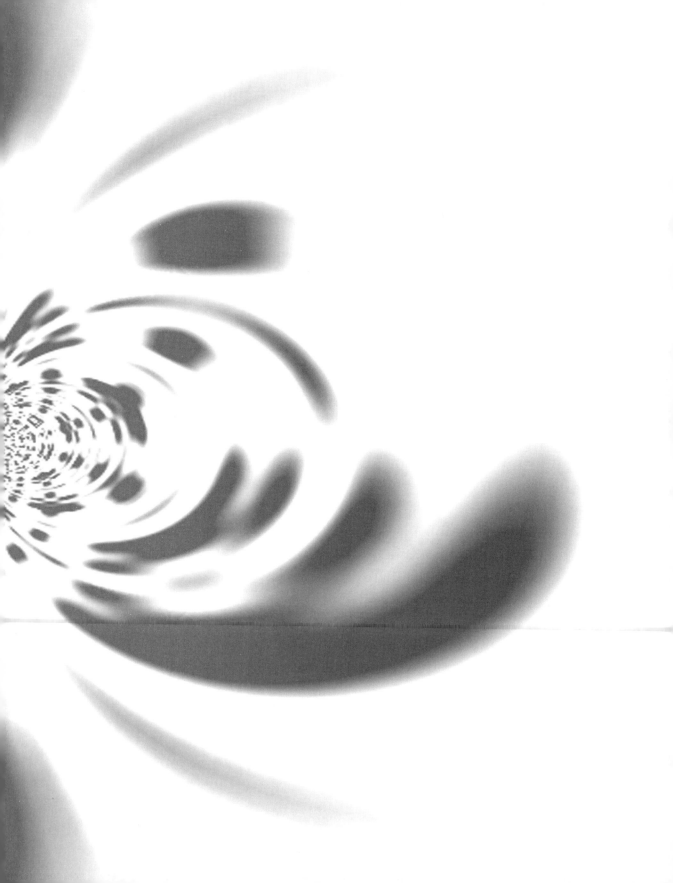

The Buttons

The following is a list of the buttons used in Character Studio and Bones Pro as mentioned throughout Chapters 7 through 12:

Bones Pro

 Bind to Space Warp

 Deselect All Bones

 Deselect All Vertices

 Deselect Unlinked

 Deselect Vertices in the Zone(s) of Selected Bones

 Draw Bones On/Off

 Draw Mesh On/Off

 Edit Bones' Influence Interactively

 Edit Influence of Selected Bones

Exclude Selected Vertices from Selected Bones

 Select Unlinked

 Exclude Unlinked from Selected Bones

 Select Vertices by Region

 Invert Bones Selection

 Select Vertices in the Zone(s) of Selected Bones

 Invert Vertices Selection

 Space Warps

 Reset Exclusion

 Toggle Vertex Display Mode

 Select All Bones

 Visualize Bones' Influence

 Select All Vertices

Character Studio

 Animate

 Arc Rotate

 Attach to Node

 Bend Links Mode

 Biped Playback

 Center of Mass

 Copy Posture

 Copy Selected Footsteps

 Create Keys for Inactive Footsteps

 Create Footsteps (append)

 Create Multiple Footsteps

 Create Panel Systems

 Cross Section Editor

 CS Cross Sections

 CS Draw Control Points

 CS Insert Bulge Angle

 CS Previous Link

 CS Select and Scale Control Point

 CS Slice

 Deactivate Selected Footsteps

 Figure Mode

 Filters in Track View

Footstep Track

 Jump

 Key Mode

 Load File

 Motion Panel

 Opposite Tracks

 Paste Posture

 Paste Posture Opposite

 Right Arm Anchor

 Rubber-Band

 Run

 Save File

Select by Link

Select by Link

 Select Object Space Object

 Set Key

 Symmetrical Tracks

 Walk

Appendix B

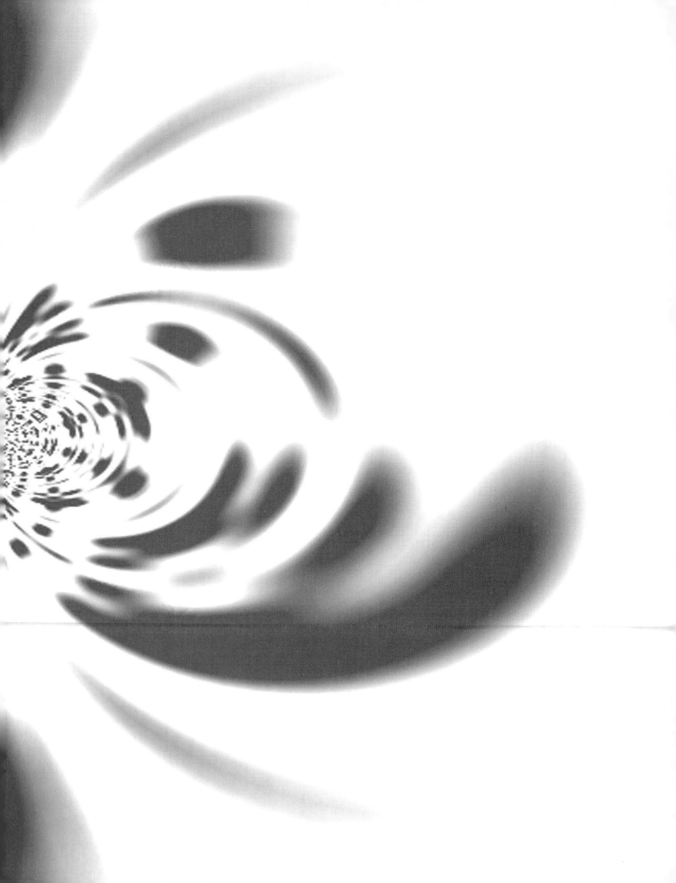

Resources

This guide should point you to a variety of resources in print and online that will help you in producing your own character animation. This list is not meant to be exhaustive—no such list can be—but it does list many sites and resources that I found valuable when writing this book.

Web Sites

Human Simulation

The Center of Human Modeling and Simulation
www.cis.upenn.edu.

Center for Human Simulation
www.uchsc.edu/sm/chs/

Facial Animation
mambo.ucsc.edu/psl/fan.html

Graphics, Visualization & Usability Center,
Georgia Institute of Technology College of Computing
http://www.cc.gatech.edu/gvu/
This is a great educational site for those of you seeking technical information on dynamic movement and simulations. To learn more about this top-ranked research and teaching facility, read the file GTI_GVU.txt in the Animata\qtmovies folder on the CD-ROM. And check out their animations from this site in the *animata\qtmovies* folder on the CD-ROM.

Welcome to FaceMaker
zeppo.cs.ubc.ca:5656/
Experimental online interactive facial animation tool.

Eadweard Muybridge

Eadweard Muybridge Home Page
www.linder.com/muybridge.html

Eadweard Muybridge
eagle.online.discovery.com/DCO/doc/
1012/world/science/muybridge/
navpage.html

Eadweard Muybridge of Kingston Upon Thames
www.king.ac.uk/kingston/museum/
muytext0.html

Pacific Interactive Media presents New Media Pioneers
www.linder.com/newmedia.html

Primates

The Gorilla Resource Center
www.brueggersnw.com

Mountain Gorilla Home Page
larch.ukc.ac.uk:2001/gorillas/

The Virtual Gorilla Exhibit Project at Zoo Atlanta
www.cc.gatech.edu/grads/a/Don.Allison/
gorilla/gorilla.html

Primate Information Home Page
www.primate.wisc.edu/pin/

3D Studio MAX Support

Kinetix: The Home of Interactive 3D Multimedia
www.ktx.com/

VIERTE ART (MAX plug-in developer)
www.vierte-art.com/

Support for 3D Studio MAX
www.complete-support.com/

The MAXimum resource page!
www.heathcomm.no./max/

Animetix
www.animetix.com

Diaquest
www.diaquest.com

Digimation
www.digimation.com

Photron
www.photron.com

Sisyphus
www.sisyphus.com

Spacetec
www.spacetec.com

4DVision
www.4dvision.com

Truevision
www.truevision.com

Animation Houses

(Colossal) Pictures
www.colossal.com

Disney Software
www.disney.com

Rhythm & Hues Studios
www.rhythm.com

J. Goodman Library
www.rhythm.com/~goodman/Library/
library.html
John Goodman's personal Web site (he's
the Technical Director at Rhythm &
Hues).

R/GA Digital Studios
www.rga.com/index.html

Pacific Data Images
www.pdi.com/

Deep Blue Sea
www.deepbluesea.com/

3D Model Sources

**3D CAFE(tm) (3D Mesh Model
Geometry and Graphical Imaging)**
www.baraboo.com/3dcafe/

3D Site
www.3dsite.com/3dsite/

Acuris Home Page
www.acuris.com

Avalon Public Domain
www.viewpoint.com/avalon

CGW: Cool Connections: 3D Models
www.cgw.com/cgw/Connections/
models.html

Mesh Mart Home Page
cedar.cic.net/~rtilmann/mm/

**Stephens Seefeld's 3D Studio
and Max Archive**
www.ozemail.com.au./~grind/

Viewpoint DataLabs
www.viewpoint.com/

Zygote Home Page
www.zygote.com

Miscellaneous Animation and Art Reference Sources

David Goodnow's "How Birds Fly"
www.us.net/birds

**Graphics groups, UNC-Chapel Hill
CS Department**
www.cs.unc.edu/graphics/

**Computer Animation Home Pages
at AAST**
www.bergen.org/AAST/Computer-
Animation/

CineWebSite: Animation
www.cinesite.com/

Animation Art by Bob Clampett
www.cartoon-factory.com/wb_bc.html

The Digital Directory
www.digitaldirectory.com/
animation.html

UCSC Computer Graphics
mambo.ucsc.edu/psl/cg.html

The Ray Tracing Home Page
arachnid.cs.cf.ac.uk/Ray.Tracing/

The World Wide Web Virtual Library:
Computer Graphics and Visualization
www.dataspace.com/WWW/vlib/comp-
graphics.html

ACM SIGGRAPH Online!
siggraph.org/

The Dragon Wing
www.cs.ubc.ca/nest/imager/contribu-
tions/forsey/dragon/top.html

MOVIEWEB: Home Page
www.movieweb.com/

Sony Pictures Entertainment
Home Page
www.spe.sony.com/Pictures/index.html

AFI OnLine
www.afionline.org/

Motion Capture

Bio-vision Home Page
www.bio-vision.com

4Dvision
www.4dvision.com

Bookstore

Amazon.com Books! Earth's
Biggest Bookstore
www.amazon.com

Magazines

PlanetStudio
livedv.com/PlanetStudio/

3D Artist
www.3dartist.com

Digital Video
www.livedv.com

Computer Graphics World
www.cgw.com

Papers and Articles

Lasseter, John. "Principles of Traditional Animation Applied to 3D Computer Animation." *Siggraph 1987*, Proceedings of the Conference on Computer Graphics and Interactive Techniques. ACM-0-89791-227-6/87/007/0035.

Pelachaud, Catherine, Norman I. Badler, and Marie-Luce Viaud. "Final Report to the National Science Foundation of the Standards for Facial Animation Workshop." *University of Pennsylvania School of Engineering and Applied Sciences. Computer and Information Science Department.* Oct. 1994.

Robertson, Barbara. "Hair-Raising Effects." *CGW Magazine,* Oct. 1995. The "New Wave" in 3D hair generation.

Robertson, Barbara. Feature: "Toy Story: A Triumph of Animation." *CGW Magazine,* Aug. 1995. Insights into the making of *Toy Story.*

Robertson, Barbara. "Jumanji's Amazing Animals." *CGW Magazine,* Jan. 1996. A behind-the-scenes article telling how they made the 3D animals in the movie.

Spedding, G.R.. "Hydro- and Aerodynamics of Animal Swimming and Flight." [Online], Available at: www.usc.edu. May 21, 1996. An interesting report on animal swimming and flight.

Books

Bammes, Gottfried. *The Artist's Guide to Animal Anatomy.* UK: Transedition Books, 1994. ISBN: 1-898250-36-7. This is a translation from the original German text. It can be rather hard to understand in some areas, but it has great drawings to use as a resource.

Blair, Preston. *Cartoon Animation.* California: Walter Foster Publishing, Inc., 1994. ISBN: 1-56010-084-2. This is another wonderful animation book to have as a resource.

Corson, Richard. *Stage Makeup.* New Jersey: Prentice-Hall, 1986. ISBN: 0-13-840521-2. This is a fun book that gives you an insight into the physical characteristics that give a face character. Good for studying nose types, eyes, mouth types, and hair.

Faigin, Gary. *The Artist's Complete Guide to Facial Expression.* New York: Watson-Guptill, 1990. ISBN: 0-8230-1628-5. This is one of those must-have books for anyone interested in animating facial expressions.

Goodnow, David. *How Birds Fly.* Maryland: Periwinkle Books Inc., 1992. ISBN: 0-9634244-0-8. This is a great book for those who are interested in the details of bird flight; includes beautiful time-lapsed photos.

Hamm, Jack. *Drawing the Head and Figure.* New York: Perigee Books, 1982. ISBN: 0-399-50791-4. This is a very useful book for visualizing the human form in different positions. Although originally written for 2D figure drawing, this book has helpful information for the 3D artist as well.

Hince, Peter. *Figures: The Concise Illustrator's Reference Manual.* New Jersey: Quatro Books, 1995. ISBN: 0-7858-0515-X. A little book that's easy to carry. It is a good reference for how poses look from different angles.

Hince, Peter. *Nudes: The Concise Illustrator's Reference Manual.* New Jersey: Quatro Books, 1995. ISBN: 0-7858-0514-1. A little book to show nude figures from different angles.

Kent, Sarah. *Composition*. New York: Dorling Kindersley Publishing, 1995. ISBN: 1-56458-612-X.

Morrison, Mike. *Becoming a Computer Animator*. Indiana: Sams Publishing, 1994.
ISBN: 0-672-30463-5.

Muybridge, Eadweard. *Horses and Other Animals in Motion*. New York: Dover Publications, 1985.
ISBN: 0-486-24911-5.
These motion studies, photographed by Muybridge in the last century, are very helpful for basic animal movement.

Muybridge, Eadweard. *The Male and Female Figure in Motion*. New York: Dover Publications, 1984.
ISBN: 0-486-24745-7.
This group of Muybridge's motion studies of male and female bodies in motion are very helpful to 3D artists who need to visualize how the body moves.

Noake, Roger. *Animation Techniques*. New Jersey: Chartwell Books, 1988.
ISBN: 1-55521-331-6.

Peck, Stephen Rogers. *Atlas of Human Anatomy for the Artist*. New York: Oxford University Press, 1951.
ISBN: 0-19-503095-9.
A great resource for human anatomy. Wonderful line drawings and pictures make this more understandable for the artist without a medical degree.

Thomas, Frank and Ollie Johnston. *The Illusion of Life*. New York: Hyperion, 1981. ISBN: 0-7868-6070-7.
This is a truly wonderful book. Considered in most animator's circles, to be the cel animator's bible, it has a wealth of information for many areas of 3D as well. It's a beautiful book to use and to read. I highly recommend this one for your resource library.

White, Tony. *The Animator's Workbook*. New York: Watson-Guptill, 1988.
ISBN: 0-8230-0229-2.
This is a great resource for 2D cel animation techniques. Although it was written with 2D in mind, 3D artists will find a lot of helpful information, especially for cartooning in 3D.

Zetti, Herbert. *Sight Sound Motion, Applied Media Aesthetics*. California: Wadsworth Publishing Co., 1973.
ISBN: 0-534-00238-2.

Magazines

These magazines are of interest to animators. See the Web sites list above for some of these.

3-D Artist
Columbine, Inc.
P.O. Box 4787
Santa Fe, NM 87502
(505) 982-3532
$5/issue (Subscription price not given.)
Bimonthly

3D Design
Miller Freeman, Inc.
600 Harrison St.
San Francisco, CA 94107
(415) 905-2200
$3.95/issue or $29.95/year
Monthly

Advanced Imaging
PTN Publishing Co.
445 Broad Hollow Road
Melville, NY 11747-4722
(516) 845-2700
No charge to qualified professionals.
All others $60/year
Monthly

American Cinematographer
ASC Holding Corporation
1782 N. Orange Dr.
Hollywood, CA 90028
(800) 448-0145
$5.00/issue or $35/year
Monthly

Animation
30101 Agoura Court, Suite 110
Agoura Hills, CA 91301
(818) 991-2884
$4.95/issue or $45/year
Monthly

Animerica
Viz Communications, Inc.
P.O. Box 77010
San Francisco, CA 94107
(415) 546-7073
$4.95/issue or $58/year
Monthly

Cinefantastique
7240 W. Roosevelt Rd.
Forest Park, IL 60130
(708) 366-5566
$5.95/issue or $48/year
Monthly

Cinefex
P.O. Box 20027
Riverside, CA 92516
$8.50/issue or $26/year
Quarterly

Cinescape
Cinescape Group, Inc.
1920 Highland Ave., Suite 222
Lombard, IL 60148
(708) 268-2498
$4.99/issue or $29.95/year
Monthly

Computer Artist
PennWell Publishing
One Technology Park Drive
P.O. Box 987
Westford, MA 01886
(508) 392-2166
$4.95/issue or $14.95/year
Bimonthly

CGW (Computer Graphics World)
10 Tara Blvd., 5th Floor
Nashua, NH 03062-2801
(918) 835-3161
$4.95/issue or $40/year
Monthly

Digital Imaging
Micro Publishing Press, Inc.
2340 Plaza del Amo, Suite 100
Torrance, CA 90501
(310) 212-5802
Free to qualified professionals.
All others $24.95/year
Bimonthly

Digital Video Magazine
IDG Company
600 Townsend St., Suite 170 East
San Francisco, CA 94103
(800) 998-0806
$4.95/issue or $29.97/year
Monthly

New Media
Hyper Media Communications
901 Mariner's Island Blvd., Suite 365
San Mateo, CA 94404
(415) 573-5170
Free to new media pros.
All others $4.95/issue or $52/year
Monthly

PC Graphics & Video
Avanstar Communications
222 Rosewood Dr.
Danvers, MA 01923
(800) 346-0085

Wired Magazine
Wired Ventures Ltd
P.O. Box 191826
San Francisco, CA 94119-9866
(415) 222-6200
$4.95/issue or $39.95/year
Monthly

Miscellaneous

Digimation Animation Catalog
1000-L Riverbend Blvd.
St. Rose, LA 70087
(800) 854-4496
Quarterly catalog

VCE Inc.
(Pyromania)
13300 Ralston Ave.
Sylmar, CA 91342-7608
(800) 242-9627

Viewpoint Catalog
Viewpoint DataLabs Int'l
625 South State St.
Orem, Utah 84058
(800) DATASET
www.viewpoint.com

New Third-Party Plug-In Applications for 3D Studio MAX

4DPAINT - 4DPAINT—Available from
4DVISION LLC at $1,495 U.S. list.
Contact: Scott Susmann,
9303) 759-1024; scot@4dvision.com

Sculptor NT—Available from
4DVISION LLC at $495 U.S. list.
Contact: Scott Susmann,
(303) 759-1024; scot@4dvision.com

MetaREYES Metaballs NT—Available
from 4DVISION LLC at $595 U.S. list.
Contact: Scott Susmann,
(303) 759-1024; scot@4dvision.com

Puppeteer NT—Available September 1996 from 4DVISION LLC at $795 U.S. list.
Contact: Scott Susmann, (303) 759-1024; scot@4dvision.com

RayMax—Available August 1996 from ABSOLUTE Software GmbH, Dammtorstr. 34 B, 20354 Hamburg, Germany
Contact: Ruediger Hoefert, 100136,1105@compuserve.com

GAMUT-SGm—Available from Animetix Technologies, Inc. at $995 U.S. list.
Contact: Adam Walters, (604) 730-5627; adamw@axionet.com

GAMUT-PSm—Available July 1 from Animetix Technologies, Inc. at $995 U.S. list.
Contact: Adam Walters, (604) 730-5627; adamw@axionet.com

GAMUT-DXm—Available from Animetix Technologies, Inc. at a price to be announced.
Contact: Adam Walters, (604) 730-5627; adamw@axionet.com

3D/AV Digital Production Suite— Available from Diaquest at $795 U.S. list.Contact: Howard Gutstadt, (510) 526-7167; howard@diaquest.com

3D/Digital Disk Available from Diaquest at $795 U.S. list.
Contact: Howard Gutstadt, (510) 526-7167; howard@diaquest.com

Sand Blaster—Available from Digimation at a price to be announced.
Contact: David Avgikos, (504) 468-7898; sold@digimation.com

Fractal Flow—Available from Digimation at a price to be announced.
Contact: David Avgikos, (504) 468-7898; davida@digimation.com
http://www.digimation.com

Image Master—Available from Digimation at a price to be announced.
Contact: David Avgikos, (504) 468-7898; davida@digimation.com
http://www.digimation.com

Bones Pro—Available from Digimation at $795
Contact: David Avgikos, (504) 468-7898; davida@digimation.com;
http://www.digimation.com

LenZFX MAX—Available from Digimation at a price to be announced.
Contact: David Avgikos, (504) 468-7898; davida@digimation.com;
http://www.digimation.com

SpaceArm 3D Digitizer SpaceSculpt Interface—Available from FARO Technologies, Inc. Call for pricing.
Contact: Jon Houston, (800) 736-0234; houstonj@faro.com

SPRN DLL—Available now over CompuServe via credit card no.
Contact: netnice GbR, Horst Brueckner, +49-9195-946612, CIS 100015.1534 @compuserve.com

PRIMATTE S-100 for 3D Studio MAX—Available from P.E. Photron at $400 U.S. list.
Contact: Scott Gross, (408) 261-3613; sgross@photron.com

MaxParticles II/All-Purpose-Emitter—Available from Sisyphus Software and from Independent Kinetix and Graphics Software Dealers at a recommended price of $70.
Contact: Eric Peterson, (210) 543-0665; CIS 74461,157 or 74461.157@compuserve.com

MaxTrax—Available from Sisyphus Software and from Independent Kinetix and Graphics Software Dealers at a recommended price of $70.
Contact: Eric Peterson, (210) 543-0665; CIS 74461,157 or 74461.157@compuserve.com

Max'Plode (MaxParticles III)—Available from Sisyphus Software and from Independent Kinetix and Graphics Software Dealers at a recommended price of $75.
Contact: Eric Peterson, (210) 543-0665; CIS 74461,157 or 74461.157@compuserve.com

MaxParticles 1—Available from Sisyphus Software and from Independent Kinetix and Graphics Software Dealers

at a recommended price of $70.
Contact: Eric Peterson, (210) 543-0665; CIS 74461,157 or 74461.157@compuserve.com

MaxSolids—Available from Sisyphus Software and from Independent Kinetix and Graphics Software Dealers at a recommended price of $50.
Contact: Eric Peterson, (210) 543-0665; CIS 74461,157 or 74461.157@compuserve.com

SpaceWare AniMotion—Available from Spacetec IMC at $495 U.S. list.
Contact: Stas Mylek, (508) 970-0330, ext. 123; stas@spacetec.com

TARGA 1000 Pro & 3D/AV Digital Production Suite—Available from Truevision and Diaquest at $3,495 through Dec. 31.
Contact: Truevision, (408) 562-4200 or (800)-522-TRUE; info@truevision.com

Hardware for High-End Graphics Use

TDZ Series of multiprocessor workstations are ideal for 3D Studio MAX work. For information, contact:

Intergraph Corporation
290 Dunlop Blvd.
Huntsville, AL 35824
(205) 730-2000

Index

D

E

F

N

O

P

Q

R

HOW BIRDS FLY

A book by David Goodnow
Reveals the mysteries of bird flight with sequences of high-speed photos.
A valuable resource for artists and animators.

ISBN: 0-9634244-0-8
Periwinkle Books Inc. • Columbia, MD
http://www.us.net/birds

© 1996 Frank Robbins

ISETA 250
Modeled by Pedro P. Uz

Modeled by Pedro P. Uz of R.E.M. Infographica, S.A.

Character Animation
with **3D STUDIO**
MAX
Gallery

Mesh objects like this cartoonlike razor-back hog are available to you on the CD-ROM. You can see from this little fellow that secondary motion can help show speed and movement.

3D Models provided by Viewpoint Datalabs International, Inc.

The Conga Line shown here is my version of the cover image created by Michael Girard of Unreal Pictures. It shows the flexibility of Character Studio: you can animate any two-legged creature realistically and replace creatures of different stature in an existing scene flawlessly. Check out the AVI on the CD-ROM in the *animata\avi* folder.

3D Models provided by Viewpoint Datalabs International, Inc.

Proper anatomy, proportion, movement, and balance give your 3D models a more life-like appearance. Character Studio was used to pose this mesh character and capture the tension in her movements.

Note the intricate detail of this hairy little 3D bee: even the transparency of the wings makes the bee more realistic.

3D Models provided by Viewpoint Datalabs International, Inc.

Martin Foster '96   for the film   "Jungle Boy"

The three leopard pictures here were produced by Martin Foster for the movie *Jungle Boy*. Although similar to the work done by Rhythm & Hues in the movie *Babe*, these images were created in 3D Studio MAX. Be sure to view the animation of this sequence in the *animata\avi* folder on the CD-ROM.

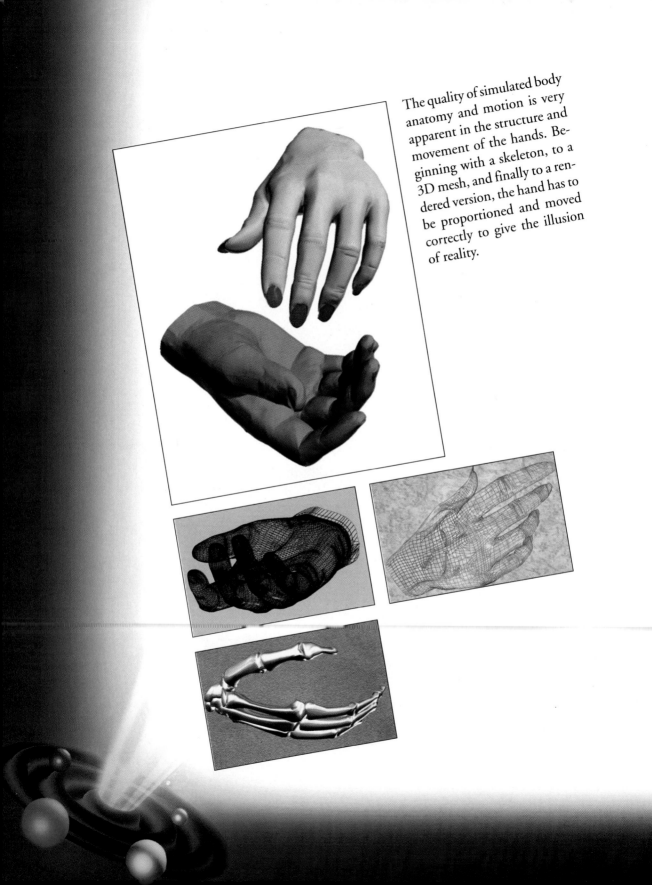

The quality of simulated body anatomy and motion is very apparent in the structure and movement of the hands. Beginning with a skeleton, to a 3D mesh, and finally to a rendered version, the hand has to be proportioned and moved correctly to give the illusion of reality.

In both the upper and lower illustrations, the biped skeletons were animated exactly the same except for the balance factor. The boy and the green biped have both been animated with a balance factor of 0.0 while the girl and the blue biped have a balance factor of 2.0. In the top illustration, the action is at frame 0, the Biped animation below is at its peak at frame 55 where the greatest differences can be seen.

This playground image is from the "Atlanta in Motion" animation presented in 1996 SIGGraph Electronic Theater. All animation in this amazing sequence was created using dynamic simulation (but not 3D Studio MAX) by Professor Jessica Hodgins and her students in the Graphics, Visualization, & Usability Center in the Georgia Tech College of Computing. Don't miss this great animation in the *animata\QTmovies* folder on the CD-ROM.

Another image from "Atlanta in Motion" by Professor Jessica Hodgins and her students at the Graphics, Visualization, & Usability Center in the Georgia Tech College of Computing. To learn more about this dynamite research and teaching facility read the file GTI_GVU.txt in the *animata\QTmovies* folder on the CD-ROM.

Figure 3

Marvelous Mootilda is shown here with her mesh and Bones Pro Skeleton. The Bones Pro MAX Influence Editor lets you visualize and adjust the influence of each bone over the mesh surrounding it. Note the difference between Figure 1 with no absolute control by any bone over the vertices (they're all green), Figure 2 with minor control (some are red), and Figure 3 with total control (all are red).

3D Models provided by Viewpoint Datalabs International, Inc.

Figure 1

Figure 2

Mootilda in all her glory. You can create a whole herd from a single mesh with Bones Pro MAX Snapshot Plus. It's faster than breeding.

3D Models provided by Viewpoint Datalabs International, Inc.

Body language is vital to convey the emotional content of a scene. In Character Studio, you can adjust the vertical dynamics and center of gravity to fit the stance you give your figure.

3D Models provided by Viewpoint Datalabs International, Inc.

The Biped skeleton deforms the figure's mesh as it moves. The baby's skin stretches and moves with the biped to give natural movement without breaking at the joints.

3D Models provided by Viewpoint Datalabs International, Inc.

Biped can create realistic (or fantastic) bipedal movement to any two-legged creature, robot, or whatever.

The robot mesh, courtesy of Stephen Seefeld, is on the CD-ROM in the *scenes\misc* folder. Rendering, setting, and effects by Andrew Reese.

The griffon uses Character Studio and Bones Pro MAX together to give the you the ease of footstep animation with the ability to deform the wings for flight.

The griffon mesh, courtesy of Stephen Seefeld, is available on the CD-ROM in the *scenes\misc* folder.

In this 3D Studio MAX signature image, note that Character Studio lets you disengage the vertical dynamics that keep a Biped's feet on the ground, so that you can animate babies flying through the air.